Discrete Representation of Spatial Objects in Computer Vision

Computational Imaging and Vision

Volume 11

Discrete Representation of Spatial Objects in Computer Vision

by

Longin Jan Latecki

Department of Computer Science,
University of Hamburg,
Hamburg, Germany

KLUWER ACADEMIC PUBLISHERS

DORDRECHT / BOSTON / LONDON

A C.I.P. Catalogue record for this book is available from the Library of Congress.

ISBN 978-90-481-4982-7

Published by Kluwer Academic Publishers,
P.O. Box 17, 3300 AA Dordrecht, The Netherlands.

Sold and distributed in the U.S.A. and Canada
by Kluwer Academic Publishers,
101 Philip Drive, Norwell, MA 02061, U.S.A.

In all other countries, sold and distributed
by Kluwer Academic Publishers,
P.O. Box 322, 3300 AH Dordrecht, The Netherlands.

Printed on acid-free paper

To my parents and my sister

Contents

Acknowledgments

A major part of this work was done while I was supported by a *Habilitandenstipendium* (a post-doctoral research grant) from the German Research Foundation (DFG). I would like to acknowledge this support as well as helpful advice from Prof. Christopher Habel, who also suggested the possibility of the *Habilitandenstipendium* and in whose working group (AB Wissens- und Sprachverarbeitung, Fachbereich Informatik, Univ. Hamburg) the work was mainly carried out.

Also the hospitality and collaboration of Prof. Azriel Rosenfeld (Center for Automation Research, University of Maryland at College Park, USA), Prof. Yung Kong, and Prof. Ari Gross (Department of Computer Science at Queens College, CUNY, New York, USA) is gratefully acknowledged. During the *Habilitandenstipendium* I additionally visited Prof. Frank Prokop (University of Wollongong, Australia) and Prof. Rober Melter (Long Island University, USA).

My work was influenced by many helpful comments and advice from Prof. Ulrich Eckhardt (Institut für Angewandte Mathematik, Universität Hamburg), Prof. Siegfried Stiehl (FB Informatik, Univ. Hamburg) and Christopher Conrad (Institut für Angewandte Mathematik, Univ. Hamburg). Further, I greatly appreciate the helpful discussions with Prof. Ralph Kopperman (CUNY, New York), Prof. Paul Meyer (CUNY, New York), and Prof. Atsushi Imiya (Chiba University, Japan) as well as comments from Prof. Akira Nakamura (Meiji University, Kawasaki, Japan) and Rolf Lakämper (Institut für Angewandte Mathematik, Univ. Hamburg). I also would like to mention my university teachers Dr. Piotr Zarzycki and Dr. Adam Mysior.

Finally, I want to express my special thanks to my colleagues at the FB Informatik, Univ. Hamburg, in particular to Thomas Barkowsky, Steffen Egner, Prof. Christian Freksa, M. N. Khenkhar, Simone Pribbenow, Ralf Röhrig, Geoff Simmons, and Christoph Schlieder. Most of the joint work with these researchers is documented in many common publications.

Chapter 1

Introduction

A fundamental task of knowledge representation and processing is to infer properties of real objects or situations given their representations. In spatial knowledge representation, and, in particular, in computer vision, real objects are represented in a pictorial way as finite sets (also called discrete sets), since computers only can handle finite structures. The discrete sets result from a quantization process, in which real objects are approximated by discrete sets. This is a standard process in finite element models in engineering. In computer vision, this process is called sampling or digitization and is naturally realized by technical devices like CCD cameras or scanners. Consequently, a fundamental question addressed in spatial knowledge representation is: which properties inferred from discrete representations of real objects correspond to properties of their originals, and under what conditions is this the case? In this book, we present a comprehensive answer to this question with respect to important topological and certain geometrical properties.

The description of geometric and, in particular, topological features in discrete structures is based on graph theory, which is widely accepted in the computer science community. A graph is obtained when a neighborhood relation is introduced into a discrete set, e.g., a finite subset of $\mathbf{Z}^2$ or $\mathbf{Z}^3$, where $\mathbf{Z}$ denotes the integers. On the one hand, graph theory allows investigation into connectivity and separability of discrete sets (for a simple and natural definition of connectivity see Chapter 2 or Kong and Rosenfeld [82], for example). On the other hand, a finite graph is an elementary structure that can be easily implemented on computers. Discrete representations are analyzed by algorithms based on graph theory, and the properties extracted are assumed to represent properties of the original objects. Since practical applications, for example in image analysis, show that this is not always the case, it is necessary to relate properties of discrete representations to the corresponding properties of the originals. Since such relations allow us to describe and justify the algorithms on discrete graphs, their characterization contributes directly to the computational investigation of algorithms on discrete structures. This computational investigation is an important part of the research in computer science, and in computer vision in particular (Marr [110]), where it can contribute to the development of more suitable and reliable algorithms for extracting required shape properties from discrete representations.

It is clear that no discrete representation can exhibit all features of the real original. Therefore, one has to accept compromises. The compromise chosen depends on the specific application and on the questions which are typical for that application. Real objects and their spatial relations can be characterized using geometric features. Therefore, any useful discrete representation should model the geometry faithfully in order to avoid wrong conclusions. Topology deals with the invariance of fundamental geometric features like connectivity and separability. Topological properties play an important role, since they are the most primitive object features and our visual system seems to be well-adapted to cope with topological properties.

However, we do not have any direct access to spatial properties of real objects. Therefore, we represent real objects, as commonly accepted from the beginning of mathematics and recently in computer vision, as bounded continuous subsets of the Euclidean space $\mathbb{R}^3$, and their 2D views (projections) as bounded continuous subsets of the plane $\mathbb{R}^2$, which satisfy some additional conditions. Hence, from the theoretical point of view of knowledge representation, we will relate two different pictorial representations of objects in the real world: a discrete and a continuous representation. This is schematically illustrated in Figure 1.1, where both continuous and discrete representations are *analogical* in the sense that they represent the real object in a pictorial way. We model the representing space for discrete representations (i.e., the space that contains analogical discrete representations) as the set $\mathbf{Z}^2$ (or $\mathbf{Z}^3$) of points with integer coordinates in the plane $\mathbb{R}^2$ (or space $\mathbb{R}^3$) on which some adjacency relations are defined.

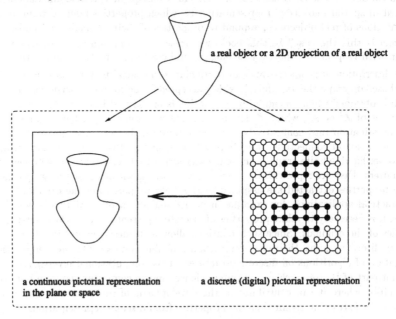

a real object or a 2D projection of a real object

a continuous pictorial representation in the plane or space

a discrete (digital) pictorial representation

Figure 1.1: Our main goal is the description of the relation between two different representations of real objects, the discrete and the continuous representations.

The main goal of this book is the description of the relation between two different pictorial representations of real objects, the discrete and the continuous representations. To describe this relation it is necessary to examine properties of both representations thoroughly. To compare continuous and discrete representations of a real object, their properties will be extracted (made explicit) in the form of predicates. For example, both representations in Figure 1.1 are "connected" sets. The extraction of properties can be viewed as a mapping from an analogical representation to a propositional representation in the form of predicates, i.e., in the form of symbolic descriptions. This mapping is applied to the continuous as well as to the discrete representation.

To extract the properties (such as connectedness) from continuous and discrete representations, it is necessary to have mathematical theories that allow us to describe the meaning of these properties precisely. We will use standard Euclidean geometry and topology for the description of continuous representations in $\mathbb{R}^2$ or $\mathbb{R}^3$. For the description of discrete representations in $\mathbf{Z}^2$ or $\mathbf{Z}^3$, we use graph theory as the basic theory, but it is also necessary to specify the graph structures on $\mathbf{Z}^2$ and $\mathbf{Z}^3$. In addition to graph theory, standard Euclidean geometry and topology is also used to describe the discrete spaces, since we view $\mathbf{Z}^2$ (or $\mathbf{Z}^3$) as canonically embedded in the plane $\mathbb{R}^2$ (or space $\mathbb{R}^3$), and it can be useful to calculate the Euclidean distance of two points with integer coordinates, for example. Depending on whether a theory is used to describe a continuous or discrete representing space, we will distinguish between *continuous* and *discrete theories*. This work contributes mainly to the development of discrete theories, but it also features a further development of continuous theories. The development of discrete theories, which has a long mathematical tradition, is a fundamental part of research in computer science.

Although there are considerations which suggest that maybe some other representations (e.g., using rational numbers) are more suitable to describe real objects than the continuous representation, we will use the continuous representation, since only the continuous theory yields the rich mathematical language necessary for shape description of spatial objects. Therefore, we will assume that the continuous theory describes the shape properties of real objects. Since the results presented will also allow us to relate two different discrete representations on a discrete and a rational representations of a real object, they can also be used when an alternative representation of a real object is presumed. In this case, the continuous theory would be the metalanguage of the alternative theory. The questions related to a finite, discrete, dense (non-continuous), and continuous nature of representations are addressed in Habel [62].

According to Stiehl [147] (see also Ballard and Brown [14], in computer vision one can distinguish four main categories of representations:

1. *"generalized images, which are in iconic or analogical representation (e.g., discrete arrays of edge elements, intrinsic images with explicit depth or surface orientation of visible surfaces, processing cones with a multi-resolution hierarchy of images);*

2. *segmented images, which are again in analogical representation (e.g. line segments and their junctions, regions of spectral uniformity, scale-space representation of zero-crossing);*

3. *geometric representations, which are also in analogical form, of two- and three-dimensional shape; and*

4. *relational structures, viz. complex symbolic descriptions of image and world structure,
   in an analogical/propositional representation (e.g., semantic nets)."*

We will use representations of category 1 (e.g., a digital gray-value picture in form of a square grid) and category 2 (e.g., a segmented digital binary picture, where the object of interest is given by the set of black pixels) as the discrete representations. The extraction of object properties can be viewed as a mapping from representations in categories 1 and 2 to a symbolic representation in form of predicates, which belongs to category 4. Therefore, our work can be classified as belonging to digital pattern recognition in the area of computer vision.

However, the analysis of geometric properties directly in discrete representations is not only useful in pattern recognition but also in general in spatial knowledge representation. Discrete representations are one of the most natural representations for modeling spatial objects in computers, since they are naturally obtained by segmenting sensor images, like images obtained using a CCD camera or computer tomography. Consequently, it is relatively simple to construct discrete representations, even if the segmentation is manually driven. For example, the 3D digital representation for the anatomy atlas VOXEL-MAN (Höhne et al. [67]) is obtained by interactive segmentation of CT or MRI images (Höhne and Hanson [66]). The direct, spatially intrinsic 3D voxel representation of human organs also has many processing advantages like viewing the constituents of the anatomy from any direction, simulating X-ray images, or surgical interventions. In robot navigation, a discrete representation of a bird's eye view of a terrain map can be obtained from a laser range scanner or sonar sensors. As argued in Elfes [40], such representations are more suitable to handle sensor distortion and uncertainty than classical geometric representations like polygonal object descriptions. From the cognitive point of view, discrete representations represent spatial objects and their relations in an intrinsic way, and are used as part of computational imagery. Glasgow and Papadias [50] distinguish three kinds of representations for computational imagery, which *"can be defined as the ability to represent, retrieve, and reason about spatial and visual information ..."*. Two of these representations called *spatial* and *visual representations* are realized in the form of discrete representations. While, in the visual representations, spatial objects are represented in a form similar to their digital images, in the spatial representations, spatial objects are represented by symbolic annotations in occupancy arrays that preserve some relevant spatial and topological relationships of the image features, but not necessarily relative sizes and distances.

Our discussion of digital representation applies also to quadtrees and octrees, since they can be viewed as special data structures for discrete representations that are organized in a tree-like hierarchical structure (Samet [139]). Clearly, quadtrees, octrees and other hierarchically organized occupancy arrays have additional properties, which we will not discuss here, since they permit multi-resolution representation of spatial objects (see Strat and Smith [150]).

Recent efforts in knowledge representation in artificial intelligence and computer science have been moving towards coding spatial knowledge not just propositionally, but also in the form of *pictorial representations*, that are mostly realized as discrete representations. Kosslyn [89], Lindsay [107], and Habel [60] show many advantages in using pictorial representations for spatial inferences. These advantages have led to the development of a new research field on diagrammatic reasoning (see Kulpa [91], Glasgow, Narayan, and Chandrsekaran [51], and in particular Barwise and Etchemandy [15]). There exist formalisms for diagrammatic reasoning that use discrete representations (not necessarily in form of a square raster), e.g., Funt [48] and Furnas [49]. Among the most important of these advantages is the direct (i.e., intrinsic) reproduction of the shape, location and spatial configuration of objects under consideration. This can be difficult in propositional formalisms, where spatial knowledge is described by logical predicates or mathematical equations. In some cases, this may even be impossible, since a large number of spatial properties must be expressed with predicates, and it may be that not all properties that are relevant to the problem in question have been made explicit using predicates. In contrast, pictorial representation formats are intrinsically spatial, i.e., spatial properties of represented objects are automatically inherited from the structure in which they are represented. Therefore, in pictorial representations, we need not make all relevant assumptions explicit, which is necessary in propositional representations of spatial knowledge. It is reasonable to conclude, then, that for many tasks, pictorial representations can be more suitable than propositional representations. A general discussion of intrinsic representations can be found in Palmer [119] and Freksa [46].

To drive and control spatial inferences directly using discrete representations, it is necessary to relate digital concepts described in graph theory to their continuous counterparts, since pictorial inferences are based on the interaction between pictorial and propositional representational formats. (Examples that illustrate the process of such spatial (pictorial) inferences are given in Section 1.6.) It is also important for spatial inferences to identify (a) the minimal resolution and (b) shape properties invariant under digital image transformations, like resolution changes or rotations. An example of an invariance question is whether a concave part of an object boundary will remain concave after decreasing the image resolution. To be able to answer such questions, it is necessary to develop a digital invariance theory, which allows us to determine allowable digital image transformations. Its usefulness may be compared to the study of projective invariants, a field that has gained considerable attention recently within the computer vision community. Digital invariance theory allows us to measure the accuracy of discrete representations by relating discrete to continuous representations, and determining the minimal resolution that guarantees invariance of the geometric properties under this relation.

The main difficulty with discrete (or digital[1]) representations is that they are only approximations of the original objects and are only as accurate as the cell size allows. For example, this is the case in computer graphics, where the digitization process is simulated based on some mathematical formulas. If digitization is done by real sensor devices, then there is an additional difficulty with distortion, e.g., blurring and noise of CCD cameras. Since digital geometric concepts are defined for idealized, non-noisy digital images, in order to use these concepts as shape classifiers for real digital images, it is necessary to extend their definitions to fit real images that are distorted due to such effects as blurring and noise.

The difficulties with inaccuracy and distortion result in a problem of identification of digital representations of the same object: Two digital representations A and B of a spatial

---

[1]The adjectives "discrete" and "digital" are used as equivalent concepts here.

object may not be equal on the pixel (or voxel) level although they "look" very similar. In order to recognize that A and B represent the same object, it is necessary to compare them on a higher level based on shape features on which the pixel (or voxel) distortions are less influential. This can be done by relating shape features of the underlying continuous object to the corresponding features obtained from a digital representation of this object. The relation between features of a continuous object and its digital representation can be split into two sub-relations:

R_1 the relation between a continuous object and its idealized digital representation created by a mathematical model of a digitization process with no influence of sensor distortion, and

R_2 the relation between the idealized digital representation and the digital representation obtained by segmenting an image of a real sensing device with influence of distortion effects like blurring and noise.

Whereas it is sufficient to only consider relation R_1 in many areas of computer science, like computer graphics and CAD systems, for problems of image analysis like object recognition and image database classification both kinds of relation between features of the real object and its digital representations are necessary. Relation R_2 is also important for direct matching of a prototypical digital representation of an object to regions in a digital image without any feature analysis. For instance, several methods exist for direct comparison between the spatial representations of digital symbols in the analysis of image documents (e.g., Kia et al. [74]). In Section 1.6, digital representations are analyzed in various applications. Their advantages and relevant features for spatial reasoning are pointed out.

We are interested in the comparison of features of a segmented object in a digital representation to the features of the underlying continuous object. Although the graph structure forms the basis for defining geometric properties, in this structure itself it is not possible to relate the geometric properties to their continuous counterparts, since the geometric features are originally based on the well-known "natural" continuous structure of Euclidean space and on its axiomatic description. There are actually four approaches to defining a continuous analog of graph-theoretic, geometric concepts of discrete structures, and thus, to relate properties of digital representations to their continuous originals:

- **Graph-based approach:** A digital analog of a continuous concept is defined based on a discrete theory, usually graph theory. Then the properties of a continuous concept, described by continuous theories, are compared to the properties of a digital analog of this continuous concept, which are described by discrete theories, e.g., it is shown using graph-theoretic tools that some particular properties of the digital concept are the same as the corresponding properties of its continuous original.

- **Axiomatic approach:** A common axiomatic theory that describes both continuous and discrete structures is developed. Axioms have to be chosen in such a way that the digital structure is assigned properties that are as close as possible to the corresponding properties of standard topology and geometry. An ideal case is when the resulting properties and definitions coincide with the standard ones in $\mathbb{R}^n$. In this case, all consequences of the axioms are the same independently of the continuous or discrete nature of the domain, since if a given digital concept satisfies the same axioms as its continuous analog, then the implied properties are the same.

- **Embedding approach:** The discrete structure is embedded into a known continuous structure, usually Euclidean space. This is done by a construction of a continuous analog for some classes of discrete objects. In this way, properties of discrete objects can be related directly to their continuous analogs using only continuous theories.

- **Digitization approach:** This is the most natural approach in the sense that it deals with mathematical models for digitization processes of real sensor devices. This is a "dual" embedding approach in the sense that a continuous object is mapped to a discrete graph structure. In this approach it is possible to justify a given property of a digital set by the fact that there exists a continuous set with this property that digitizes to it.

These approaches have advantages and disadvantages. For example, the axiomatic approach is mathematically very elegant, but it is a complicated task to provide a theory which is needed in applications. The embedding approach allows us to relate a continuous analog of a digital object to the underlying continuous object using the standard topological tools of the Euclidean space directly. The problem is to find an appropriate continuous analog. Therefore, all approaches are used in image analysis and, in general, in spatial knowledge representation depending on the goals to be achieved.

The research disciplines of digital topology and geometry deal mainly with the relation of digital representations to their continuous originals. The outcome of over 30 years of research in digital topology and geometry is that continuous concepts like connectedness, connected components, arcs, simple closed curves, and Euler number have digital analogs with analog properties. These analogs and their properties are described in at least one of the four approaches. The situation is similar but more complicated for geometric concepts like convexity and linearity.

The most often used discrete representation space (graph) is a rectangular array (a raster), which can be regarded as a finite subset of $\mathbf{Z}^2$, in which adjacency relations can be defined. For example, consider the 4-adjacency and 8-adjacency relations: the four 4-adjacent points (or 4-neighbors) of the center point are illustrated in Figure 1.2.a and the eight 8-adjacent points (or 8-neighbors) of the center point are illustrated in Figure 1.2.b.[2] It is important to notice that there are two different interpretations of raster cells: as points with integer coordinates on the plane or as squares (centered at points with integer coordinates) that form a uniform cover of the plane as shown in Figure 1.2.

The set $\mathbf{Z}^2$ with a certain graph structure induced by some adjacency relations is called a *digital plane*. Analogously, $\mathbf{Z}^3$ with a certain graph structure given by some adjacency relations is called a *digital space*. Based on graph theory we can then extend the local adjacency relations to a global concept of *connectedness* of subsets of $\mathbf{Z}^2$ and $\mathbf{Z}^3$. For example,

---

[2]Definitions of basic concepts can be found in Chapter 2.

we can distinguish between 4- and 8-connectedness on $\mathbf{Z}^2$. An important property of these graph structures is the fact that each point is adjacent to a finite number of other points; thus, a graph neighborhood of every point is finite. Such graphs are called *locally finite*. In this book, we define a *digital object* or a *discrete object* to be a subset of the digital plane or space. The adjectives "discrete" and "digital" are equivalent concepts.

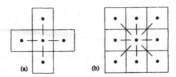

Figure 1.2: (a) shows four 4-adjacent points (or 4-neighbors) of the center point and (b) shows eight 8-adjacent points (or 8-neighbors) of the center point.

In Sections 1.1 to 1.5, we give an overview of the four approaches. We end this chapter with Section 1.6, in which a short overview of applications is presented. The reader not interested in applications can omit Section 1.6. In Chapter 2, basic digital and continuous concepts are defined and their elementary properties are stated. In Chapters 3, 4, 5, and 7, the four approaches are described in greater detail. These chapters can be read independently, since each chapter is self-contained in the sense that it contains all relevant definitions (that are not stated in Chapter 2). In Chapter 6 we describe the classes of continuous sets that will be used in Chapter 7 as input to digitization functions.

1.1 Graph-based Approach

A digital analog of a continuous concept is defined based on a discrete theory, mostly graph theory. Then it is shown using graph-theoretical tools that some particular properties of the digital concept are the same as the corresponding properties of its continuous original. For example, a digital version of a *simple closed curve* can be defined as a connected subgraph of the digital plane (with a certain minimal number of points) in which each point is adjacent to exactly two other points. Further, it can be proved that a simple closed curve separates the digital plane into exactly two components, which can be interpreted as the interior and the exterior of the curve (Rosenfeld [129]). Thus, a digital simple closed curve has exactly the same separability property as its continuous original. This property is known as the Jordan curve theorem. Rosenfeld proved this property for a special graph structure of $\mathbf{Z}^2$, which we will describe below. A 3D digital version of the Jordan curve theorem, known as the Jordan-Brouwer surface theorem, is proven in Herman [64]. Actually, Herman not only defines a Jordan surface but also introduces a set of conditions on a graph structure which allows one to prove multidimensional discrete analogs of the Jordan separability theorem for a variety of different adjacency relations.

Thus, a typical situation in defining discrete analogs of continuous concepts is the following: It is not enough to define a digital concept, but it is additionally necessary to specify the graph structure of the digital plane (or space) in which this concept should have analog properties to its continuous original. For example, there are graph structures on $\mathbf{Z}^2$ in which a simple closed curve does not satisfy the Jordan curve theorem, as we will see below. Due to the discrete nature of the graph structure, not every property required can be satisfied by a given graph structure. Another example is the fact that there is no topology on $\mathbf{Z}^2$ in which the connected sets are exactly the 8-connected sets (Chassery [25]).[3] Some other properties of continuous concepts that are not satisfied by discrete representations are related to the separability of discrete graph structures. These properties were noted early in the history of image analysis and referred to as "paradoxes".

We illustrate some of the paradoxes pointed out in Rosenfeld and Pfaltz [132] (see also Kong and Rosenfeld [82]). If 8-adjacency is used for black as well as white points in Figure 1.3.a, then the black points form a discrete analog of a simple closed curve, but they do not separate the white points, i.e., there is an 8-path between any pair of the white points, which means that the set of the white points is 8-connected. This example shows that a digital version of the Jordan curve theorem does not hold for 8-adjacency.

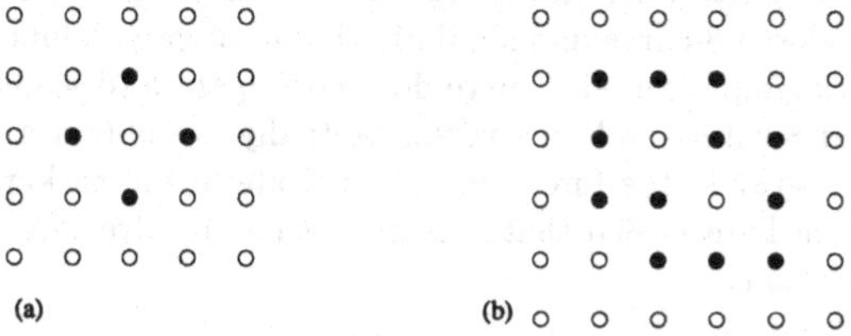

Figure 1.3: Connectivity paradoxes.

Figure 1.3.b shows that the situation is equally problematic for 4-adjacency. The black points constitute a 4-connected simple closed curve, but there exist three 4-connected components of the background. Thus, in either case, a digital version of the Jordan curve theorem does not hold. Observe also that, if 4-adjacency is used for black as well as white points in Figure 1.3.a, then the black points are totally disconnected. However, they separate the set of white points into two 4-components.

The most popular solution to these problems was the idea of using different adjacency relations for the foreground and the background: 8-adjacency for black points and 4-adjacency for white points, or vice versa (first recommended in Duda et al. [35]). If we consider 8-adjacency for the black points in Figure 1.3.a, then the set of black points forms a simple closed 8-curve which separates the white background into exactly two 4-components. Similarly, if we consider 4-adjacency for the black points in Figure 1.3.b, then the set of black points forms a simple closed 4-curve which separates the white background into exactly two 8-components. Rosenfeld [129] developed the foundations of digital topology based on this idea, and showed that the Jordan curve theorem is then satisfied.

The price we have to pay for this solution is that we have two different adjacency relations in one digital picture which depend on the objects being represented. Therefore,

---

[3]In Latecki [93] a much simpler and shorter proof of this fact is given.

the adjacency relation is not an intrinsic feature of a digital picture as a representing medium. Consequently, connected components are also not intrinsic features as is the case for $\mathbb{R}^2$ with the usual topology. Since we have one connectedness relation for the foreground (e.g., the set of black points) and another for the background (e.g., the set of white points), interchanging the foreground and the background also changes the connectedness relations of the digital picture. By the foreground we mean the objects whose properties we want to analyze, and by the background all the other objects of a digital image. Hence, the choice of foreground and of background is critical with respect to the segmentation process, especially in cases where it is not clear at the beginning of the analysis what constitutes the foreground and what constitutes the background, since this choice immediately determines the connectedness structure of the digital picture.

The situation becomes considerably worse if one wants to distinguish among different objects in the foreground (or in the background). We demonstrate this with the following example image illustrated in Figure 1.4, where the black and gray points form the foreground, and the remaining grid points the background. If we consider 8-adjacency for the foreground and 4-adjacency for the background, then the set of black points can be identified as a simple closed 8-curve and similarly the set of gray points as a simple closed 8-curve. Yet, the black simple closed 8-curve does not separate (disconnect) the points in the gray simple closed 8-curve, and vice versa. Actually, we obtain a three-color digital image this way (black, gray in the foreground, and white in the background). In Section 3.8 it is shown based on Latecki [94] that it is impossible to solve this problem using two different adjacency relations.

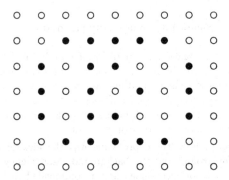

Figure 1.4: The black simple closed 8-curve does not separate the gray simple closed 8-curve, and vice versa.

In Chapter 3 (based on Latecki et al. [98]), we present a solution which allows us to avoid the connectivity paradoxes while having only one connectedness relation for the entire digital picture. We will use only 4-connectedness (which will be shown to be equivalent to 8-connectedness) for black as well as for white points. The idea is not to treat all decompositions of $\mathbb{Z}^2$ into foreground and background as digital pictures, but only a special class which define what we call "well-composed sets". This idea has a real mathematical flavor, since in most fields of mathematics we do not treat all subsets of a given space, but only a class of subsets which have "nice properties" with regard to features we are especially interested in. In our case, a binary digital picture is *well-composed* if it does not contain the patterns shown in Figure 1.5.

Figure 1.5: A 2D well-composed picture does not contain these critical configurations.

Since the pictures such as those shown in Figure 1.3 are not well-composed, their connectivity paradoxes will not occur in well-composed pictures. Thus, we only have one kind of simple closed curve in well-composed 2D pictures; these are simple closed 4-curves. At first glance, it may seem that by requiring well-composedness we restrict the variety of digital pictures. However, requiring digital pictures to be well-composed is actually a consequence of requiring that the process of digitization preserves topology, as we proved in Latecki et al. [101]. We proved that if the digitization resolution is fine enough, then the output digital picture will be well-composed and topologically equivalent to its continuous original image. We present this issue in Section 1.4 and in greater detail in Chapter 7.

Analogously, we can define a digital picture to be well-composed if every 8-component of either the foreground or the background is also 4-connected (and hence is a 4-component). This implies that 4-connectedness and 8-connectedness are equivalent. Consequently, connected components become intrinsic features, as is the case for $\mathbb{R}^2$ with the usual topology. Since 4- and 8-adjacency leads to the same connectedness relation on $\mathbb{Z}^2$, it is enough to consider only 4-adjacency. One of the consequences of this fact is the reduction of the number of links in the well-composed graph structure, which positively influences the speed of algorithms. Another consequence is that every well-composed digital picture is a planar graph, i.e., it can be embedded into the plane $\mathbb{R}^2$ in such a way that its links which represent adjacencies do not intersect. This is not the case for $\mathbb{Z}^2$ with 8-adjacency, as it is shown in Eckhardt and Latecki [38], for example. Another advantage of treating only well-composed digital pictures is that their digital topological description is much simpler, in particular as regards the Jordan curve theorem and the Euler characteristic. These facts imply that the descriptions of many algorithms used in digital picture processing can become simpler.

As we will show in Section 3.8, the concept of well-composedness extends easily to multicolor digital images (Latecki [94]). The extension of these concepts and results to 3D images is presented in Chapter 5 (Latecki [95]). The advantages of the concept of well-composedness turn out to be even greater for multicolor and 3D images. For example, we proved that the Jordan surface in a well-composed image has properties analog to its 3D continuous original. We present 3D well-composed images in the context of the embedding approach, since the 3D definitions and properties are based on an embedding function which maps 3D digital images to their continuous analogs.

Wang and Bhattacharya [160] extend well-composed pictures from the quadratic grid system to an arbitrary grid system in the plane. They also combine the concept of well-composed pictures with parameter-dependent components, such that each connected component of a well-composed picture may contain pixels of different gray values.

1.2   Axiomatic Approach

A common axiomatic theory that describes both continuous and discrete structures is developed. Certain sets or set relations are required to satisfy certain conditions (axioms), e.g., certain sets are declared to be "open sets". Axioms have to be chosen in such a way that the digital structure is assigned properties that are as close as possible to the corresponding properties of standard topology and geometry. An ideal case is when the resulting properties and definitions coincide with the standard ones in $\mathbb{R}^n$. In this way, all consequences of the axioms are the same independently of either the continuous or the discrete nature of the domain, since if a given digital concept satisfies the same axioms as its continuous analog, then the implied properties are the same. Hence it is not necessary to prove separately for discrete structures each required property of a given digital concept, as is the case in the graph-based approach. In this approach, proofs are based on axioms that describe the continuous as well as discrete structures, while in the graph-based approach, the proofs of discrete properties are based on graph theory. Clearly, graph theory can also be described using axioms. However, in the axiomatic approach the axioms are common for both discrete and continuous representations.

The ideal case is achieved in Latecki and Prokop [102] with respect to the concepts of connectivity, continuity, arcs and simple closed curves. A simple set of axioms for a *semi-proximity* relation is given that applies to continuous as well as discrete domains. Starting with an intuitive concept of "nearness" as a binary relation, semi-proximity spaces are defined. The restrictions on semi-proximity spaces are weaker than the restrictions on topological proximity spaces. Thus, semi-proximity spaces generalize classical topological spaces. Moreover, it is possible to describe the digital pictures with the most common neighborhood structures used in spatial knowledge representation, and in particular in image analysis and computer graphics, as non-trivial semi-proximity spaces, which is not possible in classical topology. Therefore, we will use semi-proximity spaces to establish a formal relationship between the "topological" concepts of image analysis and their continuous counterparts in $\mathbb{R}^n$. Using the semi-proximity relation, connectivity and continuity are defined in such a way that the standard definitions in $\mathbb{R}^n$ are special cases. One of the consequences of the semi-proximity axioms is the fact that continuous functions preserve connectivity. Moreover, an arc and a simple closed curve are defined by exactly the same definitions as in the continuous case: an arc is a homeomorphic image of a closed interval and a simple closed curve is a homeomorphic image of a circle. This implies for example, that deleting a single point disconnects an arc and deleting two different points disconnects a simple closed curve.

Many operations on 2D and 3D digital images are required to *preserve connected components*, which means they are not allowed to split a connected component or to merge two different components while transforming one digital image into another. This implies a one-to-one correspondence between components of the input and output image and their structure. For example, this requirement must be satisfied by any preprocessing step for character recognition, since an object with the structure of "8" should not be transformed into an object with a structure of "o" or "i". Thinning (or shrinking) is a kind of transformation where connected components must be preserved. Thinning a digital set B of black points in a binary picture means deleting a subset $A \subseteq B$, i.e., changing the color of points in A from black to white, with the goal to obtain a "skeleton" of set B. Thinning is a useful operation in image analysis, since in many applications it is computationally cheaper to recognize the structure of a "thinner" image, provided that the thinning algorithm did not change the structure of connected components in the image. Thinning allows for a compact representation of digital objects in the form of their skeletons.

The axiomatic approach allows us to speak about preservation of digital properties under digital transformations. For example, it is enough to show that a given digital transformation is continuous in both directions in order to be guaranteed that it preserves connected components. This fact is used in Latecki and Prokop [102] to show the connectivity preservation of thinning algorithms. The semi-proximity spaces are described in Chapter 4.

The axiomatic approach is also taken in Latecki [92], where digital images are described as so-called character one symmetric semi-topological spaces. Although the semi-proximity spaces defined in [102] as well as semi-topological spaces in [92] generalize topological spaces, they are not topological spaces in the classical sense. If the axioms chosen induce a topology in a discrete structure, then the axiomatic approach is called a topological approach. Kong and Rosenfeld [84] describe a topological approach and compare it to the graph-based approach. We will call the graph-based approach in the sense of [84] embedding approach here, since Kong and Rosenfeld actually describe in their approach embedding of graphs into the Euclidean space.

The topological approach described in [84] is presented in Khalimsky, Kopperman, and Meyer [73]. This approach is based on Alexandroff T_0 discrete spaces [6]. A topological space is an **Alexandroff discrete space** if it additionally satisfies the following axiom:

The intersection of any collection of open sets is open.

Actually, this axiom is a stronger version of the axiom of topological spaces that requires that the intersection of any finite collection of open sets is open. By the stronger intersection axiom, Alexandroff spaces are completely symmetric with respect to open and closed sets (complements of open sets) and there exists for each point a smallest open neighborhood. We additionally require that a topological space be locally finite in order to be discrete, where a space is **locally finite** if each point has a finite open neighborhood.

Khalimsky et al. [73] consider further Alexandroff T_0 discrete spaces that are additionally connected order topological spaces defined in the following way:

A **connected order topological space** *is a connected topological space X such that for any three distinct points $a, b, c \in X$, one of them, say b, separates the other two in the sense that a, c lie in two different components of $X \setminus \{b\}$.*

For example, the real line $\mathbb{R}$ with the usual topology is a connected order topological space. Khalimsky, Kopperman, and Meyer show that there is a unique connected order Alexandroff T_0 discrete topology on $\mathbb{Z}$ and call $\mathbb{Z}$ with this topology a **digital line**. They call $\mathbb{Z}^2$ that is a topological product of two digital lines a **digital plane**. In this approach, an arc is defined as a homeomorphic image of a digital interval, where, for example, a digital interval $[1, 5]$ is simply the set $\{1, 2, ..., 5\}$ with the subset topology of the digital line $\mathbb{Z}$. The definition of a digital simple closed curve is based on the well-known property of the continuous simple closed curve: C is a digital simple closed curve if $C \setminus \{x\}$ is a digital arc for every point $x \in C$. The obtained digital simple closed curve has exactly the same separation properties as its continuous analog. Using this approach Kong, Kopperman, and Meyer [85] give a proof of a 3D digital version of the separation theorem which is based on the continuous Jordan-Brouwer surface theorem.

However, the axioms of the Alexandroff T_0 discrete topology are not satisfied by the standard topology on $\mathbb{R}^n$, since the Alexandroff T_0 discrete topology is not a T_1 topology, for example. Another argument is that the Alexandroff topology cannot be *homogeneous*[4] as is proven in Latecki [92] (p. 49). Intuitively speaking, a topology is homogeneous if every point has the same neighborhood. Clearly, $\mathbb{R}^n$ with the standard topology is a homogeneous space. We also show that there is no Alexandroff topology on $\mathbb{Z}^2$ where every point has the same neighborhood. $\mathbb{Z}^2$ in which every point has the same neighborhood is the most natural graph structure in image analysis, since in a digital picture, which is a finite subset of $\mathbb{Z}^2$, the adjacency relations are not represented explicitly (e.g. as edges of a graph), but they are implicitly induced by the spatial arrangements of the points in the picture. In the digital plane defined in [73], [85] the points of $\mathbb{Z}^2$ have three different neighborhood types. Therefore, for image processing in this plane, special algorithms must be developed. This plane was independently introduced in Kovalevsky [90], where also image processing algorithms designed specially for this structure were presented.

An interesting interpretation of the Alexandroff T_0 discrete topology on $\mathbb{Z}^2$ is obtained if one considers subsets of the plane as topological points. The resulting, so-called cellular topology is based on the subdivision of the plane into cells: open squares, line segments without their endpoints (which are sides of the squares), and points (which are corners of the squares), as illustrated in Figure 1.6. The smallest neighborhood of each cell in this topology is the smallest open set in the standard Euclidean topology that contains this cell. For example, open squares are (the only) one-point open sets in this topology. This topology was presented in Alexandroff and Hopf [7] already in 1935.

Sometimes it can be useful to combine two different approaches to define continuous analogs of digital concepts. Kong and Khalimsky [81] use a combination of an axiomatic approach and an embedding approach. The presented axioms of the locally finite Alexandroff topology ([73], [85]) introduce a topological structure into a special class of locally finite graphs. In [81], a polyhedral analog for this topology is defined which is based on the cellular topology illustrated in Figure 1.6 for the 2D case. As the result, they obtain an embedding of the special class of locally finite graphs into the real plane and space.

---

[4]A topology on X is **homogeneous** if any two points in X have homeomorphic neighborhoods.

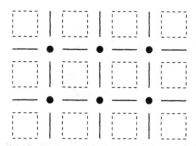

Figure 1.6: The cellular topology is based on the subdivision of the plane into cells: open squares, line segments without their endpoints (which are sides of the squares), and points (which are corners of the squares).

1.3 Embedding Approach

In this approach, a discrete structure is embedded into a known continuous structure, usually Euclidean space. Formally, the embedding is a mapping which assigns to a discrete structure a subset of Euclidean space, called a **continuous analog**. In this way, properties of discrete objects can be defined by means of their continuous analogs, e.g., a digital set is a simple closed curve if its continuous analog is a simple closed curve in the usual sense of classical topology. Using this approach it is also possible to define digital concepts in graph theory, and then to show that their continuous analogs have the same properties. If we model real objects or their 2D projections as subsets of the plane, then we can directly relate a continuous analog of a digital object to the underlying continuous object using the standard topological tools in the plane. In particular, it then makes sense to speak about homotopy equivalence between real objects and their digital versions. For example, a digital object has a hole iff (if and only if) its continuous analog has a hole.

This approach was first applied in Kong and Roscoe [80], where the Jordan-Brouwer surface theorem is proven for various digital adjacency relations. Kong [77] defines digital fundamental groups and shows that a digital fundamental group of a digital set is the same as the fundamental group of a continuous analog of the digital set. We illustrate Kong's approach in the 2D case following Kong and Rosenfeld [82]. Kong associates a set of black points in a binary digital picture P with a polyhedral subset of the plane $C(P)$, called a continuous analog of P. For example, for an (8, 4) digital picture P, where black points are 8-adjacent and white points are 4-adjacent, $C(P)$ is the union of the following polygons (see Figure 1.7):

1. A closed line segment pq is assigned to two 8-adjacent black digital points p and q.

2. A closed triangle pqr is assigned to three 8-adjacent black digital points p, q, and r.

3. A closed square $pqrs$ is assigned to four 8-adjacent black digital points p, q, r, and s.

It is easy to observe that an (8, 4) digital picture P is connected (i.e., the set of its black points is 8-connected) iff $C(P)$ is a connected subset of the plane. Eckhardt proposed

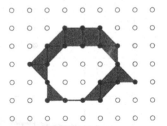

Figure 1.7: Kong's continuous analog of an (8, 4) digital picture.

an embedding approach which is based on line complexes. It is presented in Eckhardt and Latecki [38].

A different embedding approach is used in Gross and Latecki [55] to relate properties of digital output images to real input objects that are represented as continuous sets. While Kong identifies digital points with corners of squares, triangles, or line segments in the polyhedral analog, we identify digital points with the center points of squares that form a uniform cover of the plane. Consequently, a digital picture is identified with a union of squares in the continuous analog. Figure 1.8 shows the continuous analog of the same digital picture that we used to demonstrate Kong's analog (Figure 1.7). Thus, for a 2D digital picture $(\mathbf{Z}^2, S)$, a set of black pixels S is mapped onto a union of closed unit squares centered at points of S, which we denote $CA(S)$. The continuous analog $CA(S)$ formalized a natural interpretation of binary digital pictures. This approach was also applied in Pavlidis [120], for example.

We assume that either S or S^c is finite and nonempty. A **(face) boundary** $bdCA(S)$ of $CA(S)$ is defined as the union of the set of unit line segments each of which is the common edge of a square in $CA(S)$ and a square in the complement of $CA(S)$. Thus, $bdCA(S) = bdCA(S^c)$. Observe that there is only one kind of adjacency for $bdCA(S)$: two segments are adjacent if they have an endpoint in common. Hence, there is also only one kind of connectedness for $bdCA(S)$. It can be easily proven that a digital picture $(\mathbf{Z}^2, X)$ is well-composed iff $bdCA(X)$ is a compact 1D manifold (i.e., each point in $bdCA(X)$ has a neighborhood homeomorphic to $\mathbb{R}$). For instance, the digital picture in Figure 1.8 is well-composed.

In a similar way, an embedding function which maps 3D digital images to their continuous analogs is defined in Latecki [95], where black points of a 3D digital image are mapped to closed unit cubes of which they are center points. The obtained continuous analog is used to define 3D well-composed images and to prove their properties, like the Jordan-Brouwer separation theorem. We describe this 3D approach in Chapter 5. The 2D and 3D embedding approaches will play an important role in Chapter 7, since an embedding can be regarded as a dual mapping to a digitization mapping in the sense that it maps discrete objects to continuous objects.

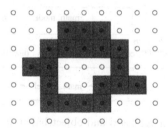

Figure 1.8: The continuous analog in which digital points are mapped to the squares of which they are centers.

1.4 Digitization Approach

A continuous object is mapped to some discrete graph structure. This mapping models in most cases some digitization process. In this approach, it is possible to show that if a digital set has a certain property, then there exists a continuous set with the same property which digitizes to the digital set. One can also directly define a digital property by stipulating that a digital set has a certain property if it is a digital image of some continuous set having the same property, provided a sufficient resolution of the digitization process.

We are interested in comparison of features of a segmented object in the digital image to the features of the underlying continuous object. In computer vision, there are well-known sampling theorems which relate a continuous signal representing spatial objects to a digital signal obtained by a digitization process (see Figure 1.9, upper part). The main concern of these theorems is the sampling rate that allows one to recover the underlying continuous signal from the digital signal. The sampling models are mostly based on Fourier or other transforms that transform signals to frequency spaces. Although frequency spaces are suitable to perform many useful image measurements and processing operations, it is an extremely complicated and mostly unsolved task to recover shape features from the Fourier transform and other frequency space transforms; for example, one of the most basic structural shape properties, connectedness, cannot be represented in the Fourier space.

We model a digitization process by a direct relation between a continuous object and a segmented object in the digital image (see Figure 1.9, lower part). This approach allows us to avoid tedious details of signal analysis. Due to this object based approach, we can directly compare the features of a continuous object and its digital image. This kind of the interpretation of digitization processes for relating topological properties is used in Pavlidis [120], Serra [140], Gross and Latecki [55], and Latecki et al. [106].

This approach has also been used in digital geometry. For example, a digital set is defined to be a digital straight line if there exists a real straight line which digitizes to the digital set. Rosenfeld [127] formulated a chord property and showed that a digital set is a digital straight line iff it satisfies the chord property. There are many algorithms and theoretical considerations which define digital lines (e.g., Debled and Reveilles [32], Dorst and Smeulders [34], [143], Freeman [45], Koplowitz and Sundar Raj [87], Koplowitz and Bruckstein [88], and Rosenfeld and Kim [134]). However, the digital lines obtained using

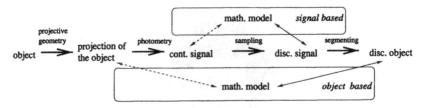

Figure 1.9: A comparison of signal based and object based approaches to relating spatial objects and their digital images.

object boundary quantization as a model of the digitization process have gained the most attention in the literature and, as a result, have been the most thoroughly studied. Yet, this model, although adequate for computer graphics, is not an adequate model of the digitization process for picture processing. In Chapter 7, we show that the results and algorithms for object boundary quantization are also valid if we assume a much more realistic digitization model that handles both blurring and arbitrary thresholding. In Chapter 7 we introduce conditions that guarantee that a real object and its digital image are topologically equivalent.

An important and common property of a continuous simple closed curve and a digital simple closed curve is that their connectivity is destroyed by the removal of any two points (see the definitions in Chapter 2). In Agrawal et al. [2] the question of preservation of this property under a digitization process is addressed. A necessary and sufficient condition on continuous simple closed curves and on the resolution of a square grid is given such that this property is preserved under intersection digitization (for a definition see Section 7.1). Furthermore, it is shown that for a simple closed curve with a finite number of extrema, there exists a fine enough square grid such that the digital image of the curve contains only one digital simple closed 4-curve; and this holds for all translations of the grid except for a set of measure zero.

In order to study the topological equivalence of a real continuous object and its digitization, which is a finite set of points, some preliminaries are in order. It is intuitively clear that the real object in Figure 1.10.a and the digital object in Figure 1.10.b have the "same topological structure". Based on the technical properties of sampling devices like a CCD camera, digital points representing sensor output are generally assumed to form a square grid and are modeled as points with integer coordinates located in the plane $\mathbb{R}^2$. By a digitization process, these points are assigned some gray-level or color values. By a segmentation process, the digital points are grouped to form digital objects. For example, the digital points are grouped by thresholding gray-level values with some threshold value, i.e., the pixels whose gray-level values are greater than some given threshold value are classified as belonging to a digital object (i.e., assigned the color black). As an output of a digitization and segmentation process, we obtain a binary digital picture $Dig(X)$ with black points representing the digital object X and white points representing the background.

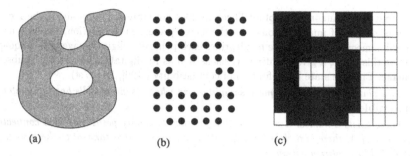

(a)   (b)   (c)

Figure 1.10: (a) A real object (represented as a subset of the plane) and its digital (discrete) representation.

Yet, it is impossible to directly compare the input object X, that is modeled as a subset of the plane, with its digital image $Dig(X)$. To make this comparison possible, we use the embedding approach. We map the digital image $Dig(X)$ to its continuous analog $CA(Dig(X))$, i.e., we identify each black point with a square centered at this point (in such a way that the squares form a uniform cover of the plane). A digital object is then represented as a union of squares which form a subset of the plane. For example, the digital set in Figure 1.10.b, a finite subset of $\mathbf{Z}^2$, is identified with the union of black squares in Figure 1.10.c, a subset of $\mathbb{R}^2$. Therefore, it makes sense to speak about topological equivalence between a real object (Figure 1.10.a) and its digital image (Figure 1.10.c). Thus, the digitization (and segmentation) process is modeled as a mapping from continuous 2D sets representing real objects to discrete sets represented as finite subsets of $\mathbf{Z}^2$, which are identified with their continuous analogs in $\mathbb{R}^2$ (finite unions of squares). Consequently, we can relate topological properties of a continuous 2D object (e.g., a projection of a 3D object) to its digital image interpreted as the union of squares centered at black points.

Serra [140] considered many kinds of digitizations. He showed that, for a certain class of planar sets, digitizations preserve homotopy. He proved this only for digitizations in hexagonal grids, where a digitization of a set A in $\mathbb{R}^2$ is the set of points in $\mathbf{Z}^2$ which are contained in A. To show non-trivial problems connected with digitizations, Serra gave the following title to one of the sections: *"To digitize is not as easy as it looks"* ([140], p. 211).

Pavlidis [120] was primarily interested in digitizations based on the square sampling grid, since ([120], p.36): *"The most common grid used in picture processing is the square grid consisting of square cells arranged as a chessboard."* His starting point was the Shannon's Sampling Theorem, which is well-known in signal processing. This theorem allows us to determine a size of the sampling interval, and thus a sampling frequency minimum, such that a continuous signal can be reconstructed from its samples. Pavlidis was interested in determining the size of the squares of the sampling grid that guarantees a reconstruction of the "shapes" of image regions ([120], Chapter 7, p. 129):

"The size of the cells of the sampling grid must be small enough so that the shapes of regions of a given color remain unaltered in reconstructing the image."

Note that the Shannon's Sampling Theorem does not state anything about the reconstruction of shapes of image regions. As the shape preservation criterion, Pavlidis used topological homeomorphism. Since he identifies each point of a digital image with a square centered at this point, a given continuous set as well as its digital image are both subsets of the plane. First we state his definition of compatibility ([120], Def. 7.4):

A closed planar set A and a square sampling grid whose (square) cells have diameter h are **compatible** *if:*

(a) There exists a number d > h such that for each boundary point x of each connected component R of A, there is a closed ball C with diameter d that is tangent to the boundary of R at x and lies entirely within R.

(b) The same is also true for the closure of the complement of A.

For example, both sets shown in Figure 1.11 are compatible with the square sampling grid. Using this definition, Pavlidis stated the following theorem ([120], Theorem 7.1):

For a planar set A, the condition of compatibility implies that A and its digitization are topologically equivalent (i.e., homeomorphic).

It is not clearly stated which digitization process is used in Pavlidis' Theorem 7.1. This theorem holds for the square grid version of the digitization model used by Serra [140], where the grid squares chosen to represent a planar set A are the squares whose centers lie in A. However, this way only a special case of a digitization process is modeled.

We consider a more general class of digitization models that are more relevant to practical applications. Consistent with real sensor output of a device like a CCD camera, a digitization is defined with respect to a grid of squares, where each square has the diagonal length r. Associated with the center of each square is a sensor. The value of the sensor output depends on the ratio of the area of the object in the square to the total area of the square. As an output of a digitization process, we obtain a gray-level (or color) digital picture with values of the pixels (picture elements) representing the values of the corresponding sensors. We assume that the gray-level values assigned to the sensors are monotonic with respect to the area of the continuous object in the sensor square. This is a standard model of the digitization process of a real CCD camera in picture processing, which is described in Pavlidis [120], for example. Of course, the image generation process of a real CCD camera is more complicated; CCD cameras consist of sensor cells which measure e.g. reflectance properties via space-time integrals, while we integrate over the image function in the squares corresponding to the sensors (Section 7.9). We also do not consider the digitization noise, but we incorporate a blurring function like Gaussian blur into our model (Section 7.10). In Section 7.12 we give experimental results supporting this digitization model.

We assume that pixels in the gray-level image are segmented to form digital objects by thresholding gray-level values with some threshold value, i.e., the pixels whose gray-level values are greater than some given threshold value are classified as belonging to a digital object (i.e., assigned a black color). Segmenting objects under this model corresponds to coloring an image point black if the ratio of the area of the object in a square centered at this point to the area of the entire square is greater than some threshold value. This is a standard model of the digitization and segmentation process for CCD cameras if we exclude digitization errors.

If we use this digitization and segmentation model, then Pavlidis' theorem is not true, as shown in the following examples. Let A be a strip of width d, where $2h > d > h$, forming a 45° angle with the square grid, as illustrated in Figure 1.11.a. A square p is black iff $area(p \cap A)/area(p) > 0.99$ and white otherwise. Then the digitization of strip A represented by the black squares is a digital 8-line, which is not homeomorphic to strip A. Note, however, that A and its digitization are homotopy equivalent. This is not the case for our second example illustrated in Figure 1.11.b, where a square p is black iff $area(p \cap A)/area(p) > 0$ and white otherwise. Here set A is not even homotopy equivalent to its digitization, represented by black squares, since A is simply connected, but its digitization is not (there is a white "hole" in it).

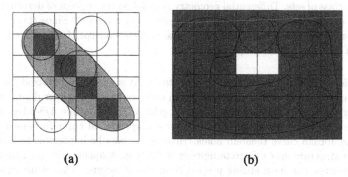

(a)   (b)

Figure 1.11: The two sets shown are compatible with the square sampling grid. However, the set and its digitization represented by the black squares are not homeomorphic in (a) and not homotopy equivalent in (b).

In Chapter 7 we present our digitization approach in greater detail. We derive conditions relating properties of real objects to the digitization resolution, i.e., the length of diagonal of a square in the square grid, which guarantee that a real object and its digital image are topologically equivalent. Loosely speaking, we show that if we double the diameter of the tangent ball used by Pavlidis, then a continuous object and its digital image will be topologically equivalent. Since we did not see how the proof of Pavlidis' theorem can imply this fact, we developed new proof methods presented in Chapter 7.

These conditions also guarantee the topological equivalence of any two digital images of a given object. Hence transformations of the camera or of the object, like translations, rotations, and reflections, will not change the topological properties of the resulting digital images. These conditions additionally allow us to determine the scaling factor such that the scaled image and the original image have the same topology. We also show that an output digital image must be well-composed if the resolution of the digitization process is fine enough to guarantee topology preservation.

1.5   Continuous Representations of Real Objects

For the digitization approach, it is necessary to explicitly characterize continuous representations of real objects, since they will be mapped to discrete representations by functions modeling digitization processes. Thus, continuous representations of real objects are the starting point for the digitization approach. Therefore, in Chapter 6 we describe the classes of continuous sets that will be used in Chapter 7 as input to digitization functions.

In Section 6.1 we define parallel regular sets, which model real objects and their 2D projections in the way commonly accepted in computer vision as subsets of $\mathbb{R}^3$ and $\mathbb{R}^2$ with "smooth" boundaries. However, we will not use the classical tools of differential geometry to define this class of sets. Differential geometry is based on the concept of derivative, which requires the calculation of limits of infinite sequences of numbers. Since this calculation cannot be transfered into discrete spaces, no analog of the concept of derivative in discrete spaces exists that has similar properties.

The considerations in Section 1.1 demonstrate that it is necessary to introduce a special graph structure into a discrete representation in order to ensure a proper digital analog of a continuous concept. For example, a square grid with changeable 4/8-adjacency or a well-composed graph allows for the definition of a simple closed curve for which a digital version of the Jordan curve theorem holds. However, it may be impossible to introduce a special graph structure into a discrete representation, e.g., a square grid, such that a given continuous concept can have analog properties in this structure. This is the case for the concept of derivative, for instance.

We give now another example for the concept of local convexity. In image analysis it is often useful to decide whether a region could be convex, given only an image of part of its boundary (due to occlusions). A set S is *convex* if for every pair of points $P, Q \in S$, the line segment PQ is contained in S. Convexity is a central concept in geometry which is used in many practical applications, since every set can be described, at least locally, in terms of convex sets. Thus, a digital version of the characterization of parts of the boundaries of convex sets could have many applications in digital image analysis. In the continuous case, a region S with boundary B can be simply defined to be convex if every point of B has a neighborhood $\mathcal{N}$ such that $S \cap \mathcal{N}$ is convex. This definition is based on the well known fact (Tietze [152]) that a planar set S is convex iff every boundary point of S has a convex neighborhood. However, this definition cannot be used in discrete structures, since in the discrete case the concept of local convexity does not characterize boundaries of convex sets as it does in the continuous case. We illustrate this for the digital set S in Figure 1.12, where for every boundary point P of S, S intersects the 8-neighborhood (i.e., 3×3 neighborhood) of P in a digitally convex set, but evidently S is not digitally convex.

The 8-neighborhood of each boundary point in S is convex by all definitions of digital convexity given in Voss [159], and it is even digitally linear (see Figure 7.21), in the sense that it is a legal digital image of a continuous half-plane obtained by the intersection digitization, as proven in Theorem 7.12. The intersection digitization will be defined in Section 7.1. Similar examples can be given for other digital neighborhoods.

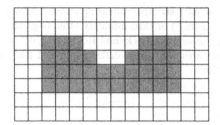

Figure 1.12: Tietze's theorem does not hold in the digital case: Every boundary point of the illustrated set S has a digitally convex 8-neighborhood in S, but evidently S is not digitally convex.

Since not every continuous property can be satisfied by a given graph structure, due to its discrete nature, it is thus necessary to determine properties of continuous concepts which can also apply to digital domains. For example, it is necessary to look for continuous characterizations of parts of boundaries of convex sets that can also apply to digital domains. In Section 6.2 (Latecki et al. [99]), we define a concept of CP_3 convexity that characterizes parts of the boundaries of convex sets. This concept promises to characterize parts of the boundaries of digitally convex sets as well, but we have not yet established analogs of CP_3 properties for digital images.

There are a number of approaches for generalizing convexity to discrete structures (e.g., see Voss [159]). One class of generalizations of convexity, due to Valentine [154], makes use of triples (or k-tuples), rather than pairs, of points. A set satisfies Valentine's property P_3 if for every triple of points P, Q, R of S, at least one of the line segments PQ, QR, or RP is contained in S. For example, a polygonal arc consisting of two non-collinear line segments is not convex, but is easily seen to have property P_3. It can be shown that if a set has property P_3, it is a union of at most three convex sets.

In Section 6.2 (based on Latecki et al. [99]) we study a property closely related to, but weaker than, P_3. We say that S has *property CP_3* ("collinear P_3") if P_3 holds for all *collinear* triples of points of S. This property turns out to characterize parts of the boundaries of convex sets; in fact, we prove that a closed curve is the boundary of a convex set, and a simple arc is part of the boundary of a convex set, iff they have property CP_3. This result appears to be the first simple characterization of parts of the boundaries of convex sets; it solves a problem studied over 30 years ago by Menger [112] and Valentine [155]. For arcs and closed curves, convexity is a very strong property; in fact, a closed curve or a nonsimple arc cannot be convex, and a simple arc is convex iff it is a straight line segment. Our weaker property CP_3, on the other hand, is shown in Section 6.2 to define very useful classes of arcs and curves.

The CP_3 property is a useful tool in Section 6.3, where we introduce *supported sets*. As stated in Latecki and Rosenfeld [104], requiring the boundaries of continuous sets to be differentiable may be too restrictive, since this excludes polygons, which are not differentiable at their vertices. A somewhat better idea is to require differentiability at all but a finite number of points; but this is not restrictive enough, because it allows arcs that can oscillate (e.g., the graph of function $x \sin \frac{1}{x}$) or turn infinitely often (e.g., the inward-turning spiral illustrated in Figure 1.13). Based on Latecki and Rosenfeld [104], we define in Section 6.3 classes of continuous planar arcs and curves called supported and tame sets that exclude all of these pathological cases.

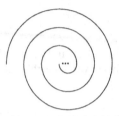

Figure 1.13: An inward-turning spiral that turns infinitely often.

1.6   Applications

Now we present some important applications in which to ensure correct outputs of algorithms, it is necessary to relate properties of discrete representations to the corresponding properties of their continuous originals. To these properties, the separability of the digital plane or space belongs as described in the Jordan curve theorem or the Jordan-Brouwer separation theorem. The separability property describes the correct behavior of such concepts as: simple closed (Jordan) curves, simple closed (Jordan) surfaces, connectivity, interior points, boundary points, and boundaries. In addition to these topological concepts, such geometric concepts as linearity, convexity, and concavity play a key role in these applications.

As argumented above, the analysis of geometric properties directly in digital representations is not only very useful in computer vision but also in general in spatial knowledge representation. Thus, we give not only examples of spatial inferences on digital representations in image analysis but also in GIS (Geographic Information Systems), CAD, and robot navigation systems.

- In computer vision and computer graphics, the boundaries of segmented objects are often used to store digital images, i.e., instead of storing each pixel of an image by specifying its color, it is sufficient to store boundary pixels and specify uniformly the colors for the insides and outsides. This procedure leads to very significant compression of memory usage. If each connected component of the object boundary forms a simple closed curve, then the Jordan curve theorem implies the correctness of the boundary encoding by such procedures. The Jordan curve theorem states that every simple closed curve separates the plane into two connected components. Digital versions of the Jordan theorem and its higher dimensional generalizations are proved, for example, in Rosenfeld [129], Morgenthaler and Rosenfeld [116], Kong and Roscoe [79, 80], Stout [149], Khalimsky et al. [73], Rosenfeld et al. [136], Herman [64], and Latecki [95] (Chapter 5).

- Discrete representations are used in robot navigation to represent the bird's eye view of robot's 2D environment map, e.g., see Figure 1.14. For example, a raster representation that realizes a configuration space of a surrounding physical environment (intrduced by Lozano-Pères [108]) is called digitized configuration space in Dean et al. [31], p. 283. The intrinsic spatial properties of raster representations with respect to object distances and directions allows to design simple and reliable processes for registration of sensor readings and for path planning in a raster representation of the environment (see Elfes [40]). Consequently, many autonomus robots use raster structures to represent their environment (e.g., robots RHINO [19] and MACROBE [13]).

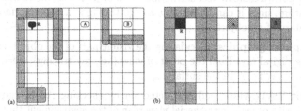

Figure 1.14: (b) a digital representation of the robot environment in (a).

The digital version of the Jordan curve theorem is also relevant in robot navigation. As stated in the description of the graph-based approach, it is not sufficient to define a digital concept, but it is additionally necessary to specify the graph structure of the digital plane in which this concept should have analog properties to its continuous original. This graph structure plays a key role in the pictorial representation of spatial knowledge, where spatial properties of represented objects are automatically inherited from the structure in which they are represented.

For example, let us assume that in a robot's spatial imagery a bird's eye view of a terrain map is given as a square grid in which the objects are identified. The task of the robot is to bring a box from its actual location to a location that is surrounded by a fence that the robot cannot cross over. The robot ought to know that his task cannot be achieved. To infer this, it is enough for the robot to identify that its starting and goal locations do not belong to the same connected component. This can be done by a connected component labeling algorithm, presupposing that the discrete representation of the fence separates the robot's digital imagery into two components. To infer this, it is necessary that the Jordan curve theorem holds in the robot's digital imagery if the pixels representing the fence form a simple closed curve. Note that the robot need not have explicit knowledge about the Jordan curve theorem.

The situation is similar in natural language understanding. Habel [61] proposes to group discrete objects that represent natural language spatial phrases to form connected paths which, in particular, can have the Jordan curve property. This property makes possible to understand sentences that describe complicated spatial relations like *"The policemen encircled the house"* (Eckhardt and Latecki [38]). If an automatic reasoning system is to be capable of understanding this sentence, then it must also understand that it is impossible to leave the house without meeting a policeman. This will be the case if the set of policemen is represented as a Jordan curve, and the representing digital space enables us to separate the house from the remainder of the world by this curve (unless one is able to move in three dimensions).

- In summary, if the Jordan curve (surface) theorem does not hold in a discrete representation, then, for example, the following processes will not yield the expected results:

  1. **Data compression:** reconstruction of an object from its boundary by a fill in algorithm, since it can be possible to "go through" a curve/surface which is the boundary of an object.

  2. **Computer graphics:** calculating the visible part of the object surface by emanating digital rays from the point of view (i.e., ray tracing), since a ray can "go through" a "hole" in the surface.

  3. **Robot navigation:** collision detection by checking the overlapping of robot routes with objects in the aerial view plan of the environment that is represented in a pictorial format, e.g., as a 2D square grid using idealized objects.

- Classification of points in a digital set as either interior or boundary points, and the definition of boundaries, can be used to justify correctness of surface tracking algorithms. Such a classification is particularly important in 3D medical imaging. For example, Kong and Udupa [86] proved correctness of a surface tracking algorithm, which is used to display a surface of a 3D object on a 2D screen in medicine and engineering. The correct behavior of this algorithm had only been conjectured, but observed nonetheless, in all uses.

  Once digital object boundaries are identified, their differential geometric properties can be extracted using, for example, local difference operators, which are assumed to recover the $n - th$ order derivatives of surfaces of real objects. To ensure that differential geometric properties recovered by the difference operators correspond to the properties of surfaces of real objects, it is necessary to relate these properties of discrete representations to the corresponding properties of their continuous originals. Further, this relation allows us to determine the required resolution of the discrete representation such that the invariance of the differential geometric properties is guaranteed.[5]

- Pictorial inferences are also used in natural language understanding (Habel [59]). Given a natural language description of a spatial situation, a digital representation is

---

[5]This example was suggested to the author by Prof. Siegfried Stiehl, University of Hamburg.

first generated, and subseqently, in the inspection phase, questions can be answered. For example, in Latecki and Pribbenow [96] it is shown that the connectedness relation is necessary to interpret the proposition *near* in contexts like the following:

"The Chinese pavilion is *in front of* the river, a dragon sculpture is *to the left of* the pavilion, and there is a café *on the other side of* the river."

In this context, the most likely negative answer to the question

"Is the café *near* the pavilion?"

follows from the fact that the *river* separates the *café* from the *pavilion*, i.e., the *café* and the *pavilion* are in two different connected components with respect to the *river*. Pictorial inferences are very suitable to derive this answer, since it is relatively easy to inspect such properties of digital representations as connected components and separability, which play an important role in the interpretation of spatial expressions. In the generation phase, prototypical digital objects in a bird's eye representation are used. For example, to answer the above question, we need digital models of a *river, café*, and *pavilion* which represent the relevant shape properties. In this case, it is necessary that a *river* prototype divide the raster representation in two connected components and that the relative size proportions of such digital prototypes are realistic.

- Topology can be seen as an invariance theory of continuous functions. Continuous functions have no direct counterparts in discrete structures. However, it seems to be useful for many applications to have such a concept as "discrete continuity". Two different versions of discrete continuity are defined in Rosenfeld [131] and in Latecki and Prokop [102] (Chapter 4). By means of a suitable definition of continuity, one is able to compare topological structures with each other, and thus, one is able to speak about digital invariance of such properties like connectedness. Another important topological invariant is the Euler number. This is, in a certain sense, the only digital invariant which can be decided locally, i.e., in parallel (Minsky and Papert [114]). This invariant has been used to prove the correctness of topology preserving thinning algorithms.

- In character recognition, letters in a document can be classified according to their topological homotopy types. Optical checking of computer chips involves determining if the chip layout has the desired homotopy type. Homotopy theory deals with properties which are invariant under continuous deformations. Translating homotopy from general topology to discrete structures raises a number of questions which have not yet been resolved in a satisfactory manner. However, there are interesting new approaches to homotopy in discrete structures, e.g., Boxer [17] defines homotopy directly for a square grid and its higher dimensional versions based on a discrete version of continuity given in Rosenfeld [131]. A definition of homotopy that is more flexible can be obtained if we base Boxer's definition on that of digital continuity defined in Latecki and Prokop [102] (Chapter 4). In Gross and Latecki [55] the classical continuous homotopy is applied to the continuous analog of a digital image obtained by modeling a digitization process (Chapter 7).

- Since there exists a large number of large databases with digital images and this number continues to grow, the application of search engines that can automatically extract relevant information about each image becomes necessary. In order to extract this information, digital image search engines must be used to annotate the image with respect to shape of digital objects, color, texture and symmetry properties. Since these databases contain images of many different kinds of spatial objects (e.g., multimedia databases on the Internet), search engines must be used that can extract, among other things, domain-independent universal shape properties of spatial objects. There are many different approaches to describe and extract shape properties of spatial objects in computer vision. However, most of them are domain specific in the sense that their application requires the specification of a set of object parameters, e.g., parametric models such as superquadrics and generalized cylinders.

Digital representations allow us to develop domain independent, universal geometric shape features of spatial objects that can be used as parts of image search engines. The structural non-parametric shape descriptions of digital representations can be based on digital geometry. Digital geometry is a theory of shape properties of objects in digital images, and therefore, it provides a suitable basis for domain-independent shape models as it describes geometric shape properties on the pixel level. Digital geometry has been developed in parallel to digital pattern recognition as a formal implementation-independent theory of geometric shape properties. Consequently, there exist digital definitions of most geometric concepts like connected components, lines, convexity, and so on (e.g., Kong and Rosenfeld [82], Melter et al. [111], Voss [159]). There also exist methods to estimate the curvature directly in discrete data (e.g., Rosenfeld and Kak [133], Worring and Smeulders [162]). The subject which has been most thoroughly studied and which plays a primary role is the identification of digital line segments. There are many tasks in image analysis that require the identification of straight line segments in a given digital image, like analysis of technical drawings and identification of man-made objects in satellite images. Some tasks additionally require the recovery of the space of real straight lines (the slope and translation) which digitize to a given digital line segment. Understanding digital lines comprises two components:

  i) determining whether a given digital set is a digital line segment, i.e., whether there exists a real straight line in $\mathbb{R}^2$ that digitizes to it, and

  ii) recovering the space of straight lines.

- In the latest development of image analysis, neural networks are frequently used to recover some of the shape properties of digital objects, which are represented in finite graph structures. It is important that this neural representation ensures the analog properties of digital concepts. For example, the definitions of digital straight lines are used as a basis for designing perceptrons for the recognition of digital straight lines in Veelaert [157]. Already back in 1969 Minsky and Papert [114] discussed the recognition of topological properties by perceptrons.

- We give now an example showing that in Geographic Information Systems (known as GIS, e.g., Frank and Kuhn [44]), it is useful to map a continuous representation of spatial objects, e.g., a vector representation of occluding polygons, to a discrete representation, e.g., a square grid. (In a *vector representation*, object boundaries are described with coordinates of boundary points.) To determine the required resolution of this digitization mapping, it is necessary to relate properties of discrete representations to the corresponding properties of their continuous originals. The problem of the resolution of the digital representation in GIS is discussed in Burrough [20], Chapter 6. A correct estimation of the required resolution is also important in model based remote sensing of aerial images.

  A commonly used operation in GIS is to compute the intersection of two (or more) spatial objects (see e.g., Faltings [42]). We assume a geographic information system in which spatial objects are represented by polygons, e.g., the coordinates of the vectors that represent the polygonal line segments are given. If we compute the intersection of two polygons A and B in a propositional formalism, then we solve for every pair of vectors, one from A and one from B, an equation system to determine their intersection point. Thus, if polygon A is represented by n vectors and B m vectors, then nm equations must be solved, which requires quadratic time in the number of vectors. However, it may be possible to reduce the time complexity by applying some sorting algorithms.

  On the other hand, if we represent the polygons directly in an intrinsically spatial structure like a square grid, then we can find the intersection polygon of polygons A and B directly, by inspecting each point of the grid. In this representation each point (cell) of the grid is assigned a set of labels indicating to which object it belongs, e.g., point with coordinates $(3,5)$ belongs to polygon A and point with coordinates $(14,5)$ belongs to polygon A as well as to B, an so on. This spatial representation lends itself quite naturally to algorithms that involve common sense reasoning, analogous to methods used by humans in diagram construction and inspection. For example, a diagram representing the two polygons is shown in Figure 1.15. Since in a square grid, each cell contains information about which objects it belongs to, each cell must be inspected only one time. Thus, the inspection of this representation can be done in a constant time determined by the number of grid points. Moreover, the inspection can be done in parallel for each cell separately in just one step. Hence, in a pictorial representation, we can solve the intersection problem in linear time, since only linear time (of order $m + n$ with respect to the number of vectors) is required to digitize the polygons to the square grid. This example also illustrates the process of pictorial reasoning. Pictorial inferences are divided into two phases. In the first, *generation phase*, spatial configurations of the objects under consideration are generated. In the second, *inspection phase*, these configurations are verified by means of inspection processes. These two phases can also be applied simultaneously, i.e., while generating an object, check if the required properties hold.

- In GIS, CAD, and navigation systems, both raster representations as well as analytical vector representations of spatial objects are used. Therefore, one of the main tasks of

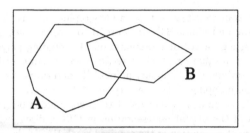

Figure 1.15: A diagram representing polygons A and B.

GIS and CAD systems is conversion between vector and raster representations (Star and Estes [145]).

The idealized digitization (relation R_1) is used for vector to raster conversion, and feature extraction from idealized digital models is necessary for raster to vector conversion. For example, vector to raster conversion is obtained by digitizing the curves in Figure 1.16(a) to the "stair-step" digital curves in Figure 1.16(c). A result of a raster to vector conversion of the digital curves by joining midpoints of occupied raster squares is illustrated by Figure 1.16(d). Thus, the application of vector to raster conversion followed by raster to vector conversion leads, among others, to the loss of the feature of linearity, which characterizes the straight line in Figure 1.16(a). If we can recover features that characterize subsets of the raster that can be images of real straight lines and ensure that the digitization process preserves these features, then the features of linearity can be used for raster to vector conversion which is capable of recovering the straight lines. This example illustrates that correct extraction of geometric features from digital representation is important for as accurate as possible raster to vector conversion in GIS.

The situation regarding topological features is analogous: For example, the two continuous lines in Figure 1.16(a) do not intersect, but their digital images in Figure 1.16(c) have a common point x. The reason is that there exists a raster square that intersects both curves, due to the size of the raster squares. This fact again implies that the reconstructed vector representation in Figure 1.16(d) is connected, while the original curves in Figure 1.16(a) are disconnected. From this example, it follows that correct extraction of topological and geometric features from digital representation depends on the resolution of the digital representation (i.e., size of raster squares).

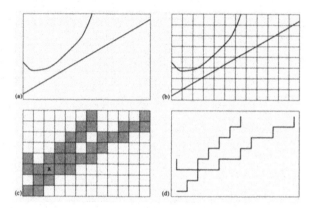

Figure 1.16: Vector–raster conversion: (a) → (c). A raster–vector conversion: (c) → (d).

Chapter 2

Basic Definitions and Propositions

2.1 Digital Concepts

In this section we review some definitions from digital topology and geometry mostly following Rosenfeld [129] and Kong and Rosenfeld [82]. Unless explicitly stated otherwise, we consider $\mathbf{Z}^2$ as the set of points with integer coordinates in the plane $\mathbb{R}^2$, and similarly $\mathbf{Z}^3$ as the set of points with integer coordinates in space $\mathbb{R}^3$ As usual we assume that all sets are subsets of a **digital plane** $\mathbf{Z}^2$ or a **digital space** $\mathbf{Z}^3$ with some adjacency (neighborhood) relations which are defined below.

A pair $(\mathbf{Z}^i, \lambda)$, where $i = 2, 3, \ldots$ will be called a **segmented (or multicolor) digital picture** if λ is a function from $\mathbf{Z}^i$ to some finite label space Λ assigning a unique label (i.e., color) to each point in $\mathbf{Z}^i$.

Given a specific color $\kappa \in \Lambda$, the set of points having color κ is denoted by X_κ, i.e., $X_\kappa = \{p \in \mathbf{Z}^i : \lambda(p) = \kappa\}$. We assume that for every color $\kappa \in \Lambda$, either X_κ or its complement X_κ^c is finite and nonempty. If we concentrate on properties of points of a certain color κ, then X_κ will be termed $(\kappa\text{-})$**foreground**, while the set of all points in the complement will be termed $(\kappa\text{-})$**background**.

If every point is assigned only one of two colors, then a multicolor digital picture is called a **binary digital picture**. Thus, we denote by $(\mathbf{Z}^i, X)$, where $X \subseteq \mathbf{Z}^i$, a i−dimensional binary digital picture $(\mathbf{Z}^i, \lambda)$, where $\lambda : \mathbf{Z}^i \to \{0, 1\}$ is given by $\lambda(p) = 1$ iff $p \in X$.

On X and its complement X^c, there is defined an adjacency relation. Every point in X is called a **foreground** or **black point** and assigned value 1; every point in $X^c = \mathbf{Z}^i \setminus X$ is called a **background** or **white point** and assigned value 0.

The **4-neighbors** (or **direct neighbors**) of a point (x, y) in $\mathbf{Z}^2$ are its four horizontal and vertical neighbors $(x + 1, y)$, $(x − 1, y)$ and $(x, y + 1)$, $(x, y − 1)$ (see Figure 1.2). The **8-neighbors** of a point (x, y) in $\mathbf{Z}^2$ are its four horizontal and vertical neighbors together with its four diagonal neighbors $(x+1, y+1)$, $(x+1, y−1)$ and $(x−1, y+1)$, $(x−1, y−1)$. If two points P and Q are n-neighbors, we also call them n-**adjacent** and write $n − adj(P, Q)$, where $n = 4$ or 8.

For $n = 4$ or 8, the n-**neighborhood** of a point $P = (x, y)$ in $\mathbf{Z}^2$ is the set $\mathcal{N}_n(P)$ consisting of P and its n-neighbors. $\mathcal{N}_n^*(P)$ is the set of all neighbors of P without P itself.

Note that $\mathcal{N}_n^*(P) = \mathcal{N}_n(P) \setminus \{P\}$. The points in $\mathcal{N}_8^*(P)$ are numbered 0 to 7 according to the following scheme:

$N_3(P)$	$N_2(P)$	$N_1(P)$
$N_4(P)$	P	$N_0(P)$
$N_5(P)$	$N_6(P)$	$N_7(P)$

Each N_i, $i = 0, \ldots, 7$, is a function from $\mathbf{Z}^2$ to $\mathbf{Z}^2$ that maps a point P to one of its neighbors according to this scheme.

Each point P in a binary digital picture $(\mathbf{Z}^2, X)$ can be assigned a number $B(P)$: Let $d_i = 1$ if $N_i(P) \in X$ and $d_i = 0$ if $N_i(P) \notin X$; then

$$B(P) = \sum_{i=0}^{7} d_i \cdot 2^i.$$

If a neighborhood configuration $\mathcal{N}_n(P)$ is given in the text, we sometimes write the number $B(P)$ in the center. Among configurations which are equivalent with respect to rotations or reflections of the digital plane, we usually take the one that has the smallest value of $B(P)$ as a representative.

If changeable 8/4 (or 4/8)-adjacency relations are used, then the following definition of a digital picture is used (Kong and Rosenfeld [82]). The reason for this more complicated definition are the connectivity paradoxes pointed out in the introduction.

A (two-dimensional) (m, n) **digital picture** is a quadruple $(\mathbf{Z}^2, m, n, B)$, where $B \subseteq \mathbf{Z}^2$ and $(m, n) = (4, 8)$ or $(8, 4)$. The points of B are called the **black points** of the picture and the points of $\mathbf{Z}^2 \setminus B$ the **white points**. Two black points in a digital picture $(\mathbf{Z}^2, m, n, B)$ are said to be **neighbors** if they are m-neighbors, and two white points or one white point and one black point are said to be **neighbors** if they are n-neighbors. Usually the set B is assumed to be finite. We call B the **foreground** and $\mathbf{Z}^2 \setminus B$ the **background** of a digital picture.

In an analogous way, we can define three-dimensional digital pictures with changeable adjacencies. A three-dimensional digital object (a finite subset of $\mathbf{Z}^3$) can be identified with a union of axis parallel unit cubes which are centered at object points (see Figure 2.1).

This gives us a simple correspondence between cubes and points in $\mathbf{Z}^3$ (i.e., each cube corresponds to its center). In this case a common **face** of two cubes centered at points $P, Q \in \mathbf{Z}^3$ (i.e., a unit square parallel to one of the coordinate planes) can be identified with the pair (P, Q). Such pairs are called "surface elements" in Herman [64], since they are constituent parts of object surfaces. If we identify cubes (voxels) with points in $\mathbf{Z}^3$ at which they are centered, the following definitions apply as well for cubes in $\mathbb{R}^3$ as for points in $\mathbf{Z}^3$.

Two cubes (voxels) are said to be **face-adjacent**, or **face neighbors**, if they share a face, or equivalently, if two of the coordinates of their centers are the same and the third

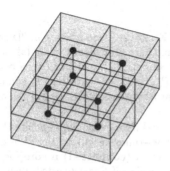

Figure 2.1: A 3D digital object can be interpreted as a union of unit cubes which are centered at object points.

coordinates differ by 1 (see Figure 2.2). Two voxels are said to be **edge-adjacent (edge neighbors, diagonally-adjacent)**, if they share an edge but not a face, i.e., if one of the coordinates of their centers is the same and the other two coordinates differ by 1. Two voxels are said to be **corner-adjacent (corner neighbors, diametrically-adjacent)** if they share a vertex but not an edge, i.e., if all three of the coordinates of their centers differ by 1.

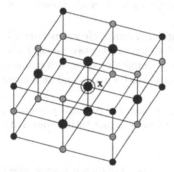

Figure 2.2: The slightly larger black balls illustrate the face neighbors (6-neighbors) of the center point x, the gray balls illustrate the edge neighbors of x, and the small black balls illustrate the corner neighbors of x.

Two voxels are said to be **6-adjacent (6-neighbors)** if they are face-adjacent. Two voxels are said to be **18-adjacent (18-neighbors)** if they are face- or edge-adjacent. Two voxels are said to be **26-adjacent (26-neighbors)** if they are face-, edge-, or corner-adjacent. Similarly as in 2D case, $\mathcal{N}_k(P)$ denotes the set containing P and all points k-adjacent to P and $\mathcal{N}_k^*(P)$ denotes $N_k(P) - \{P\}$, where $k = 6, 18, 26$. $\mathcal{N}_{26}(P)$ is also referred to as $\mathcal{N}(P)$ and called the **neighborhood** of P, whereas $\mathcal{N}_{26}(P) - \{P\}$ is referred to as $\mathcal{N}^*(P)$.

Let P, Q be any points of $\mathbf{Z}^i$, $i = 2, 3$, and $n = 4, 8$ in 2D case, and $n = 6, 18, 26$ in 3D case. We say that points P and Q are **n-adjacent** in digital picture $(\mathbf{Z}^i, \lambda)$ if P and Q are n-adjacent and have the same color, i.e., $\lambda(P) = \lambda(Q)$. By a **n-path** from P to Q we mean a sequence of points $P = P_1, P_2, \ldots, P_l = Q$ such that P_i is n-adjacent to P_{i-1}, $1 < i \leq l$. If an adjacency relation is clear from the context, we will call an n-path simply a **path**.

A digital set X is **n-connected** if for every pair of points P, Q in X, there is an n-path contained in X from P to Q. Sometimes we will say that X is **connected** if the adjacency relation is clear from the context. A **(connected) n-component** of a set S is a greatest n-connected subset of S. In particular, if S is connected, then the only component of S is S itself.

An important property of a continuous arc is that its connectivity is destroyed by the removal of one point other than an endpoint. A continuous simple closed curve has the property that deleting any of its points makes it an arc. This statements can be used for general definitions of a discrete arc and a discrete simple closed curve in any graph, which reduce to the following definitions in the case of a digital plane or space.

A finite set A is called a **(digital) n-arc** if it is n-connected, and all but two of its points have exactly two n-neighbors in A, while these two have exactly one. These two points are called **endpoints**.

A finite set C is called a **(digital) simple closed n-curve (Jordan n-curve)** if it is n-connected, and each of its points has exactly two n-neighbors in C. To avoid pathological situations, we require that an n-simple closed curve contains a certain minimal number of points, e.g., a 4-curve contains at least 8 points and an 8-curve at least 4 points [129].

By these definitions, an important and common property of a continuous simple closed curve and a digital simple closed curve is that their connectivity is destroyed by the removal of any two points.

A point of a digital set X having all of its n-neighbors also in X is called an **n-interior point**. The set of all interior points of a set X is termed the **n-interior** or **n-kernel** of X. A point of X that has an n-neighbor in the complement S^c is called an **n-boundary point**.

Again for these concepts, as for all other concepts defined above, we will drop the prefix n if the n-adjacency relation is clear from the context. For illustration purposes, we will denote the different types of points by the following symbols:

$\bullet$:   black point
o   :   (or blank position) white point
$\blacksquare$:   interior point
·   :   point of either black or white color.

2.2 Continuous Concepts

2.2.1 Topological Concepts

We begin with the definitions of topological concepts.

A **topological space** is a pair $(X, \mathcal{T})$ that consists of a set X and a collection $\mathcal{T}$ of subsets of X which are called **open sets** and satisfy the following axioms:

(1) X and $\emptyset$ are open.

(2) The union of any collection of open sets is open.

(3) The intersection of any finite collection of open sets is open.

The collection of all open sets $\mathcal{T}$ is termed a **topology** on X. A subset S of X is **closed** if its complement is open, i.e., if $S^c = X \setminus S$ is open. An open set which contains a point x of X is called a **neighborhood** of x and denoted $U(x)$. A topological space is **locally finite** if each point has a finite open neighborhood. Locally finite spaces are also called **discrete spaces**. A topology on X is **homogeneous** if any two points in X have homeomorphic neighborhoods.

A point $x \in S$ is an interior point of S if there exists an open set U such that $x \in U \subseteq S$. The set of all interior points of S is called the **interior** of S and denoted by $intS$. The interior $intS$ can also be defined as the union of all open sets that are contained in S, i.e., $intS$ is the greatest open set that is contained in S. The smallest closed set that contains S is called the **closure** of S and denoted as clS. Equivalently, the closure clS is the intersection of all closed sets that contain S. The closure operator is a function $cl : P(X) \to P(X)$, where $P(X)$ denotes the power set of the set X. The closure operator can be used to define a topology on X if we define a set $S \subseteq X$ to be closed iff $clS = S$.

In the year 1937 Čech [26] gave the following axioms to characterize the **weak closure operator** on a set X:

1. $cl\emptyset = \emptyset$,

2. for every $A \in P(X)$: $A \subseteq clA$,

3. for every $A, B \in P(X)$: $A \subseteq B \Rightarrow clA \subseteq clB$.

In Arnaud et al. [11] pretopological spaces are introduced as situation models in economics. Their definition is based on the weak closure operator.

Later Čech [27] (Chapter 14, p. 237) defined a stronger version of his closure operator. We say that $cl : P(X) \to P(X)$ is a **Čech (strong) closure mapping** on a set X if

(I) $cl\emptyset = \emptyset$,

(II) for every $A \in P(X)$: $A \subseteq clA$,

(III) for every $A, B \in P(X)$: $cl(A \cup B) = clA \cup clB$.

The Čech strong closure mapping does not define topological spaces. However, if we add the following axiom IV to I, II, and III, then the obtained closure operator defines exactly topological spaces.

(IV) for every $A \in P(X)$: $cl(clA) = clA$

Topological spaces are classified according to their separation properties in the following way: A topological space X is

T_0 if for any two different points in X, at least one has a neighborhood that does not contain the other;

T_1 if for any two different points x and y in X, there exists a neighborhood of x not containing y and a neighborhood of y not containing x;

T_2 if for any two different points x and y in X, there exists a neighborhood of x and a neighborhood of y which are disjoint. T_2–spaces are also called **Hausdorff spaces**.

Let S be a subset of X. In the **relative (or subset) topology** induced in S by the topology in X, the open sets are all sets $U \cap S$ with U open in X. One easily sees that this is indeed a topology in S. A set which is open in the relative topology of S is a **relatively open set** in S.

The set $S \subseteq X$ is called **connected** if there is no decomposition $S = S_1 \cup S_2$ such that $S_1 \cap S_2 = \emptyset$, both S_1, S_2 are relatively open in S, and $S_1, S_2 \neq \emptyset$. A **(connected) component** of a set X is a greatest connected subset of X.

A closed and bounded subset of $\mathbb{R}^n$ is called **compact**.

Let X and Y be two topological spaces. A function $f : X \to Y$ is called **continuous** if the inverse image of any open subset of Y is open in X. A bijection $f : X \to Y$ is called a **homeomorphism** if f and the inverse image f^{-1} are both continuous.

A **(proper) arc** $A \subseteq \mathbb{R}^n$, for $n = 2, 3, ...$, is a homeomorphic image of an interval of nonzero length: $A : [a, b] \to \mathbb{R}^2$, where $a < b$. The points $p = A(a)$ and $q = A(b)$ are called the **endpoints** of arc A; A is said to **join** p and q, and is sometimes denoted by $arc(p, q)$. If the endpoints of an arc are identified (i.e., $A(a) = A(b)$), the arc becomes a **simple closed curve** (or a **Jordan curve**), and can be regarded as having no endpoints. A simple closed curve can also be defined as a homeomorphic image $C : S^1 \to \mathbb{R}^n$ of a circle of nonzero radius r. A simple closed curve and a single point are sometimes called **nonproper** or **degenerate arcs**.

A set $P \subseteq \mathbb{R}^n$ is called a **path** if it is a continuous image of a closed interval I. A point p of a path P is a **multiple point** if p is the image of two (or more) distinct points of I. A point which is not a multiple point will be called a **simple point**.

For example, all points of a proper arc are simple points. Note also that a path P that contains only simple points is an arc, since then the function from I to P is also one-to-one, and a continuous one-to-one function on a closed interval is a homeomorphism onto its image.

A set S is **arc-connected** if for every pair of points $p, q \in S$, there is an arc joining p and q contained in S. A closed arc-connected subset of $\mathbb{R}^2$ will be sometimes called a **figure**.

Let P be an arc which is the image of the closed interval $I \subseteq \mathbb{R}$ by the homeomorphism $f : I \to \mathbb{R}^n$, and let J be a closed subinterval of I. The image $f(J)$ will be called a **subarc** of P. Note that the restriction of f to J is a homeomorphism: $J \to \mathbb{R}^2$; hence a subarc of an arc is an arc.

We now state some propositions which are useful in the proofs of some theorems in this book. Most of them are stated without proof, because they are well-known, basic facts about arcs and closed curves.

Proposition 2.1 *Every closed arc-connected subset of an arc is a subarc.* ∎

Proposition 2.2 *Every closed arc-connected proper subset of a simple closed curve is an arc.* ∎

Proposition 2.3 *A subset of an arc is connected iff it is arc-connected.* ∎

Proposition 2.4 *Three non-degenerate closed subarcs of an arc cannot pairwise intersect in a single point.*

Proof: Let $S = f(I)$ be an arc, and let $A, B, C \subseteq S$ be non-degenerate closed subarcs which pairwise intersect in a single point. Then $f^{-1}(A), f^{-1}(B), f^{-1}(C)$ would be three non-degenerate closed subintervals of I which pairwise intersect in a single point, which is impossible. ∎

Proposition 2.5 *Let S be an arc, and let $A, B, C \subseteq S$ be three non-degenerate closed line segments. Then A, B, C cannot pairwise intersect in a single point.*

Proof: This follows from Propositions 2.1 and 2.4. ∎

Proposition 2.6 *Let S be an arc which is the image of the closed interval $I \subseteq R$ by the homeomorphism $f : I \to \mathbb{R}^2$. Then for every three points $a, b, c \in I$ we have $b \in [a, c]$ iff $f(b) \in f([a, c]) = \text{arc}(f(a), f(c))$.* ∎

Note that by this proposition, the order of the points on S is the same as or the reverse of the order of the points on I.

Proposition 2.7 *Let S be an arc which is the image of the closed interval $I \subseteq R$ by the homeomorphism $f : I \to \mathbb{R}^2$. If $b \in \mathrm{arc}(a,c) \subseteq S$, then $\mathrm{arc}(a,b) \cap \mathrm{arc}(b,c) = \{b\}$.*

Proof: By Proposition 2.6, $f^{-1}(b) \in [f^{-1}(a), f^{-1}(c)]$ (or its reversal). Hence the intervals $[f^{-1}(a), f^{-1}(b)]$ and $[f^{-1}(b), f^{-1}(c)]$ can have only $f^{-1}(b)$ in common. Applying f to both sides proves the proposition. ∎

Proposition 2.8 *Let S be an arc and let $\mathrm{arc}(a,b)$ and $\mathrm{arc}(a,c)$ be subarcs of S such that $b \notin \mathrm{arc}(a,c)$. Then either $\mathrm{arc}(a,c) \subseteq \mathrm{arc}(a,b)$ or $\mathrm{arc}(a,c) \cap \mathrm{arc}(a,b) = \{a\}$. (See Figure 2.3.)*

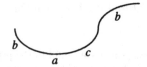

Figure 2.3:

Proof: Let $S = f(I)$, where f is a homeomorphism. By Proposition 2.6, $f^{-1}(b)$ cannot lie between $f^{-1}(a)$ and $f^{-1}(c)$. If $f^{-1}(c)$ is between $f^{-1}(a)$ and $f^{-1}(b)$, then $\mathrm{arc}(a,c) \subseteq \mathrm{arc}(a,b)$. If $f^{-1}(a)$ is between $f^{-1}(b)$ and $f^{-1}(c)$, we have $\mathrm{arc}(a,c) \cap \mathrm{arc}(a,b) = \{a\}$ by Proposition 2.7. ∎

Proposition 2.9 *A proper subarc of an arc S cannot have the same endpoints as S.* ∎

Proposition 2.10 *The union of two arcs which are disjoint except for one endpoint is an arc. If they are disjoint except for both endpoints, their union is a simple closed curve.* ∎

Proposition 2.11 *Deleting one point (other than an endpoint) from an arc, or two points from a simple closed curve, disconnects it.* ∎

We now define manifolds; for example, a 2D manifold in $\mathbb{R}^n$ "looks" locally like a planar open set. A subset X of $\mathbb{R}^n$ is a **1D, 2D, or 3D manifold** if each point in X has a neighborhood homeomorphic to $\mathbb{R}$, $\mathbb{R}^2$, or $\mathbb{R}^3$, correspondingly. A closed set $A \subseteq \mathbb{R}^n$ is a **bordered 2D manifold** if every point in A has a neighborhood homeomorphic to a relatively open subset of a closed half-plane. A closed set $A \subseteq \mathbb{R}^n$ is a **bordered 3D manifold** if every point in A has a neighborhood homeomorphic to a relatively open subset of a closed half-space.

Now we briefly review the concept of homotopy equivalence. Let X and Y be two topological spaces. Two functions $f, g : X \to Y$ are said to be **homotopic** if there exists a continuous function $H : X \times [0,1] \to Y$, where $[0,1]$ is the unit interval, with $H(x,0) = f(x)$ and $H(x,1) = g(x)$ for all $x \in X$. The function H is called a **homotopy** from f to g. Intuitively, a homotopy H from f to g represents a continuous deformation of function f to g.

Sets X and Y are called **homotopy equivalent** or of the same **homotopy type** if there exist two functions $f : X \to Y$ and $g : Y \to X$ such that $g \circ f$ is homotopic with the identity over X (id_X) and $f \circ g$ is homotopic with the identity over Y (id_Y).

As a consequence of the properties of homotopy equivalence between sets X and Y, there is a complete correspondence between connected components of X and Y and the corresponding components are homotopy equivalent. The Euler characteristics, as well as the fundamental groups of X and Y, are the same (see e.g., Naber [117]).

2.2.2 Geometric Concepts

The line segment joining two points x and y will be denoted by xy. A set S is called **convex** if for every two points in S the line segment joining them is contained in S.

Evidently, a convex set is arc-connected. Note also that if S is convex, then for any three non-collinear points in S the triangle determined by them (with its interior) is contained in S. Thus, if S contains three non-collinear points, it has a nonempty interior. This proves

Proposition 2.12 *A convex set with empty interior must be a line, a ray, or a line segment.* ∎

Proposition 2.13 *The closure of a convex set is convex.*

Proof: Let A be a convex set whose closure clA is not convex. Then there exist two points $a, b \in clA$ such that the line segment ab is not contained in clA. Therefore, there exists a point $c \in ab$ and $\varepsilon > 0$ such that $B(c,\varepsilon) \cap A = \emptyset$ (see Figure 2.4), where $B(c,\varepsilon)$ denotes the ball (i.e., a disk) having center c and radius ε.

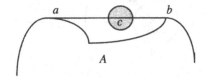

Figure 2.4:

If we take $0 < \delta < \varepsilon$, then two points x and y exist such that $x \in B(a,\delta) \cap A$ and $y \in B(b,\delta) \cap A$, because $a, b \in clA$. The line segment xy cannot be contained in A, since $xy \cap B(c,\varepsilon) \neq \emptyset$ and $B(c,\varepsilon) \cap A = \emptyset$. Hence A cannot be convex. ∎

In the book of Yaglom and Boltyanskii [164], the following two characterizations of convex sets are given:

Theorem 2.1 *A bounded figure in* $\mathbb{R}^2$ *is convex iff every straight line passing through an arbitrary interior point of the figure intersects the boundary of the figure in exactly two points* (see [164], p. 7). ∎

A straight line L passing through a boundary point p of a set $S \subseteq \mathbb{R}^2$ is called a **supporting line** (or a **line of support**) of S at p if S is contained in one of the closed half-planes into which L divides $\mathbb{R}^2$.

Theorem 2.2 *A bounded figure in* $\mathbb{R}^2$ *is convex iff through each of its boundary points there passes at least one supporting line* (see [164], p. 12). ∎

In order to characterize connected subsets of the boundaries of convex sets, it is enough to give such a characterization for arcs and simple closed curves, since by Proposition 2.12, a bounded convex set with empty interior is a line segment, and the boundary of a bounded convex set with nonempty interior is a simple closed curve, as we shall now prove.

Theorem 2.3 *The boundary of a bounded convex set with nonempty interior is a simple closed curve.*

Proof: Every point in $\mathbb{R}^2$ can be described as a pair (r, θ), where r is the distance to the origin and θ is an angle, $0 \le \theta < 2\pi$. The function $f : \mathbb{R}^2 \setminus \{(0,0)\} \to B$, $f((r, \theta)) = (1, \theta)$, where B is the unit circle, is continuous and onto B.

Now let S be the boundary of a bounded convex set C with nonempty interior. Translate C so that the origin is in its interior. Function f restricted to S, $f : S \to B$, is "1-1" and "onto", by Theorem 2.1 (see Figure 2.5). Since S is a boundary of a bounded set, it is bounded and closed, hence compact. Thus f is a homeomorphism between S and the unit circle, since it is a continuous bijection on a compact set. ∎

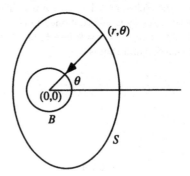

Figure 2.5:

By Propositions 2.2 and 2.12, we thus have

Corollary 2.1 *A closed arc-connected proper subset of the boundary of a bounded convex set is an arc.* ∎

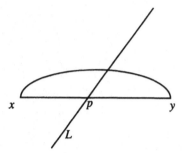

Figure 2.6:

Proposition 2.14 *For any pair of distinct points $x, y \in \mathbb{R}^2$, every straight line that intersects the line segment xy also intersects every $\mathrm{arc}(x, y)$ (see Figure 2.6).*

Proof: Let $f : I \to \mathrm{arc}(x, y)$ be a continuous function from the closed interval I onto $\mathrm{arc}(x, y)$ mapping the endpoints of I onto x and y. Obviously, the straight line M that contains x and y intersects every $\mathrm{arc}(x, y)$ at least in x and y. Let L be any straight line that intersects xy in a single point p. Let π_L be the projection of $\mathbb{R}^2$ along L onto M. The composition $\pi_L \circ f : I \to M$ is a continuous function mapping the endpoints of I onto x and y. Therefore, $\pi_L \circ f$ takes on every intermediate value between x and y on line M, i.e., every value on xy, and in particular value p. This implies that L intersects $\mathrm{arc}(x, y)$ in at least one point. ∎

Definitions of differential geometric concepts can be found in Stoker [148], for example.

Chapter 3

Graph-based Approach

In this approach, it is possible to show that some particular properties of a digital concept are the same as the corresponding properties of its continuous original. The considerations in Chapter 1 demonstrate that it is necessary to introduce a special graph structure into a discrete representation in order to ensure the required properties of a digital analog of a continuous concept. Thus, while defining a digital analog, one must specify at the same time in which graph structure this analog is defined. For example, if one defines a digital analog of a simple closed curve as a subgraph of the digital plane $\mathbf{Z}^2$ in which each point is 4-adjacent to exactly two other points, then the Jordan curve theorem holds for this curve in a graph with changeable 4/8-adjacency or in a well-composed graph. However, as demonstrated in Chapter 1, the Jordan curve theorem does not hold for the simple closed 4-curve in a graph with only one 4-adjacency relation. If we use the changeable 4/8-adjacency, we have 4-connectedness for the foreground and 8-connectedness for the background. Consequently, connected components are not intrinsic features of the digital representation and the neighborhoods of points are not homogeneous as it is the case for $\mathbb{R}^2$ with the usual topology.

In this chapter, we define well-composed digital representations. Neighborhoods in a well-composed representation are homogeneous and connected components are intrinsic features. Thus, in a well-composed graph structure not only the concept of Jordan curve has analog properties to its continuous original with respect to separation, but additionally the neighborhoods and connected components have analog properties to their continuous originals. Additionally, every well-composed graph is a planar graph, since only 4-adjacency links must be considered, i.e., it can be embedded into the plane $\mathbb{R}^2$ in such a way that its links do not intersect.

These features imply that many basic algorithms used in image processing become simpler on well-composed pictures. We will investigate the process of thinning as an example of the usefulness of the concept of well-composedness. We will show that the thinning process (sequential as well as parallel) is greatly simplified and also that the resulting skeletons have a very simple structure if the input set is well-composed. We will show that simple thinning algorithms can be defined for well-composed sets which generate really "thin" skeletons which are "one point thick", and we also formally define what this means. Consequently, the problem of irreducible "thick" sets disappears in well-composed pictures. We will also show that skeletons have a graph structure and we define what this means.

Restricting thinning to well-composed sets leads to an interesting situation. Although we delete points in fewer configurations, the resulting skeletons are thinner, since only 1/3 as many neighborhood configurations need be considered to decide if a given point can be deleted. In general, there are 18 types of 3 × 3 neighborhoods of simple points (other than endpoints), which generate 108 neighborhood configurations by rotations and reflections; of these, only 7 types are neighborhoods of simple points (other than endpoints) in well-composed sets, which generate only 36 configurations.

If a set lacks the property of being well-composed, the digitization process that gave rise to it must not have been topology preserving. As we will prove in Section 7.3 (Chapter 7), if the resolution of a digitization process is fine enough, the output digital picture must be well-composed. This gives us the right to "repair" a non-well-composed picture, since if the neighborhood of a point is not well-composed, it must be due to noise. Since well-composedness is a local property, i.e., it depends on the colors of single picture points, it can be decided very efficiently in parallel whether a given set is well-composed. Therefore, a picture can be "repaired" by adding (or subtracting) single points by parallel algorithm (Section 3.7). The other possibility, which is more promising for applications, would be to impose local conditions on the segmentation process which ensure that the obtained segmented image is well-composed.

In Sections 3.1 – 3.7 we define 2D binary well-composed pictures and show their properties based on Latecki et al. [98]. In Section 3.8 we extend the concept of well-composedness to 2D multicolor images (Latecki [94]).

3.1   Well-Composed Digital Images

First we define a well-composed graph structure on $\mathbf{Z}^2$. The main idea is not to allow configurations as shown in Figure 3.1 to occur in a well-composed digital picture. All of the following sets are subsets of a digital picture $(\mathbf{Z}^2, S)$.

Figure 3.1: The critical configurations that appear in non-well-composed images.

Definition: S is **weakly well-composed** if any 8-component of S is a 4-component.

Definition: S is **well-composed** if both S and its complement S^c are weakly well-composed.

Examples are shown in Figures 3.2 and 3.3. Since sets like the two sets of black points in Figure 1.3 cannot be well-composed, the connectivity paradoxes described in the introduction simply do not occur for well-composed sets. In Section 3.2 we will prove the Jordan curve theorem for well-composed sets. The following definition gives a local characterization of well-composed sets, as we show in Theorem 3.1.

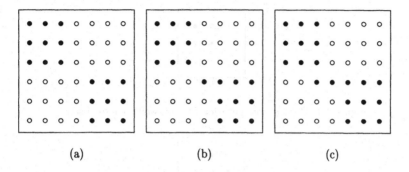

(a)   (b)   (c)

Figure 3.2: The sets in (a) and (c) are well-composed; the set in (b) is neither well-composed nor weakly well-composed.

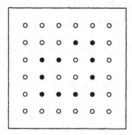

Figure 3.3: A weakly well-composed set which is not well-composed.

Definition: S is **locally 4-connected** if $S \cap (\mathcal{N}_8(P))$ is 4-connected for every point $P \in S$. (Recall that point P also belongs to $\mathcal{N}_8(P)$.)

For example, the set of black points in Figure 3.4 is not 4-connected. So, "S is locally 4-connected" means that the critical configuration shown in Figure 3.4 cannot occur in the 8-neighborhood of any point of S.

Theorem 3.1 *S is well-composed iff S is locally 4-connected.*

The proof follows from Propositions 3.1 to 3.4 below.

Proposition 3.1 *If S is locally 4-connected, then S^c is locally 4-connected.*

Proof: We show that if S^c is not locally 4-connected, then S is not locally 4-connected. If S^c is not locally 4-connected, then we can find a point $Q \in S^c$ with an 8-neighborhood like the following (Q is the white point in the middle):

Figure 3.4: Critical configuration for non-well-composed sets.

Then the 8-neighborhood of the point $N_4(Q) \in S$ (the black point on the left) is as in Figure 3.4. Hence S is not locally 4-connected.   ∎

Proposition 3.2 *If S is locally 4-connected, then S is weakly well-composed.*

Proof: If S is not well-composed, then a part of S is as in Figure 3.4; but then S is not locally 4-connected.   ∎

Proposition 3.3 *If S is locally 4-connected, then S is well-composed.*

Proof: This follows from Proposition 3.1 and Proposition 3.2 applied to S and S^c.   ∎

Proposition 3.4 *If S is well-composed, then S is locally 4-connected.*

Proof: If S is not locally 4-connected, than we can find a point of S with an 8-neighborhood as in Figure 3.4. But in this case, either S or S^c is not weakly well-composed: If there is a 4-path in S connecting the two black points in Figure 3.4, then the two white points are 8-adjacent but not 4-connected. Hence S^c is not weakly well-composed. If there is no 4-path in S connecting these two black points, then S is not weakly well-composed.   ∎

Remark. The fact that S is weakly well-composed does not imply that S is locally 4-connected; see Figure 3.3.

Let us now note the following simple but important fact that 4-connectedness and 8-connectedness are equivalent for well-composed sets; this is an immediate consequence of the definition of well-composedness:

Proposition 3.5 *A well-composed set S is 4-connected iff S is 8-connected.*

Proposition 3.6 *Every 4-component of a well-composed set S is an 8-component of S and vice versa.*

Proof: The vice versa part of this proposition is just the definition of well-composedness. Now if X is a 4-component of S, and there exists an 8-component Y of S such that X is a proper subset of Y, then the 8-component Y would not be a 4-component of S, a contradiction. ∎

3.2 Jordan Curve Theorem and Euler Characteristic

The Jordan curve theorem holds for well-composed sets, i.e. if we consider only subsets of $\mathbf{Z}^2$ which are well-composed, then every simple closed curve is well-composed, and therefore we have no problems with the paradoxes presented in the introduction. Observe that a well-composed, simple closed curve is always a 4-curve.

Theorem 3.2 (Jordan curve theorem) *The complement of a well-composed, simple closed curve always has exactly two components.*

Proof: Let C be a well-composed, simple closed curve. Rosenfeld [129] proved that if we consider 8-adjacency for C and 4-adjacency for C^c (or vice versa), then C^c has exactly two components. Our Theorem follows easily from his theorem: Since C is well-composed, it is 4- as well as 8-connected (Proposition 3.5). Due to Proposition 3.6, every 4-component of C^c is also an 8-component and vice versa. Hence C^c has exactly two components.

We can also prove this theorem directly following Rosenfeld's proof [129, 130], which is based on a standard proof of the theorem for polygons. We sketch only the main parts of it here: Let C be a well-composed, simple closed curve, and $P \notin C$; we say that $P = (x, y)$ is "inside" C if the half-line $H_p = \{(z, y) \mid x \leq z\}$ crosses C an odd number of times, and "outside" C otherwise (H_p may meet C in a sequence of consecutive points; such a sequence is a "crossing" if C enters the sequence from the row above H_p and exits to the row below H_p, or vice versa).

The main part of the proof is establishing that neighboring points of C^c are either both inside or both outside C^c. This part can be easily shown for well-composed sets. Hence points in the same component of C^c are either all inside or all outside. The theorem follows from this and the fact that the inside and outside of a curve are both nonempty. ∎

Kong and Rosenfeld [83] showed that if we use 4- (or 8-) connectedness for both a set and its complement, the Euler characteristic cannot be computed by counting local patterns. It is well known (Minsky and Papert [114]) that the Euler characteristic is locally computable if we use changeable 8/4- (or 4/8) connectedness. We will show that the Euler characteristic is also locally computable for well-composed sets.

Definition: Let S be a digital set. If S^c has n_0 components and S has n_1 components, then $\gamma(S) = n_1 - n_0 + 1$ is called the **Euler characteristic** of S.

Theorem 3.3 *The Euler characteristic is locally computable for well-composed sets.*

Proof: Minsky and Papert [114, Chapter 5.8.1] proved this theorem using 4-adjacency for black points and 8-adjacency for white points. We show that our theorem follows easily from their theorem.

Let S be a well-composed set. Then every 4-component of S is an 8-component of S and vice versa (Prop. 3.6). The same holds for components of S^c. Therefore, the theorem holds for every well-composed set.

We can also prove this theorem directly by following their proof. We then have even fewer cases to consider, since some of the sets treated by Minsky and Papert are not well-composed.   ∎

3.3   Thinning

Thinning is a common pre-processing operation in digital image processing. Its goal is to reduce a set S to a "skeleton" in a "topology-preserving" way. Rosenfeld [128] stated three requirements that a 2D thinning algorithm should satisfy:

(α) Connectedness is preserved, for both the objects and their complement.

(β) Curves, arcs, and isolated points remain unchanged.

(γ) Upright rectangles, whose length and width are both greater than 1, do not remain unchanged.

In this section we present a sequential algorithm, and in Section 3.6 a parallel algorithm, which fulfill these requirements. In addition, these algorithms preserve well-composedness and produce really thin sets (a concept which we will also define precisely). We begin with the definition of endpoints:

Definition: A black point P is **n-endpoint** if it has exactly one black n-neighbor in $\mathcal{N}_8^*(P)$, where $n = 4$ or 8.

There exists only one type of 8-endpoints characterized by the fact that they have exactly one 8-neighbor. There exist two different types of 4-endpoints which are endpoints in well-composed sets, namely those having exactly one 8-neighbor which is a 4-neighbor and configuration 3 in Figure 3.5 (both of these configurations can occur as endpoints of 4-arcs).

Before we give the standard 2D definition of a simple point [129, 82], we want to remind the reader that when 8-connectedness is used for the foreground, and 4-connectedness for the background, one speaks of 8-simple points, and in the opposite case one speaks of 4-simple points.

Definition: A black point p is said to be **n-simple** if

C1 p is n-adjacent to only one black n-component in $\mathcal{N}_8(p) \setminus p$ and

C2 p is m-adjacent to only one white m-component in $\mathcal{N}_8(p)$,

where $(n, m) = (8, 4)$ or $(4, 8)$.

For example, in Figure 3.5 configurations of all 8-simple points (except 8-endpoints) are shown. The algorithms for checking whether a point is simple in 2D, as well as in 3D images, are presented in Latecki and Ma [103].

Observe that a point $P \in S$ is n-simple in S iff $\mathcal{N}_8^*(P)$ contains just one n-component of S which is n-adjacent to P and P is an m-boundary point, where $(n, m) = (8, 4)$ or $(4, 8)$.

Simple points are used in thinning algorithms:

Definition: (n-) Thinning a digital set means repeated removal of n-simple points, but not n-endpoints from it. A digital set is termed n-**irreducible** if its only n-simple points are n-endpoints. An irreducible set obtained from a set by means of thinning is called its **skeleton**.

One step in a sequential thinning algorithm consists of removal of a single simple point. One step in a parallel thinning algorithm consists of the simultaneous removal of some set of simple points. It is required that after application of a thinning algorithm the connectedness of a set and of its complement are not changed (Rosenfeld's condition (α)). This is usually easy to prove for sequential thinning [82, 129], but more difficult for parallel thinning. The special treatment of endpoints guarantees that Rosenfeld's condition (β) is fulfilled.

The concept of not allowing deletion of 4-endpoints is justified by the fact that if we allow their deletion, the following "spikes" (see Tamura [151]) are reduced to two-point sets by any sequential thinning method that proceeds in a TV-scan-like sequence (row by row from top to bottom). On the other hand, when we fail to delete such "spikes", the skeleton may have "spurious" branches.

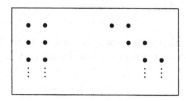

If we want thinning to preserve well-composedness, only 4-simple points which are not endpoints can be deleted. Note that the "spike" on the right remains unchanged by 4-thinning (as it should be, since it is a 4-arc). The "spike" on the left should be reduced,

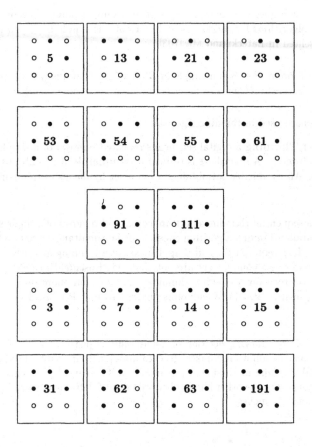

Figure 3.5: Configurations of all possible 8-simple points (except 8-endpoints). The middle point of configuration 3 is a 4-endpoint but not an 8-endpoint.

by Rosenfeld's condition (γ). In fact, as can be easily seen, it becomes "thinner" but not "shorter".

If we use changeable 8/4-connectedness, there are 18 types of 8-neighborhood configurations of 8-simple points (no including endpoint configurations), which generate 108 8-neighborhood configurations of 8-simple points by rotations and reflections ([37]). Figure 3.5 shows all 18 types of 8-simple points.

An important advantage of dealing only with well-composed sets in thinning processes is the fact that we have to treat only 7 types of 4-simple point neighborhoods (without endpoints): 7, 14, 15, 31, 62, 63 and 191 (see Figure 3.5). This corresponds to 36 neighborhood configurations obtained by rotations and reflections. This fact makes thinning algorithms simpler.

The idea of deleting only 4-simple points in thinning an 8-connected object dates back to Rutovitz in 1966 [138] and was proposed by different authors ([109, 146, 165]); however, they did not use the concept of well-composed sets. In general, if we delete only 4-simple points to thin any subset of $\mathbf{Z}^2$, we have problems with 8-components, since 4-simple points are not necessarily 8-simple, as the following configuration shows:

$$
\begin{array}{ccc}
\bullet & \circ & \bullet \\
\bullet & \mathbf{P} & \circ \\
\bullet & \circ & \bullet
\end{array}
$$

Obviously, at least one of the critical configurations shown in Figure 3.1 appears in such a situation. Thus, if we use well-composed sets, these problems cannot occur. In fact, in well-composed sets every 4-simple point is 8-simple.

Another very important property of well-composed sets is given in the following theorem. As already noted, in a well-composed set we can only have 4-simple points, since every component of a well-composed set is 4-connected. Therefore, thinning a well-composed set means removal of 4-simple points that are not endpoints.

Theorem 3.4 *Sequential 4-thinning is an internal operation on well-composed sets, i.e., applying sequential 4-thinning to a well-composed set results in a well-composed set.*

Proof: If we delete any 4-simple point from a well-composed set, we obtain a well-composed set. To prove this, it is enough to show that if we can connect two points Q and R by a 4-path in a well-composed set X, then we can still connect Q and R by a 4-path after deleting any simple point P (different from Q and R) from X. The reason is that if we have any 4-path A in a well-composed set X passing through a simple point P, then the two direct neighbors of P in A belong to $\mathcal{N}_8^*(P)$. Since $\mathcal{N}_8^*(P) \cap X$ is 4-connected, we can connect these two direct neighbors by a path in $\mathcal{N}_8^*(P) \cap X$. Therefore, we can modify any path in X passing through a simple point P to a path with the same endpoints in $X \setminus P$. ∎

We conclude that thinning is an internal operation on well-composed sets if and only if only 4-simple points are deleted. It is easy to see that if we eliminate any 8-simple point which is not 4-simple, the resulting set will no longer be well-composed (see Figure 3.5).

One of the most important goals of thinning is to obtain a skeleton of the input set. Therefore, the resulting set, which cannot be further reduced by thinning, should not have any interior points. However, thinned irreducible sets can have many kernel components of arbitrarily large sizes as shown in Eckhardt and Maderlechner [37]. The first example of a "large" kernel component was given by Arcelli in 1981 ([10]; see Figure 3.6).

For well-composed sets the situation is very simple, since there is only one type of kernel component, namely a set with only one point, as will be shown in Theorem 3.5. This type of interior point cannot be further eliminated, since it indicates a very useful property, namely that we have an intersection of two lines at this point, i.e. locally the following situation:

Eliminating such interior points would mean that a skeleton could not have such intersections of two line segments, which is an unrealistic assumption.

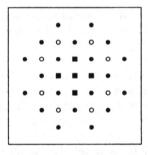

Figure 3.6: Arcelli's set with five interior points

Theorem 3.5 *Any 8-connected component of the kernel of a 4-irreducible well-composed set contains at most one point.*

Proof: We prove this by showing that it is not possible to have two adjacent interior points within a well-composed irreducible set.

Without loss of generality we may assume that we consider interior points having boundary points as direct neighbors. We distinguish two cases (in the pictures given in the proof, the one on the left gives the start situation and the one on the right gives the situation constructed during the proof):

a) P and Q are two directly neighboring interior points such that the points $N_2(P)$ and $N_2(Q)$ are not interior points. If $N_1(Q)$ were black then $N_2(Q)$ necessarily is a (4-) simple point or an interior point. So, $N_1(Q)$ must be white. Since $N_2(Q)$ cannot be simple and since the set is required to be well-composed, $N_2(N_2(Q))$ is black. The same argument holds for P. Now, $N_2(Q)$ becomes 4-simple, a contradiction.

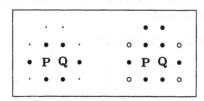

b) Assume now that there are two indirectly neighboring interior points P and Q. Without loss of generality $Q = N_1(P)$ and $N_0(P)$ is not an interior point. This means that $N_0(N_0(P))$ or $N_7(P)$ is white. If one of these neighbors is black, then $N_0(P)$ is simple; hence they both are white. Now $N_0(N_7(P))$ must be black, for otherwise $N_0(P)$ would again be simple. The configuration thus obtained is no longer well-composed.

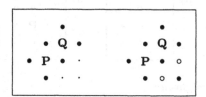

■

Definition: The **crossing number** (see e.g., Hilditch [65, page 411]) is the number of white-black (0–1) transitions in the (cyclic) sequence $N_0(P), N_1(P), \ldots, N_7(P), N_0(P)$.

Remark. For well-composed sets, the crossing number is equal to the number of black 4-components in $\mathcal{N}_8^*(P)$, since the crossing number is equal to the number of black 4-components in $\mathcal{N}_8^*(P)$ if all 8-components in $\mathcal{N}_8^*(P)$ are directly connected to P. This is the case if the critical configurations shown in Figure 3.1 are not contained in $\mathcal{N}_8(P)$.

3.4 Irreducible Well-Composed Sets

We now investigate sets having the property of being 4-irreducible and well-composed. Such sets can be obtained by applying a 4-thinning process to a well-composed set (see Theorem 3.4).

Irreducible sets obtained by ordinary thinning can contain all point configurations which are not simple. There are 148 such configurations (256 configurations of 3×3 neighborhoods minus 108 configurations of simple points that are not endpoints); they are generated by 33 neighborhood types. The situation is more favorable if thinning algorithms are applied to well-composed sets.

Theorem 3.6 *For a point P in a 4-irreducible well-composed set, only the following neighborhood configurations (as well as symmetric configurations, obtained from them by 90° rotations and reflections) are possible:*

1. One direct black neighbor *(4-endpoint)*

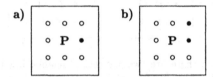

2. Two direct black neighbors

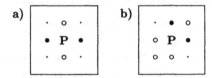

3. Three direct black neighbors

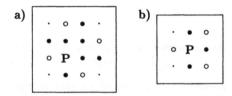

4. Four direct black neighbors

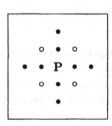

Proof: The proof is by enumeration of all possible cases, showing that if P occurs in any other configuration, it must be a 4-simple point, which is not possible in a 4-irreducible set.

1. Let $N_0(P)$ be black. $N_3(P)$ and $N_5(P)$ cannot be black, since then the set would not be well-composed. If $N_1(P)$ were black, then P is a simple point and we have case 1b. The same holds for $N_7(P)$. If $N_1(P)$ and $N_7(P)$ are white, we have case 1a. Therefore, the two configurations shown above are the only possible configuration types with one direct black neighbor.

2. This case is obvious.

3. Let $N_0(P)$, $N_2(P)$, and $N_6(P)$ be black. If $N_1(P)$ and $N_7(P)$ are white, then we have case 3b. If only one of them is white, say $N_7(P)$, then we have case 3a. Since $N_0(P)$ cannot be simple, $N_0(N_0(P))$ must be black and $N_1(N_0(P))$ must be white. Since $N_1(P)$ cannot be simple, $N_2(N_1(P))$ must be black and $N_3(N_1(P))$ must be white.

4. In this case P is an interior point. Assume that $N_1(P)$ is black (see the picture below, where the set on the left represents the start situation, and the set on the right represents the situation constructed during the proof).

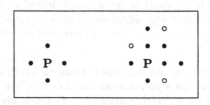

If $N_7(P)$ were black, then $N_0(P)$ is either an interior point, which contradicts Theorem 3.5, or else it is necessarily simple. The same argument applies to $N_3(P)$, so $N_3(P)$ and $N_7(P)$ must be white. $N_0(N_0(P))$ is not white, since otherwise either $N_0(P)$ would be simple ($N_7(N_0(P))$ white) or the set would not be well-composed ($N_7(N_0(P))$ black). Again, by symmetry, $N_2(N_2(P))$ is black. $N_2(N_1(P))$ must be white, since otherwise $N_1(P)$ would be simple. Now, regardless of the color of $N_0(N_1(P))$, $N_1(P)$ is always simple (since the set is assumed to be well-composed). It is now easily seen that the configuration is as shown above. ∎

Remark. If P is an interior point of an irreducible well-composed set, then we have locally only the configuration presented in part 4 of the Theorem. So, P can be treated as an intersection point of a vertical and a horizontal line segment.

3.5 Graph Structure of Irreducible Sets

The goal of thinning is formulated by different authors as obtaining a set which is "one pixel thick" (*"... a single pixel wide ... "* in Pavlidis [121, p. 143], *"... until all that remains is lines which are one point wide ... "* in Hilditch [65, p. 407], *"Thus, a final step might be necessary to reduce the set of the skeletal pixels to the unit width skeleton"* in Arcelli and Sanniti di Baja [9, p. 411], *"A unitary skeleton is a single pixel thickness skeleton, in which each of its pixels is connected to not more than two adjacent pixels unless it represents a treepoint"* in Abdulla et al. [1, p. 13]), *"Overall, these applications employ thinning (a) to reduce line images to medial lines of unit width, (b) to enable objects to be represented as simplified data structures (e.g. by chain-coding) ... "* in Davies and Plummer [30].

Bearing in mind Arcelli's example (Figure 3.6), one might wonder how to give this requirement a precise meaning. Using the concept of well-composed sets, we can now propose the following definition:

Definition: A digital set is **one pixel thick** if it is well-composed and 4-irreducible.

Thus, we may give Theorem 3.5 an alternative formulation:

Theorem 3.7 *The skeleton of a well-composed set is one pixel thick.*

On the other hand, by "thinness" is meant intuitively that the skeleton should have a "graph-like" structure, as is expressed in the informal definition in Abdulla et al. [1] or Davies and Plummer [30]. Since any digital set which is equipped with a neighborhood relation is a graph, we should make this concept more precise by formalizing the concept of a "graph-like structure".

Definition: For any point P the **8-connection number** $C_8(P)$ is the number of black 8-components in $\mathcal{N}_8^*(P)$ and the **4-connection number** $C_4(P)$ is the number of black 4-components in $\mathcal{N}_8^*(P)$ which are directly connected to P. Obviously $C_8(P)$ is never greater than $C_4(P)$.

Definition: A **n-graph point** of a digital set is a point having the property that its n-connection number equals the number of its black n-neighbors, where $n = 4$ or 8. A digital set is termed a **n-graph** if all of its points are n-graph points, where $n = 4$ or 8.

The 8-skeleton of a digital set is not necessarily an 8-graph. The following set is 8-irreducible, but P is not an 8-graph point:

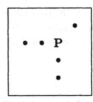

The same negative assertion holds for the 4-skeleton. In configuration 3.a of Theorem 3.6, point P is not a 4-graph point. However, if this configuration is 8-thinned, we obtain the following configuration which consists entirely of 8-graph points:

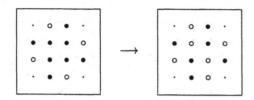

Definition: We define a point of a digital set to be a **4/8-graph point** if it is either a 4-graph point or an 8-graph point. A **4/8-graph** is a digital set consisting entirely of 4/8-graph points. Now we can formulate the ideas of the last part of this section in the following Theorem:

Theorem 3.8 *If a 4-irreducible well-composed set is postprocessed by 8-thinning applied to all configurations of type 3a of Theorem 3.6, the resulting set is a 4/8-graph.*

3.6 Parallel Thinning on Well-Composed Sets

In sequential thinning, where only one simple point is deleted at each step, connectivity is evidently preserved. Parallel thinning, on the other hand, may not preserve connectivity. For example, if the points in the central column of the following set are deleted simultaneously, the set becomes disconnected. In order for parallel thinning algorithms to be topologically correct, one must avoid such situations.

When we investigate parallel thinning methods on well-composed sets, we are faced with an additional dilemma. Parallel elimination of points, even if it is designed so as to be topologically correct, may destroy well-composedness of sets, as shown by the example in Figure 3.7. Here simultaneous elimination of two 4-simple points yields a set which is not well-composed.

Our goal in this section is to construct a parallel thinning algorithm for well-composed sets that is topologically correct and preserves well-composedness. We also want the resulting skeletons to be "thin", i.e. we want their kernel components to be as small as possible, as is the case for sequential thinning of well-composed sets. The simplest possibility is to use a 4-phase thinning algorithm as described by Rosenfeld in [128]. This algorithm removes only one type of border point at each phase: north border points are removed in the first phase, east in the second, and then south and west border points (where, for example, a north border point of S is one whose second neighbor is in S^c). Rosenfeld showed that this algorithm is topologically correct. If we allow only 4-simple points to be deleted, this

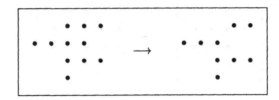

Figure 3.7: Parallel 4-thinning is not necessarily an internal operation on well-composed sets.

algorithm also preserves well-composedness, and the resulting skeletons are 4-irreducible. Therefore, Theorem 3.5 also holds for this 4-phase thinning. However, 4-phase algorithms are not very efficient, since only 1/4 of the possible points can be deleted in one phase. It is also possible to thin well-composed sets using one-phase parallel algorithms. However, such algorithms must examine a relatively large neighborhood of every point, since it is well known (Rosenfeld [128]) that a parallel thinning algorithm based on a 3 × 3 neighborhood cannot preserve connectedness.

We will now present a parallel thinning method for well-composed sets which minimizes the number of phases while at the same time minimizing the size of the neighborhoods used. It is a two-phase method consisting of one marking phase and one elimination phase. In the first phase the candidates for elimination are marked, and in the second phase these candidates are eliminated if they fulfill a simple condition described below.

In Eckhardt and Maderlechner [37] the concept of a perfect point was introduced.

Definition: A point Q of a digital set is termed **perfect** if

- Q has a direct neighbor which is an interior point, say $N_{2k}(Q)$, where $k \in \{0, 1, 2, 3\}$.

- The direct neighbor of Q which is opposite the interior point $N_{2k+4 \pmod 8}(Q)$ is white.

For example, if Q in the following configuration is black, then it is perfect.

Definition: The **south neighborhood** of a point P is

$$\mathcal{SN}(P) = \{P, N_4(P), N_5(P), N_6(P), N_7(P), N_0(P)\} :$$

In a similar way the **north neighborhood** of P can be defined.

In the first step of a parallel thinning algorithm, we will use the cross neighborhood of P to mark with "c" direct neighbors of P that are perfect points as candidates for deletion. In the second step, only points marked "c" can be deleted. While deleting the marked points, we must take care that in the following situations, at most one of the points marked "c" can be deleted:

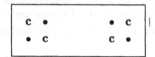

Parallel Thinning Algorithm

Let S be a set of black points to be thinned and let P be any point in S.

First Step Candidates for deletion are marked.

If P is a perfect point, then P is marked c (candidate for deletion).

Second Step Deletion of marked points.

If a point P is marked c and no critical configuration shown below occurs in the south neighborhood of P, then P is deleted (i.e., its color is changed from black to white).

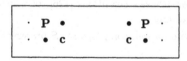

In the first step exactly the perfect points are marked as candidates, which are automatically simple points in a well-composed set, as the following Proposition states.

Proposition 3.7 *Every candidate point in a well-composed set is a simple point.*

Proof: Since the point is a candidate point, we have the following situation (possibly rotated by a multiple of 90°):

Whatever color the points marked "·" have, the candidate point "c" is obviously simple, since the set is well-composed. ∎

Since every candidate is a perfect point, we are also guaranteed that the spikes shown in Section 3.3 will be left unchanged. Note also that endpoints are preserved from deletion, since points which are deleted are simple and perfect, and a perfect point has a direct neighbor which is an interior point.

The condition in the second step of this algorithm prevents deletion of a candidate if there is a critical configuration involving another candidate to the south. However, it cannot be that the deletion of every candidate will be prevented by this condition, since there always is a candidate having no critical configuration to the south. Therefore, the number of interior points decreases after every application of this algorithm. Hence, after we finish applying the algorithm, there are no 4-simple perfect points in the resulting set. Now we prove that the algorithm preserves both well-composedness and connectivity.

Theorem 3.9 *The two-step parallel thinning method described above is an internal operation on well-composed sets.*

Proof: Well-composedness is destroyed only when a critical configuration occurs and both candidates (marked with "c") are deleted. This is prevented by deleting only candidates having no diagonal neighbors to the south which are also candidates.   ∎

Theorem 3.10 *The two-step parallel thinning method is topologically correct on well-composed sets.*

Proof: The proof is based on Ronse's conditions [126], of which a simplified version for well-composed sets is the following:

A parallel thinning algorithm on a well-composed set S preserves connectedness of the set and its complement if

(1) only simple points are deleted and

(2) for any two 8-adjacent points P and Q of S, P is simple after Q has been deleted, and Q is simple after P has been deleted.

By Proposition 3.7, only simple points can be candidates, and therefore only simple points can be deleted. So it remains to show the second condition.

Assume that P and Q are both candidates and direct neighbors. The only possibility for such a situation is indicated in the configuration below (up to rotations by multiples of 90°).

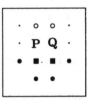

If, for example, $N_6(Q)$ is an interior point and $N_2(Q)$ is white, then $N_6(P)$ must be an interior point and $N_2(P)$ must be white. It is now easy to see that P will be simple in $S \setminus \{Q\}$, and that the same holds with P and Q interchanged.

Let P and Q be diagonal neighbors. Note that both points have to be simple and perfect in S in order to be deleted. In this case deletion of a diagonal neighbor cannot disconnect or delete a black 4-component in the 8-neighborhood of either P or Q. Therefore, P will be simple in $S \setminus \{Q\}$, and the same holds with P and Q interchanged. ∎

Theorem 3.11 *The 4-kernel of a well-composed set which contains no 4-simple perfect points is either empty or consists of 8-isolated components having one of the following forms:*

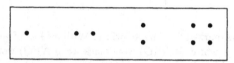

Proof: The proof follows from Propositions 3.8 and 3.9 below: In a horizontal or vertical line there can at most be two adjacent kernel-boundary points. The configuration in which the kernel contains two successive kernel-boundary points in a diagonal line such that one of their two common direct neighbors is not an interior point is impossible. Thus if the kernel contains two successive kernel-boundary points in a diagonal line, then their two common direct neighbors are also interior points. In this case the four kernel points form a square. ∎

Definition: A point in the kernel of a set is termed **a kernel-boundary point** if it has at least one direct neighbor which is not in the kernel.

Proposition 3.8 *If the 4-kernel of S contains three successive kernel-boundary points in a horizontal or vertical line then S contains a point which is (4- and 8-) simple and perfect.*

Proof: We have the following situation:

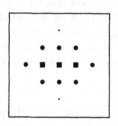

At least one of the points marked "·" is necessarily white, since otherwise the middle point would not be a kernel-boundary point. ∎

Proposition 3.9 *If the (4-)kernel of S contains two successive kernel-boundary points in a diagonal line, and one of their two common direct neighbors is not an interior point, then either S is not well-composed or it contains a point which is (4- and 8-) simple and perfect.*

Proof: We have the following situation:

At least one of the points marked "·" must be white. Without loss of generality assume that the lower "·", call it Q, is white. If $N_3(Q)$ were black, then $N_2(Q)$ would be simple; hence both Q and $N_3(Q)$ are white. If $N_4(Q)$ were black, the set would not be well-composed; if it were white, $N_2(Q)$ would be simple.   ∎

If the parallel thinning method described above is applied repeatedly to a well-composed set, the final remaining set does not contain any points which are simple and perfect. This set might contain kernel components as in Theorem 3.11. We will now show that the application of a sequential 4-thinning process to this remaining set results in a 4-irreducible well-composed set which satisfies Theorem 3.5 and which automatically has all the properties described in Sections 3.4 and 3.5. In this sequential thinning process each point in the set is examined once, and if it is simple, it is eliminated.

Theorem 3.12 *Assume that a well-composed set S contains no points which are simple and perfect. If the sequential 4-thinning process is applied to S, examining each point of S just once, the resulting set is 4-irreducible.*

Proof: There can be points of S which are simple but not perfect. We will show that after the sequential 4-thinning process is applied to S, no 4-simple points remain in the resulting set (which is also well-composed). It is clear that after the sequential 4-thinning process is applied to S, all simple points in S either have been deleted or are no longer simple. We now have to show that no point in the resulting set can become simple. More precisely, we have to show that the following situation is impossible: There is a point $P \in S$ that is not 4-simple in S, and there is a set $SP \subset \mathcal{N}_8(P)$ of 4-simple points in S such that P is 4-simple in $S \setminus SP$.

We distinguish two cases:

1. The 4-connection number $C_4(P)$ is equal to 1 with respect to S. In this case, P has at most one white indirect neighbor and since P is not simple in S, it must be an interior point. Therefore we have (up to 90° rotations) the following situation:

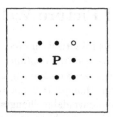

All points $N_{2i}(N_{2i}(P))$, $i = 0, 1, 2, 3$, must be black, since otherwise $N_{2i}(P)$ would be simple and perfect. Thus, $N_{2i}(P)$, $i = 2, 3$, are interior points. By the same argument $N_2(N_3(P))$, $N_4(N_3(P))$, $N_4(N_5(P))$, and $N_6(N_5(P))$ are black. Thus we have a kernel component containing five points (P and $N_i(P)$, $i = 3, 4, 5, 6$,), which contradicts Theorem 3.11.

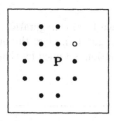

2. $C_4(P) > 1$ with respect to S. The point P should be 4-simple with respect to the set $S \setminus SP$. Therefore, it has in this set one of the configurations 7, 14, 15, 31, 62, 63 or 191 in Figure 3.5. Configurations 63 and 191, however, are not possible since $C_4(P) > 1$ with respect to S. By the same argument configuration 62 is not possible since the set S is well-composed. To obtain configuration 31, SP consists of only one point, the 6-neighbor of P. Since this latter point must be simple, it would have to be perfect, a contradiction. There remain only configurations 7, 14 and 15. We start with configuration 15.

Since $C_4(P) > 1$, $N_6(P)$ and possibly $N_5(P)$ are black in S, and the points $N_4(P)$ and $N_7(P)$ are necessarily white.

If $N_5(P)$ is black, then $N_6(P)$ is not 4-simple. As a consequence, $N_6(P)$ must be eliminated as the last point in SP. For $N_6(P)$ to be eliminated, it must be simple in $S \setminus \{N_5(P)\}$. But then $N_6(P)$ is an endpoint (configuration 3).

A similar argument applies to configuration 14 with point $N_6(P)$ as the last point in SP to be eliminated. In case of configuration 7, we can apply the same argument either to $N_6(P)$ or to $N_4(P)$ as the last point in SP. ∎

3.7   Making a Digital Picture Well-Composed

It may happen that an output of a real digitization process is not a well-composed digital picture. In this case we can locally "repair" it to obtain a well-composed picture. If a picture is not well-composed, then there is an 8-component of it which is not a 4-component. Consequently, repairing this situation changes the topology of the set. Our goal will be to repair a picture while keeping the unavoidable changes minimal. The other possibility, which is more promising for applications, would be to impose local conditions on the segmentation process which guarantee that the obtained segmented image is well-composed.

Theorem 3.13 *The following parallel algorithm makes a well-composed picture from a given picture by adding a minimal number of points.*

Repairing Algorithm
In the following pictures the possible local configurations are presented (up to rotations and reflections). The left hand configuration gives the original situation, the right hand configuration gives the repaired situation obtained by changing white points to black.

1.

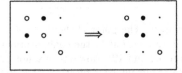

2.

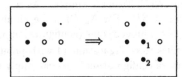

At least one of the points '*' must be black.

3.

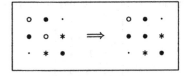

4. (a)

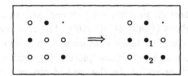

It may happen that here a new critical configuration occurs. This is the case if and only if the following situation (in the larger neighborhood) is given:

(b)

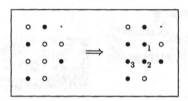

Proof: If in cases 3 and 4.a we only add the black point marked '1', then a new critical configuration occurs. Therefore we have to add the black point marked '2'.

If in case 4.b we only add the black point marked '1', then a new critical configuration occurs. Therefore we have to add the black point marked '2'. But adding point marked '2' causes again the critical situation which disappears when point marked '3' is added.

In remaining cases no further critical situations occur. ∎

Remark. This method is invariant up to 90° rotations and reflections. If full invariance does not matter, we can repair a given picture to obtain a well–composed picture by adding fewer points. This can be achieved by considering only configurations given above and their reflections at a vertical axis (this is equivalent to considering only south–neighborhoods).

We can also repair any set to obtain a well–composed set by deleting black points. An algorithm for this purpose can be formulated if black and white points are changed. This is due to the duality of well–composedness (i.e., a set S is well–composed if and only if S^c is well–composed).

3.8 Multicolor Well-Composed Pictures

In this section, we concentrate on digital properties of multicolor pictures (i.e., segmented pictures with more than two different kinds of objects). In a multicolor digital picture, every picture point is assigned some color c (i.e., label) from a given color scale Λ. The points of the same color are grouped into components. Thus, under a multicolor picture, we understand a digital picture in which all points of one component have the same color. However, there can be many components of the same color. Such pictures are naturally created by any segmentation process, e.g., by segmenting points based on local color differences using G-neighbors (Boult et al. [16]). For example, in Figure 3.8, there are five components of gray color, five black components, and five white components. A binary picture is a special case of a multicolor picture in which every picture point is assigned one of two colors, black or white. In the case of binary pictures the color of points have a very simple interpretation: black points form the foreground and white points form the background, or vice versa.

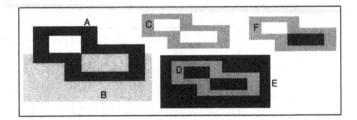

Figure 3.8: A three-color picture.

As was noted early in the history of computer vision, using the same adjacency relation for the entire digital picture leads to so-called "paradoxes", which we described in Section 1.1 of the introduction. The most popular solution to these problems for binary pictures was the idea of using different adjacency relations for the foreground and the background: 8-adjacency for black points and 4-adjacency for white points, or vice versa.

This solution is only possible for binary pictures. Figure 3.9 shows that this solution cannot work for three or more color pictures: To avoid paradoxes for black components on the gray background, black points must be 8-adjacent and gray 4-adjacent (or vice versa). If white points are 4-adjacent, then the Jordan curve theorem does not hold for the gray 4-curve A. If white points are 8-adjacent, then the Jordan curve theorem does not hold for the black 8-curve B. Thus if we want to deal with three or more colors pictures, we cannot use changeable (8, 4) or (4, 8) - adjacency to obtain the Jordan curve theorem. This argument is based on an obvious assumption that the same adjacency relation is used to group points of the same color. Similar examples can also be given for the Jordan-Brouwer surface theorem in 3D.

We present a solution which guarantees us to avoid the connectivity paradoxes for all multicolor pictures. Only one connectedness relation will be used for the entire digital picture. We will use only 4-adjacency (which will be equivalent to 8-adjacency) for every pair of points of every color. The idea is not to allow the "critical configuration" as illustrated in Figure 3.10 for black points to occur in digital pictures for any color; such pictures will be called "well-composed". Note that the critical configuration can be detected locally. Specifically, we will define a multicolor digital picture to be well-composed if every 8-component of every color is 4-connected (and hence is a 4-component).

A multicolor digital picture can be reduced to a binary picture if we temporarily concentrate on one color c and treat all points of color c as foreground and all other points

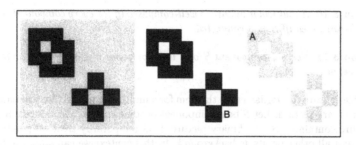

Figure 3.9: For multicolor pictures, we cannot use changeable (8, 4) or (4, 8) - adjacency to obtain the Jordan curve theorem.

Figure 3.10: Critical configuration for non-well-composed multicolor pictures.

as background. Using this reduction, all results for binary well-composed pictures will also hold for multicolor well-composed pictures.

The following definition extends the definition for binary pictures.

Definition: A multicolor digital picture $(\mathbf{Z}^i, \lambda)$ is **well-composed** if for every color $c \in \Lambda$, every 8-component of color c is also a 4-component.

Since sets like presented in Figure 3.9 cannot be well-composed, the connectivity paradoxes just described cannot occur for multicolor well-composed pictures. Below we show that the Jordan curve theorem holds for multicolor well-composed pictures. The following definition gives a local characterization of well-composed pictures, as we show in Theorem 3.14.

Definition: A set S of all points having the same color $c \in \Lambda$ is **locally 4-connected** if $S \cap (\mathcal{N}_8(P))$ is 4-connected for every point $P \in S$. (Recall that point P also belongs to $\mathcal{N}_8(P)$.)

Clearly, if S is locally 4-connected, then the critical configuration presented in Figure 3.10 cannot occur in the 8-neighborhood of any point of S.

The following theorems are stated without proof. Their proofs follow from the corresponding theorems stated above for binary pictures.

Theorem 3.14 *A multicolor digital picture is well-composed iff every component of every color is locally 4-connected.* ∎

Let us now note the following simple but important facts that 4-connectedness and 8-connectedness are equivalent for multicolor well-composed pictures, which are immediate consequences of the definition of well-composedness:

Proposition 3.10 *A multicolor picture is well-composed iff for every component S of every color, S is 4-connected iff S is 8-connected.* ∎

Proposition 3.11 *Every 4-component S of a well-composed picture is an 8-component of S and vice versa.* ∎

To be able to state the Jordan curve theorem for a multicolor picture, we will temporarily treat it as a binary picture. Let S be a component of some color c. We reduce a multicolor digital picture containing S to a binary picture if we temporarily treat all points of S as foreground and all other points as background. In this context we can state the following theorem.

Theorem 3.15 (Jordan curve theorem) *The complement of a simple closed curve in a multicolor well-composed picture always has exactly two components.* ∎

The proof follows from the corresponding theorem stated for binary pictures, since using the above reduction, all results for binary well-composed pictures will also hold for multicolor well-composed pictures. Note that a simple closed curve in a well-composed picture is always a 4-curve.

Kong and Rosenfeld [83] showed that if we use 4- (or 8-) connectedness for both a set and its complement, the Euler characteristic cannot be computed by counting local patterns. It is well known Minsky and Papert [114] that the Euler characteristic is locally computable if we use changeable 8/4- (or 4/8) connectedness. The next theorem shows that the Euler characteristic is also locally computable for multicolor well-composed pictures.

Theorem 3.16 *Let S be a component in a multicolor well-composed picture. Then the Euler characteristic of S is locally computable.* ∎

The proof of Theorem 3.16 follows directly from the proof of the corresponding theorem for binary pictures.

Of course, similarly as it is the case for binary pictures, not every multicolor picture is well-composed. If it is not, we have to change the color of a few critical points to obtain a well-composed picture. Here we profit from the fact that well-composedness can be detected locally. For example, the picture in Figure 3.8, which is clearly not well-composed, can be transformed to a well-composed picture shown in Figure 3.11 by changing the color of four points. This can be done by applying the algorithm presented in Section 3.7 to every color c. If we concentrate on color c, we can treat all points of color c as the foreground black points and all points of all other colors as the background white points. This process surely influences the connectedness of objects, but we do this at every critical point explicitly, and therefore we can use additional sources of information to decide the color of a critical point. On the other hand, digital pictures are passed through preprocessing steps, like noise removal or smoothing, which can be designed to produce well-composed pictures.

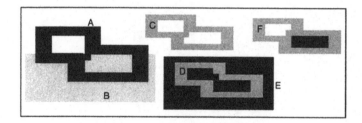

Figure 3.11: A well-composed version of the multicolor picture.

Chapter 4

Axiomatic Approach

Starting with an intuitive concept of "nearness" as a binary relation, semi-proximity spaces (sp-spaces) are defined. The restrictions on semi-proximity spaces are weaker than the restrictions on topological proximity spaces. Thus, semi-proximity spaces generalize classical topological spaces. We will use semi-proximity spaces to establish a formal relationship between the topological concepts of digital image processing and their continuous counterparts in $\mathbb{R}^n$. This is possible, since $\mathbb{R}^n$ with the usual topology and digital images with their usual structure are sp-spaces. Examples of different semi-proximity relations on digital images are given which induce the usual connectedness on digital images. This is not possible in classical topology.

It is shown that semi-proximity continuous functions can be more flexible than metric and topologically continuous functions on digital images while still preserving the usual connectedness. Useful examples of a semi-proximity continuous function are given which can map points with 8-distance one onto points with 8-distance two and which still preserve the 8-connectedness of the digital image. Semi-proximity continuous functions can be used for characterizing well-behaved operations on digital images such as thinning. It will be shown that the deletion of a simple point can be treated as a semi-proximity continuous function. These properties and a great variety of sp-relations on digital images implies that sp-continuous functions can be used to divide digital images into classes, which can be useful in the difficult task of shape description.

Since the semi-proximity relation on digital images reflects basic properties of the spatial concept "near", a digital structure with this relation can be useful in spatial reasoning, in particular, for pictorial inferences based on digital picture generating and inspection processes.

4.1 Semi-proximity Characterization of Discrete Spaces

Topology has been developed to formulate and treat continuity. This can be demonstrated by the following quotation from the translation [5] of Alexandroff [4] (p. 8, No. 8):

"A topological space is nothing other than a set of arbitrary elements (called points of the space) in which a concept of continuity is defined. Now this concept of continuity is based on the existence of relations, which may be defined as local neighborhood relations - it is precisely these relations which are preserved in a continuous mapping of one figure onto another."

A basic property of continuous functions is that the continuous image of a connected set is connected. This property can be useful in digital image processing, since most transformations of digital images must preserve connectedness. If transformations of digital images are represented by continuous functions, then we are guaranteed that they preserve connectedness. In image processing, there is a natural well-defined concept of connectedness that is based on the local neighborhood relations of digital images. Thus, the concept of digital continuity should also be based on the local neighborhood relations.

The most useful transformations of digital images are those which preserve connectedness in both directions, since they do not split or merge different components of an image. (Formally, we will say that a function preserves connectedness in both directions, if both the image and the inverse image of a connected set is connected.) If transformations of digital images were represented by functions continuous in both directions, then they would preserve connectedness in both directions. However, in order to define continuity in the inverse direction in classical topology, the inverse function must exist, and thus the original function must be one-to-one. So in classical topology a definition of continuity in the inverse direction does not exist for functions that are not invertible. Since most transformations of digital images are not one-to-one, the definition of continuity in the inverse direction for functions which need not be one-to-one would be a useful concept in digital image processing.

Rosenfeld [131] uses the natural metrics of digital images in the framework of classical topology to define continuous functions between digital images (see also Boxer [17]). Thus, a function in Rosenfeld's approach must also be a homeomorphism, and thus one-to-one, in order to be guaranteed to preserve connectedness in both directions. On the other hand, if a function on $\mathbf{Z}^2$ is one-to-one, then it is continuous iff it is a composition of the basic transformations on $\mathbf{Z}^2$, i.e., translation, rotation by $\pm 90°$ or by $180°$, and vertical, horizontal, or diagonal reflection (Rosenfeld [131]). This result is a consequence of the fact that a function is continuous in Rosenfeld's sense iff two points with distance one are mapped onto points with distance zero or one. Thus, this definition seems to be too restrictive for many applications in digital image processing. This limitation on the types of continuous functions available also applies to topologically continuous functions on $\mathbf{Z}^2$ which can be defined in the topology described in Khalimsky et al. [73] and Kovalevsky [90].

A semi-proximity structure is used to define continuous functions on digital images. Such functions can map points with distance one onto points with distance two or more. Thus, semi-proximity continuous functions are more flexible than metric or topologically continuous functions, yet they still preserve the usual kinds of connectedness of digital images. A function between semi-proximity spaces can be defined in a natural way to be continuous in both directions (bicontinuous), even if the function is not one-to-one.

The key property is the fact that bicontinuous functions between semi-proximity spaces preserve connectedness in both directions. This fact and the variety of semi-proximity relations which can be defined on digital images indicate that semi-proximity continuous functions can be used to characterize well-behaved operations on digital images and to assist in the difficult task of shape description.

Moreover, semi-proximity spaces establish a formal relationship between topological concepts of digital image processing and their continuous counterparts in $\mathbb{R}^k$ (Section 4.6). Since $\mathbb{R}^k$ with the usual topology is a semi-proximity space for every $k = 1, 2, \ldots$ and every digital image can be described as a semi-proximity space in such a way that digital connectedness and semi-proximity connectedness are equivalent, it makes sense to define semi-proximity continuous functions between $\mathbb{R}^k$ and digital images. It is impossible using classical topology, to define continuous functions between $\mathbb{R}^k$ and digital images, since the digital images which are most commonly used in applications cannot be described as topological spaces. For example, in Chassery [25] it is shown that there is no topology on $\mathbf{Z}^2$ in which connectedness is equivalent to 8-connectedness. In Latecki [93] a much simpler and shorter proof is given which requires only the consideration of a four-point subset of $\mathbf{Z}^2$.

This chapter is based on Latecki and Prokop [102]. In Sections 4.2 and 4.3, semi-proximity spaces, connectedness, and continuity are defined. It is also proved that a semi-proximity bicontinuous function, which need not be one-to-one, preserves connectedness in both directions. In Sections 4.4 and 4.5, some basic definitions of digital topology are reviewed, digital metric continuity is defined, and some useful descriptions of digital images as semi-proximity spaces are given. In Section 4.7, some examples of semi-proximity continuous functions on digital images are given. It is shown in Section 4.8 that semi-proximity continuity can be used to describe connectivity preserving thinning. In Section 4.9 properties of semi-proximity and other digital continuous functions are discussed. Finally, in Section 4.10, it shown that every nearness space in the sense of Herrlich [63] is a semi-proximity space.

4.2 Semi-Proximity Spaces

1908 Riesz [125] introduced proximity structures. In the early fifties Efremovič rediscovered the subject (see Naimpally and Warrack [118], Engelking [41]). The axioms for Riesz and Efremovič proximity structures were developed to axiomatize the properties of the relationship between sets A and B in a metric space which could be defined by stating that

$$A \text{ is close to } B \text{ (i.e., } A\delta B) \text{ iff } D(A, B) = inf\{d(x, y) : x \in A, y \in B\} = 0,$$

where d is the usual Euclidean distance function. The five axioms of Efremovič are now widely accepted as a definition of a proximity structure. The topologies generated by proximity structures are always completely regular. So, in defining a 'nearness' relation which is suitable for studying problems associated with digital images, where the topological spaces considered will not be completely regular, we will consider a generalization of a proximity structure, called a semi-proximity, which uses only four of the axioms for a proximity structure. Further, semi-proximity spaces generalize Herrlich's definition of nearness spaces defined in Herrlich [63]. Finally, we will show that underlying each semi-proximity space there is a Čech closure mapping and, conversely, that Čech closure mappings can be used to construct semi-proximity spaces. It should be noted that Čech [27] refers to semi-proximity relations which arise from a semi-uniformity as proximity relations.

Definition: A relation δ on the power set of X, denoted $P(X)$, which for all $A, B, C \in P(X)$ satisfies:

(p1) $(A \cup B)\delta C \Leftrightarrow A\delta C$ or $B\delta C$,

(p2) $A\delta B \Rightarrow A \neq \emptyset$ and $B \neq \emptyset$,

(p3) $A \cap B \neq \emptyset \Rightarrow A\delta B$,

(p4) $A\delta B \Rightarrow B\delta A$,

will be called a (symmetric) **semi-proximity** on $P(X)$. If $A\delta B$ we will say that A and B are **near**. We will write $A \not\delta B$ if A and B are not near. Finally, if X is a set and δ is a semi-proximity relation on $P(X)$, then (X, δ) will be called a **semi-proximity space** or **sp-space**.

For completeness, we note that $cl : P(X) \to P(X)$ is a **Čech (strong) closure mapping** if (Čech [27], Chapter 14, p. 237)

(I) $cl\emptyset = \emptyset$,

(II) for every $A \in P(X)$: $A \subseteq clA$,

(III) for every $A, B \in P(X)$: $cl(A \cup B) = clA \cup clB$.

The following theorem establishes the relationship between semi-proximity and Čech closure spaces. It also follows from this theorem that every topological space is a semi-proximity space, since every topological space is a Čech closure space.

Theorem 4.1 *If δ is a semi-proximity relation on $P(X)$, then $cl : P(X) \to P(X)$ given by*

$$clA = \{x \in X : A\delta\{x\}\}$$

is a Čech closure mapping on $P(X)$.

Conversely, if $cl : P(X) \to P(X)$ is a Čech closure mapping and δ_1 and δ_2 are given for every $A, B \in P(X)$ by

(i) $A\delta_1 B \Leftrightarrow clA \cap clB \neq \emptyset$ and   (ii) $A\delta_2 B \Leftrightarrow (A \cap clB \neq \emptyset$ or $clA \cap B \neq \emptyset)$,

then (X, δ_1) and (X, δ_2) are semi-proximity spaces.

Proof: Let δ be a semi-proximity relation on $P(X)$. By (p2), $cl\emptyset = \emptyset$. By (p3), $A \subseteq clA$. Finally, $cl(A \cup B) = \{x \in X : A \cup B\delta\{x\}\} = $ (by (p1))
$= \{x \in X : A\delta\{x\} \text{ or } B\delta\{x\}\} = \{x \in X : A\delta\{x\}\} \cup \{x \in X : B\delta\{x\}\} = clA \cup clB$.

Let now $cl : P(X) \to P(X)$ be a Čech closure mapping. Then (p1), (p2), and (p4) are easily verified for δ_1, while (p3) follows from

$$A \cap B \subseteq cl(A \cap B) \subseteq clA \cap clB.$$

For δ_2, we show first (p1): $(A \cup B)\delta_2 C \Leftrightarrow (A \cup B) \cap clB \neq \emptyset$ or $cl(A \cup B) \cap C \neq \emptyset \Leftrightarrow$ $(A \cap clB \neq \emptyset$ or $B \cap clB \neq \emptyset)$ or $(clA \cup clB) \cap C \neq \emptyset \Leftrightarrow (A \cap clB \neq \emptyset$ or $clA \cap C \neq \emptyset)$ or $(B \cap clB \neq \emptyset$ or $clB \cap C \neq \emptyset) \Leftrightarrow (A\delta_2 C$ or $B\delta_2 C)$, which implies (p1). The condition (p2) follows easily by considering cases. The condition (p3) follows from the fact that $A \cap B \subseteq A \cap clB$ and $A \cap B \subseteq clA \cap B$. Clearly, (p4) holds for δ_2. ∎

4.3   Connectedness and Continuity in SP-Spaces

In this section we define the concepts of connectedness and continuity in semi-proximity spaces. We will precede each analogous definition with "sp" for semi-proximity. It should be noted that for T_1 topological spaces, sp-connectivity and sp-continuity agree with their topological counterparts.

Definition: Let (X, δ) be a semi-proximity space and let $Z \subseteq X$. A pair of non-null subsets A, B of X such that $Z = A \cup B$ and $A \not\delta B$ is called an **sp-separation** of Z. The set Z is **sp-connected** in (X, δ) if there is no sp-separation of Z in (X, δ), otherwise Z is **sp-disconnected**. In particular, a semi-proximity space X is sp-connected if there is no sp-separation of X in X.

Let (X, cl) be a topological space, where cl is the closure operator generating the topology on X. If we consider the sp-relation defined by

$$A\delta B \Leftrightarrow A \cap clB \neq \emptyset \text{ or } clA \cap B \neq \emptyset,$$

then sp-connectedness agrees with the usual definition of connectedness in topological spaces. Further, if (X, cl) is a Čech closure space, then sp-connectedness agrees with Čech connectedness.

We will adopt the convention that if we are working in a semi-proximity space, we will write *A, B is a separation for a set Z* instead of the technically correct statement *A, B is a sp-separation for a set Z*. A similar convention will be adopted for all *sp* terms defined in this chapter.

Definition: Let (X, δ_1) and (Y, δ_2) be semi-proximity spaces.

A function $f : X \to Y$ is **sp-continuous** if

$$(\forall A, B \in P(X))(A\delta_1 B \Rightarrow f(A)\delta_2 f(B)).$$

A function $f : X \to Y$ is **inverse sp-continuous** if

(i) $(\forall A, B \in P(X))(f(A)\delta_2 f(B) \Rightarrow f^{-1}(f(A))\delta_1 f^{-1}(f(B)))$ and

(ii) the inverse image of every point in $f(X)$ is connected.

A function $f : X \to Y$ will be called **sp-bicontinuous** if it is continuous and inverse continuous.

Note that if $f : X \to Y$ is a function from X onto Y, then f is inverse sp-continuous iff

(i) $(\forall C, D \in P(Y))(C\delta_2 D \Rightarrow f^{-1}(C)\delta_1 f^{-1}(D))$ and

(ii) the inverse image of every point in Y is connected.

Clearly, the definition of sp-continuity agrees with the usual definition of continuity in proximity spaces. We show now that this is also the case for classical topological spaces. Let (X, cl) be a topological space, where cl is the closure operator generating the topology on X. If the sp-relation is defined by

$$A\delta B \Leftrightarrow A \cap clB \neq \emptyset \text{ or } clA \cap B \neq \emptyset,$$

then for T_1 topological spaces, sp-continuity agrees with the usual definition of continuity. Moreover, if $f : X \to Y$ is an sp-bicontinuous bijection between T_1 topological spaces, f is a topological homeomorphism. This is actually true for R_0 Čech closure spaces, where a closure space is R_0 if cl satisfies the condition

$$(R_0) \ (\forall a, b \in X)(a \in cl\{b\} \Leftrightarrow b \in cl\{a\}).$$

The most important property of an sp-bicontinuous function, which is proved in Theorem 4.4, is that it preserves connectedness in both directions. It is this property of bicontinuous functions along with the fact that they need not be one-to-one which make them an interesting tool in digital image processing. Theorem 4.2 will show that the continuous image of a connected semi-proximity space is connected. Theorem 4.3 will show that an inverse continuous function preserves connectedness in the inverse direction.

Lemma 4.1 *Let (X, δ) be a semi-proximity space.*

$$(\forall A, B \in P(X))(A\delta B \text{ and } A \subseteq C \text{ and } B \subseteq D \Rightarrow C\delta D).$$

Proof: By (p1), $A\delta B \Rightarrow (A \cup C)\delta B \Rightarrow C\delta B$.
By (p1) and (p4), $C\delta B \Rightarrow C\delta(B \cup D) \Rightarrow C\delta D$.   ∎

Theorem 4.2 *Let (X, δ_1) and (Y, δ_2) be semi-proximity spaces and $f : X \to Y$ be a continuous function. If X is connected, then $f(X)$ is connected.*

Proof: Let X be connected.

$f(X)$ disconnected $\Rightarrow \exists C, D \subseteq Y, C \neq \emptyset, D \neq \emptyset$ such that $f(X) = C \cup D$ and $C \not{\delta_2} D \Rightarrow X \subseteq f^{-1}(f(X)) = f^{-1}(C) \cup f^{-1}(D)$. If $f^{-1}(C)$ and $f^{-1}(D)$ are non-empty and X is connected, then $f^{-1}(C)\delta_1 f^{-1}(D)$. By continuity of f, $f(f^{-1}(C))\delta_2 f(f^{-1}(D))$. However, by Lemma 4.1, $f(f^{-1}(C)) \subseteq C$ and $f(f^{-1}(D)) \subseteq D \Rightarrow C\delta_2 D$, which is a contradiction. ∎

Theorem 4.3 *Let (X, δ_1) and (Y, δ_2) be semi-proximity spaces and $f : X \to Y$ be inverse continuous. If $f(X)$ is connected, then X is connected.*

Proof: Let $f(X)$ be connected and X be disconnected. There exist $B \neq \emptyset$, $B' \neq \emptyset$ subsets of X such that $X = B \cup B'$ and $B \not{\delta_1} B'$. Since $f(X)$ is connected and $f(X) = f(B) \cup f(B')$, we obtain $f(B)\delta_2 f(B')$. By inverse continuity of f,

$$f(B)\delta_2 f(B') \Rightarrow f^{-1}(f(B))\delta_1 f^{-1}(f(B')).$$

If $f^{-1}(f(B)) = B$ and $f^{-1}(f(B')) = B'$, we have a contradiction. So, at least one of these equalities does not hold. For example, let B be properly contained in $f^{-1}(f(B))$. This means that there exists $y \in f(B)$ such that $f^{-1}(\{y\}) \cap B' \neq \emptyset$. Since $y \in f(B)$, we also know that $f^{-1}(\{y\}) \cap B \neq \emptyset$. The fact that $f(X) = B \cup B'$ implies that $f^{-1}(\{y\}) = (B \cap f^{-1}(\{y\})) \cup (B' \cap f^{-1}(\{y\}))$. From Lemma 4.1 it follows that

$$B \cap f^{-1}(\{y\}) \not{\delta_1} B' \cap f^{-1}(\{y\}),$$

which means that $f^{-1}(\{y\})$ is not connected. This is a contradiction. ∎

As a simple consequence of Theorems 4.2 and 4.3, we obtain that if f is bicontinuous, then f preserves connectedness in both directions.

Theorem 4.4 *Let (X, δ_1) and (Y, δ_2) be semi-proximity spaces and $f : X \to Y$ be bicontinuous. X is connected $\Leftrightarrow f(X)$ is connected.* ∎

Theorem 4.5 follows easily from the definitions and the properties of the image and inverse image functions.

Theorem 4.5 *Let (X, δ_1), (Y, δ_2) and (Z, δ_3) be semi-proximity spaces and $f : X \to Y$ and $g : Y \to Z$ be functions.*

(i) *If f and g are continuous, then $g \circ f$ is continuous.*

(ii) *If f and g are inverse continuous, then $g \circ f$ is inverse continuous.*

(iii) *If f and g are bicontinuous, then $g \circ f$ is bicontinuous.* ∎

The following example shows that an sp-bicontinuous function between topological spaces need not be an open mapping. Let $f : [0,2] \to [0,1]$, $f(x) = min(x,1)$, be a function between closed intervals of real numbers. We treat an intervals as a sp-space with δ defined by $A\delta B \Leftrightarrow A \cap clB \neq \emptyset$ or $clA \cap B \neq \emptyset$, where cl is the usual closure operator. Then f is sp-bicontinuous, but it is not open (any open set in $(1,2]$ is mapped onto $\{1\}$).

4.4   Metric Continuity

The following definition of metric continuity is taken from Rosenfeld (1986). Rosenfeld has adopted the standard metric definition of continuity for digital pictures. However, to define metric continuity, Rosenfeld considers only metrics which fulfill the following conditions:

(i) for all $x, y \in \mathbf{Z}^n$, such that $x \neq y$, $d(x,y) \geq 1$ and

(ii) if $x = (x_1, ..., x_n)$ and $y = (y_1, ..., y_n)$, then $d(x,y) = 1$ iff there exists j, $1 \leq j \leq n$, such that $|x_j - y_j| = 1$ and $x_i = y_i$ for all $i \neq j$.

Obviously, the familiar Euclidean metric on $\mathbf{Z}^2$ and 4-distance which correspond to 4-adjacency on $\mathbf{Z}^2$ satisfy these conditions. However, the 8-distance based on 8-adjacency on $\mathbf{Z}^2$ does not satisfy condition (ii). Since digital pictures are equipped with natural metrics satisfying conditions (i) and (ii), metric continuity is a useful but restrictive property. Let r and s be natural numbers and let d_r and d_s be two metrics on $\mathbf{Z}^r$ and $\mathbf{Z}^s$, respectively, which fulfill conditions (i) and (ii). A function $f : (\mathbf{Z}^r, d_r) \to (\mathbf{Z}^s, d_s)$ is **metric continuous at a point** $p \in \mathbf{Z}^r$ if

$$(\forall \epsilon \geq 1)(\exists \delta \geq 1)(\forall q \in \mathbf{Z}^r)(d_r(p,q) \leq \delta \Rightarrow d_s(f(p), f(q)) \leq \epsilon).$$

A function $f : (\mathbf{Z}^r, d_r) \to (\mathbf{Z}^s, d_s)$ is **metric continuous** if it is metric continuous at every point $p \in \mathbf{Z}^r$.

Although Rosenfeld refers to such functions as continuous, we will use the term *metric continuity* to avoid possible confusion with sp-continuity. The definition of metric continuity is analogous to the familiar epsilon-delta definition of continuity for real valued functions. It is easy to show (see Rosenfeld [131]) that the definition of metric continuity is equivalent to the following one:
A function $f : (\mathbf{Z}^r, d_r) \to (\mathbf{Z}^s, d_s)$ is **metric continuous at a point** $p \in \mathbf{Z}^r$ if

$$(\forall q \in \mathbf{Z}^r)(d_r(p,q) \leq 1 \Rightarrow d_s(f(p), f(q)) \leq 1).$$

A simple consequence of this property is that metric continuous functions preserve metric connectedness, where a set X is **metric connected** in (Z^r, d_r) if $(\forall p, q \in X)$ there exists a sequence of points $p = p_1, p_2, ..., p_n = q$ such that $d_r(p_i, p_{i-1}) \leq 1$, $1 < i \leq n$.

For the 4-distance on $\mathbf{Z}^2$, the corresponding metric connectedness is equivalent to 4-connectedness. The following theorem, which along with its proof is found in Rosenfeld [131], indicates that metric continuity may be too restrictive for many applications in digital image processing.

Theorem 4.6 *If* $f : \mathbf{Z}^2 \to \mathbf{Z}^2$ *is metric continuous and one-to-one, then* f *is a translation, possibly combined with a vertical, horizontal, or diagonal reflection or with a rotation by* $\pm 90°$ *or by* $180°$. ∎

4.5 Semi-Proximity Relations on Digital Pictures

We will now show that there is a natural way to define a Čech closure operator on $\mathbf{Z}^k$, and that connectivity in the corresponding semi-proximities agrees with the usual connectivity of digital pictures.

In this chapter, if two points x and y are n-neighbors or $x = y$, we will say that they are **n-adjacent** and write $n - adj(x, y)$ or simply $adj(x, y)$. In the definition given in Chapter 2, we did not require that $x = y$.

Let $\mathcal{N}(x)$ be some m-neighborhood of $x \in \mathbf{Z}^k$. If we define closure cl on the power set $P(\mathbf{Z}^k)$ by

$$(\forall Y \in P(\mathbf{Z}^k))(clY = \{x \in \mathbf{Z}^k : \mathcal{N}(x) \cap Y \neq \emptyset\}),$$

then cl is a Čech closure operator on $\mathbf{Z}^k$. Thus, by Theorem 4.1, cl determines two semi-proximity relations δ_1 and δ_2 on $\mathbf{Z}^k$ given by

(i) $A\delta_1 B \Leftrightarrow clA \cap clB \neq \emptyset$ and (ii) $A\delta_2 B \Leftrightarrow (A \cap clB \neq \emptyset$ or $clA \cap B \neq \emptyset)$.

Observe that, for δ_i with $i = 1$ or 2, we have

$$(\forall A, B \in P(\mathbf{Z}^k))(A\delta_i B \Leftrightarrow (\exists a \in A, b \in B)\{a\}\delta_i\{b\}).$$

Thus, δ_1 has the following simple characterization in terms of the neighborhoods of points:

$$(\forall A, B \in P(\mathbf{Z}^k))(A\delta_1 B \Leftrightarrow ((\exists a \in A, b \in B)\mathcal{N}(a) \cap \mathcal{N}(b) \neq \emptyset).$$

Similarly, δ_2 has a point-wise characterization given by:

$$(\forall A, B \in P(\mathbf{Z}^k))(A\delta_2 B \Leftrightarrow ((\exists a \in A, b \in B)a \in \mathcal{N}(b) \vee b \in \mathcal{N}(a))).$$

Since in digital pictures

$$a \in \mathcal{N}(b) \Leftrightarrow b \in \mathcal{N}(a) \Leftrightarrow m - adj(a, b),$$

we obtain a simple equivalence for δ_2 in terms of adjacency given by:

$$(\forall A, B \in P(\mathbf{Z}^k))(A\delta_2 B \Leftrightarrow (\exists a \in A, b \in B)m - adj(a, b)).$$

Thus, δ_2 is just an extension of m-adjacency to sets. Using this definition, it is easy to observe that the sp-connectedness induced by δ_2 is exactly the m-connectedness on $\mathbf{Z}^k$ for every m-adjacency relation. This is an important property, since m-connectedness is an intuitive analog of the continuous concept of connectedness in digital pictures.

In contrary, if we define δ_1 using 4- or 8-neighborhoods, then δ_1-connectedness does not induce m-connectedness on $\mathbf{Z}^k$: if we consider the two point set in Figure 4.1.a, then it is δ_1-connected but not m-connected.

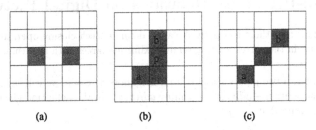

(a)   (b)   (c)

Figure 4.1: (a) The two point set is δ_1-connected but not m-connected. (b) $a\gamma b$. (c) $a \not\gamma b$.

The most commonly used digital pictures are $(\mathbf{Z}^k, m, n, B)$ pictures with changeable (m, n)-connectedness, where B is the set of black points (see Section 2.1). We will now define an sp-relation which is suitable for describing such pictures. We will begin by defining a relation γ for points in B of $(\mathbf{Z}^k, m, n, B)$:

(γ) $(\forall x, y \in B)(x\gamma y)$ iff $(\exists p \in B)((m - adj(x, p)$ and $n - adj(p, y))$
or $(n - adj(x, p)$ and $m - adj(p, y)))$.

Note that γ is reflexive, since if $x = y$, then $x\gamma y$, because p can equal either x or y. This follows from the fact that for any k-adjacency, if $a = b$, then $k - adj(a, b)$. For example, if B is the set of black points given in Figure 4.1.b with 8-adjacency in $(\mathbf{Z}^2, 8, 4, B)$ and $a, b \in B$, then $a\gamma b$, since there is $p \in B$ such that $8 - adj(a, p)$ and $4 - adj(p, b)$. This is clearly not the case for a and b in Figure 4.1.c. The extension of g to the sets of black points is straightforward:

$$(\forall A, C \in P(B))(A\gamma C) \text{ iff } (\exists x \in A, y \in C)(x\gamma y).$$

By checking (p1) - (p4) of the definition of a semi-proximity space, it can easily be shown that (B, γ) is a semi-proximity space.

Theorem 4.7 *Let* $A \subseteq \mathbb{Z}^k$ *with* m*-adjacency in* $(\mathbb{Z}^k, m, n, A)$, *where* $m < n$ *and let* (A, γ) *be a semi-proximity space defined by the condition* (γ). *We have the following implications:*
A is m*-connected* $\Rightarrow$ *A is sp-connected* $\Rightarrow$ *A is* n*-connected.*

Proof: First we will show that sp-connectedness implies n-connectedness. Let A be n-disconnected and let C, D be an n-separation of A. This implies that there is no n-path in A joining any point in C to some point in D. Thus, C, D is also an sp-separation of A.

Assume now that A is sp-disconnected and C, D is an sp-separation of A. It is clear that $(\forall x \in C, y \in D)(x \not\gamma y)$. Thus, C, D is also an m-separation of A. If this were not the case, then $(\exists x \in C, y \in D)(\exists m - path(x, y) \subseteq A)$. Since an m-path is a finite sequence of points, we obtain $(\exists c \in C, d \in D)(c, d \in m - path(x, y)$ and $m - adj(c, d))$. But this implies that $C\gamma D$, a contradiction.   ∎

4.6 A Semi-Proximity Relation between $\mathbb{R}^n$ and $\mathbb{Z}^n$

Using semi-proximity spaces we can establish a formal relationship between the topological concepts of digital image processing and their continuous counterparts. For example, a set $\alpha \subseteq \mathbb{Z}^k$ is a digital arc if α is an sp-bicontinuous image of a closed interval with usual topology. Similar characterizations can be given for digital simple curves and digital surfaces. This is impossible in classical topology, since the digital images which are most commonly used in applications cannot be described as topological spaces. Chassery [25] showed that there is no topology on $\mathbb{Z}^2$ in which connectedness is equivalent to 8-connectedness (see also Latecki [93] for a much shorter and simpler proof, which requires only the consideration of a four-point subset of $\mathbb{Z}^2$).

By the results in Section 4.1, $(\mathbb{R}, \delta)$ is a semi-proximity space having the usual topology of the real numbers $\mathbb{R}$ if we define

$$(\forall A, B \in P(\mathbb{R}))(A\delta B \text{ iff } A \cap clB \neq \emptyset \text{ or } clA \cap B \neq \emptyset),$$

where cl is the usual closure operator. By the results in Section 4.5, $\mathbb{Z}^k$ with m-adjacency is a semi-proximity space if we define

$$(\forall A, B \in P(\mathbb{Z}^k))(A\delta_m B) \Leftrightarrow (\exists a \in A, b \in B) \, m - adj(a, b)).$$

Therefore, it makes sense to define sp-continuous functions between $(\mathbb{R}, \delta)$ and $(\mathbb{Z}^k, \delta_m)$.

Note that this is the first formal link between the most commonly used digital pictures and $\mathbb{R}$ which is based on an axiomatic theory. In the approach presented in Khalimsky et al. [73] and Kovalevsky [90], $\mathbb{Z}^k$ can be treated as a T_0 topological space. However, the structure of $\mathbb{Z}^k$ obtained this way is not the one most commonly used in digital pictures with 4, 8, 6, or 26 adjacency relations.

Theorem 4.8 will show that a digital arc can be described as a sp-bicontinuous image of a closed interval with the usual topology. We recall now the definition of a digital arc which is the most commonly used in computer vision and computer graphics (see Section 2.1):

Definition: A finite set $\alpha \subseteq \mathbf{Z}^k$ is an **m-arc** connecting point p with q if α is m-connected and each point in $\alpha \setminus \{p, q\}$ has exactly two m-neighbors in α, while the **endpoints** p and q have exactly one.

A finite set $C \subseteq \mathbf{Z}^k$ is a **simple closed m-curve** if C is m-connected and all points in C have exactly two m-neighbors in C. To rule out degenerate cases the usual restriction on the minimal number of points in a simple closed curve is assumed: a 4-curve has at least eight points and an 8-curve at least four points, and so on for every m-adjacency relation.

Theorem 4.8 *A finite set $\alpha \subseteq \mathbf{Z}^k$ is an m-arc iff α is an sp-bicontinuous image of a closed interval with the usual topology, i.e., $(\exists f : (I, \delta) \to (\mathbf{Z}^k, \delta_m))(f(I) = \alpha$ and f is sp-bicontinuous), where $(I, \delta) \subseteq (R, \delta)$ is a closed interval.*

Proof:
"$\Rightarrow$" An m-arc α connecting p with q can be regarded as a sequence of points $p = p_1, p_2, ..., p_n = q$ such that p_i is a m-neighbor of p_{i-1}, $1 < i \leq n$. Let $([0, n], \delta) \subseteq (\mathbb{R}, \delta)$ be an interval and let $f : ([0, n], \delta) \to (\mathbf{Z}^k, \delta_m)$ be defined

$$f([0, 1]) = p_1 \text{ and } f((i, i + 1]) = p_i \text{ for } i = 1 \text{ to } n - 1,$$

where $(i, i + 1]$ is a half open - half closed interval. Clearly $f([0, n]) = \alpha$. It is easy to see that f is sp-bicontinuous, since all points in $\alpha \setminus \{p, q\}$ have exactly two m-neighbors in α, while the endpoints p and q have exactly one, and we have a similar situation for the relation δ among the intervals $[0, 1]$, $(i, i + 1]$, where $i = 1$ to $n - 1$.

"$\Leftarrow$" Let $f : (I, \delta) \to (\mathbf{Z}^k, \delta_m)$ be an sp-bicontinuous function such that $f(I) = \alpha$, where $(I, \delta) \subseteq (R, \delta)$ is a closed interval. Since f is an sp-bicontinuous function, $f(I) = \alpha$ is m-connected. Note that $(\forall x \in \alpha)(f^{-1}(x)$ is connected); therefore $f^{-1}(x)$ is a subinterval of I (we treat points in $\mathbb{R}$ as (degenerate) intervals). Now, $I = \bigcup_{x \in \alpha} f^{-1}(x)$ is the union of a collection of pairwise disjoint intervals; every interval in this collection is δ-near exactly two other intervals in I; except for exactly the two subintervals of I which contain the endpoints of I, say these are $f^{-1}(p)$ and $f^{-1}(q)$. These two subintervals are δ-near exactly one other subinterval. By the sp-bicontinuity of f, we obtain that all points in $\alpha \setminus \{p, q\}$ have exactly two m-neighbors in α, while p and q have exactly one. ∎

Theorem 4.9 *A finite set $C \subseteq \mathbf{Z}^k$ satisfying the restriction on the minimal number of points is a simple closed m-curve iff C is an sp-bicontinuous image of a unit circle with the usual topology, i.e., $(\exists f : (S^1, \delta) \to (\mathbf{Z}^k, \delta_m))(f(S^1) = C$ and f is sp-bicontinuous), where $(S^1, \delta) \subseteq (\mathbb{R}^2, \delta)$ is a unit circle.*

Proof: The proof is very similar to the proof of Theorem 4.8.   ■

4.7 Examples of SP-Continuous Functions

We give some examples of sp-continuous functions on digital sets. The digital sets considered in these examples are subsets of $(\mathbf{Z}^2, 8, 4, B)$, i.e., on the set of black points B we consider 8-adjacency and on its complement 4-adjacency. We will illustrate the points of set B as gray colored squares in the following figures. We recall that for any $B \subseteq \mathbf{Z}^2$ with 8-adjacency, δ_2 is defined by

$$(\forall A, C \in P(B))(A\delta_2 C \text{ iff } (\exists a \in A, c \in C)(8 - adj(a,c))),$$

and γ is defined by

$$(\forall A, C \in P(B))(A\gamma C) \text{ iff } (\exists x \in A, y \in C)(x\gamma y), \text{ where}$$

$$(\forall x, y \in X)(x\gamma y) \text{ iff } (\exists p \in X)((8 - adj(x,p) \text{ and } 4 - adj(p,y))$$
$$\text{or } (4 - adj(x,p) \text{ and } 8 - adj(p,y))).$$

Let g be the function between the two digital pictures given in Figure 4.2, i.e., $g(x) = x'$ if $x \neq b$, and $g(b) = e'$. If we use δ_2 for both sets, then g is sp-continuous, since it is clear that $u\delta_2 v \Rightarrow f(u)\delta_2 f(v)$. Similarly, if we use γ for both sets, then g is sp-continuous.

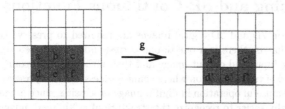

Figure 4.2: If we use δ_2 or γ for both sets, then g is sp-continuous.

Now let h be the function between the two digital pictures given in Figure 4.3, i.e., $h(x) = x'$ for every $x \neq b$, and $h(b) = e'$.

If δ_2 is used in both pictures, then h is not sp-continuous, since $b\delta_2 p$, but $h(b) \not\!\delta_2 h(p)$, i.e., $e' \not\!\delta_2 p'$. However, if we use γ for both pictures, then h is sp-continuous, since $b\gamma p$ and $h(b)\gamma h(p)$. Note that in this case h maps points with 8-distance *one* onto points with 8-distance *two* and it still preserves the 8-connectivity of the digital image.

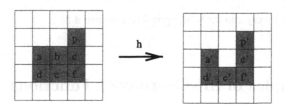

Figure 4.3: If δ_2 is used in both pictures, then h is not sp-continuous. However, if we use γ, then h is sp-continuous.

The function k shown in Figure 4.4 is defined by
$k(x) = x'$ for every $x \neq b$ and $k(b) = e'$,
is not sp-continuous for either δ_2 or γ, since it does not preserve δ_2 or γ-connectedness.

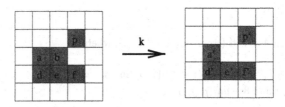

Figure 4.4: The function k is not sp-continuous for either δ_2 or γ.

4.8   Thinning and SP-Continuous Functions

Many operations on 2D and 3D digital images are required to preserve connectedness in both directions, that is, there is a one-to-one correspondence between (black and white) components of the input and output image and their structure. For example, thinning (or shrinking) is a kind of transformation where connectedness must be preserved in both directions. Thinning is a useful operation in digital image processing, since in many applications it is computationally easier to recognize the structure of a "thinner" image, provided that the thinning algorithm did not change the structure of connected components in the image. Thinning a set B of black points means deleting a subset $A \subseteq B$, i.e., changing the color of points in A from black to white. This suggests that every thinning transformation $T : B \rightarrow B \setminus A$ should preserve automatically connectedness in the inverse direction if T is appropriately defined, i.e., if X is a connected subset of $B \setminus A$, then $T^{-1}(X)$ should be a connected subset of B. Therefore, to show that a thinning transformation preserves connectedness in both directions, it is enough to show that it maps connected sets to connected sets.

According to Kong [78], a thinning algorithm (parallel or sequential) preserves connectedness (i.e., maps connected sets to connected sets) iff every set deleted by this algorithm can be ordered in a sequence such that every point is simple after all previous points are deleted. Intuitively, a point is simple if its deletion does not change locally the connected components of black and white points. Thus, this definition reduces the global problem of connectedness preservation to a local one. We show that deleting a simple point (i.e., turning its color from black to white) in a digital image $(\mathbf{Z}^2, 8, 4, Y)$ can be regarded as a sp-continuous function.

Let δ_2 and γ be as defined in Section 4.7. Since thinning can be described as a recursive deletion of simple points, we can characterize a thinning algorithm transforming a black set Y to its subset X as a sequence of sp-continuous functions $f_n : (Y_n, \delta_2) \to (Y_{n+1}, \gamma)$ for $n = 1, ..., k-1$ such that $Y_1 = Y$ and $Y_k = X$ and $Y_{n+1} = Y_n \setminus \{p_n\}$, where p_n is a simple point in Y_n. Since sp-connectedness relations induced by δ_2 and by γ both imply 8-connectedness, it follows that this thinning algorithm preserves 8-connectedness. An advantage of this approach to thinning is that the connectedness preservation of a thinning algorithm follows automatically from sp-continuity of functions f_n.

The following results are stated for 2D images with 8-connectedness relation. However, analogous results can also be proved for other connectedness relations and 3D images. We do not present them here, since their proofs require a complicated pattern analysis and our main goal is to demonstrate the advantages of the approach of viewing a thinning algorithm as a sequence of sp-continuous functions. Now we recall the standard definition of an 8-simple point (Section 3.3), which we will call a simple point in the following.

Definition: A black point p in $(\mathbf{Z}^2, 8, 4, B)$ is said to be **(8-)simple** if

C1 p is 8-adjacent to only one black 8-component in $\mathcal{N}_8(p) \setminus p$ and

C2 p is 4-adjacent to only one white 4-component in $\mathcal{N}_8(p)$.

Theorem 4.10 shows that sp-continuity can be used to characterize the deletion of simple points:

Theorem 4.10 *Let Y be a set of black points in $(\mathbf{Z}^2, 8, 4, Y)$ and $X = Y \setminus \{p\}$, where $p \in Y$. If p is simple in $(\mathbf{Z}^2, 8, 4, Y)$, then there exists an sp-continuous function*

$$f : (Y, \delta_2) \to (X, \gamma),$$

where δ_2 and γ are defined as in Section 4.7.

Proof: Recall that δ_2 is just an extension of 8-adjacency to sets, i.e.,

$$(\forall a, b \in Y)(a\delta_2 b \Leftrightarrow 8 - adj(a, b)).$$

Thus, we have

$$(\forall y \in Y)(p\delta_2 y \Leftrightarrow y \in Y \cap \mathcal{N}_8(p)).$$

Let p be simple in $(\mathbf{Z}^2, 8, 4, Y)$. Then, there exists a white 4-neighbor w of p. Assume first that w is such that there also exists a black 4-neighbor q of p such that w and q lie on the opposite sides of p (see Figure 4.5.a, where the light gray squares denote points of either color). We show that the function defined by

$$f(p) = q \quad \text{and} \quad (\forall y \in Y \setminus \{p\})(f(y) = y)$$

is sp-continuous. Since we have

$$(\forall y \in Y)(p\delta_2 y \Leftrightarrow y \in Y \cap \mathcal{N}_8(p))),$$

it remains to show that

$$(\forall y \in Y \cap \mathcal{N}_8(p))(f(y)\gamma f(p)).$$

This follows from the fact that

$$(\forall x \in X \cap \mathcal{N}_8(p))(x\gamma q),$$

which can be easily checked.

If there is no pair of 4-neighbors q and w of p such that w and q lie on the opposite sides of p and w is white while q is black, then, by the simplicity of p, all 4-neighbors of p are white and there is exactly one black 8-neighbor q of p (see Figure 4.5.b), i.e., p is an endpoint. In this case the function

$$f(p) = q \quad \text{and} \quad (\forall y \in Y \setminus \{p\})(f(y) = y)$$

is clearly continuous.   ∎

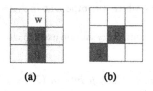

(a)   (b)

Figure 4.5:

All thinning algorithms do not delete a simple point that does not have a black 4-neighbor, since such a point has only one black 8-neighbor, and therefore it is an endpoint. Thus, only simple points that have a black 4-neighbor need be considered.

Theorem 4.10 establishes a relation between sp-continuous functions and thinning algorithms, which gives a new view of thinning as a sequence of sp-continuous mappings, so that the connectivity preservation of a thinning algorithm follows from the sp-continuity.

4.9 SP- and other Digital Continuous Functions

The example given in Figure 4.6 shows that semi-proximity continuous functions on digital images are more flexible than metric and topologically continuous functions. Consider the set of black points X on the left side in Figure 4.6. The deletion of a simple point $p \in X$ cannot be described as a continuous function in Rosenfeld's sense, since the definition of continuity in Rosenfeld [131] requires that points with distance one are mapped onto points with distance at most one and Rosenfeld's restrictions on the distance imply that only 4-neighbors are allowed to have distance one. So, two 8-neighbors must have distance greater than one. Yet the point p is at distance one to its three black 4-neighbors, and there is no other black point (onto which p could be mapped) which is at distance ≤ 1 to these three 4-neighbors. Thus, Theorem 4.10 is not true if we use the definition of metric continuous function given in Rosenfeld [131].

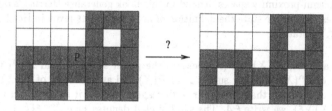

Figure 4.6: The deletion of a simple point p cannot be described as a metric continuous function.

This example also shows that the deletion of a simple point p cannot be described as a digital retraction as defined in Boxer [17], since Boxer's definition of digital retraction is based on Rosenfeld's definition of metric continuity:

Definition: A function $r : A \to B$, where $B \subseteq A$, is a **digital retraction** if r is metric continuous and $r(b) = b$ for all $b \in B$.

For the same reason, the sets X and $X \setminus \{p\}$ in Figure 4.6 are also not homotopy equivalent in the digital sense as defined in Boxer [17]: As shown above, there is no metric continuous function between X and $X \setminus \{p\}$, and there is no other set contained in $X \setminus \{p\}$ which is digital homotopy equivalent to X and $X \setminus \{p\}$, because there is no proper subset of $X \setminus \{p\}$ onto which $X \setminus \{p\}$ could be metric continuously mapped. If we base Boxer's definitions of digital retraction and homotopy on sp-continuity, then $X \setminus \{p\}$ will become a digital retract of X and the two sets will become homotopy equivalent: The function that maps p onto its south 4-neighbor and does not move the other points in X is sp-continuous if we treat X and $X \setminus \{p\}$ as digital images described in Theorem 4.10.

The definition of metric continuous functions cannot be extended by allowing greater distance between the image points, e.g., points with distance one are mapped onto points with distance at most two, since such a function would not preserve connectedness. In particular, a metric continuous function $f : (\mathbf{Z}^2, d_4) \rightarrow (\mathbf{Z}^2, d_8)$ does not preserve 8-connectedness, where d_4 denotes the 4-distance and d_8 denotes the 8-distance. On the other hand, the deletion of simple point p in Figure 4.6 cannot be described as a metric continuous function $f : (\mathbf{Z}^2, d_8) \rightarrow (\mathbf{Z}^2, d_8)$, since p must be mapped by f onto one of its black 8-neighbors, but then $f(p)$ cannot be at 8-distance one to the other black 8-neighbors of p. These limitations also apply to continuous functions in the T_0 topology on $\mathbf{Z}^2$ described in Khalimsky et al. [73] and Kovalevsky [90]. In this topology, $x \in cl\{y\} \Rightarrow d_8(x,y) \leq 1$, and therefore a topologically continuous function maps points with 8-distance one to the points with 8-distance at most one.

4.10   Semi-proximity and nearness spaces

We show that semi-proximity spaces defined in this book generalize Herrlich's definition of nearness spaces. Before we state the definition of nearness spaces given in Herrlich [63], we quote Herrlich's notation:

Let X be any set, $P^1(X) = P(X)$ denotes the power set of X, and $P^{n+1}(X)$ denotes the power set of $P^n(X)$. For any subset $\mathcal{A}$ of $P(X)$ and any subset ξ of $P^2(X)$, we write $\xi\mathcal{A}$ for $\mathcal{A} \in \xi$ and we say that $\mathcal{A}$ is **near** with respect to ξ. If it is not the case that $\xi\mathcal{A}$, i.e., $\mathcal{A} \in (P^2(X) \setminus \xi)$, we write $\overline{\xi}\mathcal{A}$. The symbol $cl_\xi A$ denotes $\{x \in X : \xi\{\{x\}, A\}\}$, where $A \subseteq X$. For $\mathcal{A}, \mathcal{B} \subseteq P(X)$, $\mathcal{A} \vee \mathcal{B} = \{A \cup B : A \in \mathcal{A} \text{ and } B \in \mathcal{B}\}$.

Definition: (Herrlich [63], Def. 1.1) A pair (X, ξ) is called a **nearness space** or **N-space** iff the following conditions are satisfied:

(N1) If $\bigcap \mathcal{A} \neq \emptyset$, then $\xi\mathcal{A}$.

(N2) If $\xi\mathcal{B}$ and for each $A \in \mathcal{A}$ there exists $B \in \mathcal{B}$ with $B \subset cl_\xi A$, then $\xi\mathcal{A}$.

(N3) If $\overline{\xi}\mathcal{A}$ and $\overline{\xi}\mathcal{B}$, then $\overline{\xi}(\mathcal{A} \vee \mathcal{B})$.

(N4) If $\emptyset \in \mathcal{A}$, then $\overline{\xi}\mathcal{A}$.

Theorem 4.11 *Every nearness space defined in Herrlich [63] is a semi-proximity space.*

Proof: Let (X, ξ) be a nearness space fulfilling (N1) - (N4). We define a relation δ on $P(X)$ by
$$A\delta B \text{ if } \xi\{A, B\}.$$
We show now that δ satisfies (p1) - (p4) in our definition of the semi-proximity relation.

(p4) is trivially satisfied, since $\{A, B\} = \{B, A\}$.

Now we show (p3): If $A \cap B \neq \emptyset$, then $\cap\{A, B\} \neq \emptyset$ implies that $\xi\{A, B\}$, which means that $A\delta B$.

To show (p2), note first that (N4) is equivalent to $(\xi\mathcal{A} \Rightarrow \emptyset \notin \mathcal{A})$. Thus
$A\delta B \Rightarrow \xi\{A, B\} \Rightarrow$ (by N4) $\emptyset \notin \{A, B\} \Rightarrow A \neq \emptyset$ and $B \neq \emptyset$.

It remains to show (p1), i.e., $(A \cup B)\delta C \Rightarrow A\delta C$ or $B\delta C$. Observe first that (N3) is equivalent to $(\xi(A \vee B) \Rightarrow \xi A$ or $\xi B)$. Let $(A \cup B)\delta C$, i.e., $\xi\{A \cup B, C\}$. Consider the set

$$\{A, C\} \vee \{B, C\} = \{A \cup B, C, A \cup C, C \cup B\}.$$

Since $\xi\{A \cup B, C\}$ and C is a subset of the following sets $C, A \cup C, C \cup B$, we obtain by (N2) that $\xi(\{A, C\} \vee \{B, C\})$. By (N3), $\xi\{A, C\}$ or $\xi\{B, C\}$. Thus $A\delta C$ or $B\delta C$. ∎

Chapter 5

Embedding Approach

By a *segmented (or multicolor)* image, we mean a digital image in which each point is assigned a unique label (e.g., a color) that indicates the object to which it belongs. By the foreground (objects) of a segmented image, we mean the objects whose properties we want to analyze, and by the background all the other objects of a digital image. If one adjacency relation is used for the foreground of a 3D segmented image (e.g., 6-adjacency) and a different one for the background (e.g., 26-adjacency), then interchanging the foreground and the background can change the connected components of the digital picture. Hence, the choice of foreground and of background is critical for the results of the subsequent analysis (like object grouping), especially in cases where it is not clear at the beginning of the analysis what constitutes the foreground and what the background, since this choice immediately determines the connected components of the digital picture.

In this chapter we describe an 3D embedding approach in which the embedding function maps foreground points of a 3D digital picture to closed unite cubes of which they are center points. The obtained continuous analog is used to define well-composed 3D pictures. The advantages of the concept of well-composedness for 3D pictures turned out to be even greater than for 2D pictures. In a well-composed picture, 6-, 14-, 18-, and 26-connected components are equal. This implies that for a well-composed digital picture, the choice of the foreground and the background is not critical for the results of the subsequent analysis. Moreover, a very natural definition of a continuous analog for well-composed digital pictures leads to regular properties of surfaces. This allows us to give a simple proof of a digital version of the 3D Jordan-Brouwer separation theorem. Additionally, in a well-composed 3D picture each connected component of the object boundary is a Jordan surface, and therefore satisfies the Jordan-Brouwer separation theorem.

5.1 Continuous Analog

In this chapter 3D well-composed pictures are defined and their properties are analyzed. Their definition is based on the concept of a continuous analog. There are actually two different approaches to define a continuous analog of a digital picture. In Artzy et al. [12], Herman [64], and Rosenfeld et al. [136], a point of a 3D digital image is interpreted as a

93

unit cube in $\mathbb{R}^3$, digital objects are interpreted as connected sets of cubes, and the surface of an object is the set of faces of the cubes that separate the object form its complement. For example, in Figure 5.1(a) a continuous analog of the eight-point digital set is the union of the eight cubes. In the graph interpretation of a digital image, a face in a surface of a continuous analog corresponds to a pair of 6-adjacent points (p, q), where p belongs to the object and q belongs to its complement (Herman [64]). A different approach is taken in Kong and Roscoe [80], where, for example, a cube belongs to a continuous analog of a (6, 26) binary digital picture if all of its eight corners belong to the digital object (set of black points), and a face of a cube belongs to the surface of a continuous analog of a digital object if the four corners of the face belong to the boundary of the digital object. For example, in Figure 5.1(b) such a continuous analog of the eight-point digital set is the single cube that has the eight points as its corners. If we treat the corners of faces as points of a (6, 26) digital picture, then the corresponding digital surface is composed of picture points. Such surfaces are analyzed in Morgenthaler and Rosenfeld [116], Kong and Roscoe [80], Francon [43], and Chen and Zhang [28, 29].

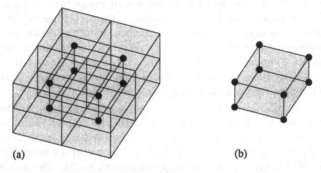

(a)   (b)

Figure 5.1: There are actually two different approaches to define a continuous analog of a digital picture.

We will interpret $\mathbf{Z}^3$ as the set of points with integer coordinates in 3D space $\mathbb{R}^3$. We will denote the set of the closed unit upright cubes which are centered at points of $\mathbf{Z}^3$ by $\mathcal{C}$, and the set of closed faces of cubes in $\mathcal{C}$ by $\mathcal{F}$, i.e., each $f \in \mathcal{F}$ is a unit closed square in $\mathbb{R}^3$ parallel to one of the coordinate planes.

A three-dimensional digital set (i.e., a finite subset of $\mathbf{Z}^3$) can be identified with a union of upright unit cubes which are centered at its points. This gives us an intuitive and simple correspondence between points in $\mathbf{Z}^3$ and cubes in $\mathbb{R}^3$. Since this correspondence plays an important role here, we will describe it formally.

The **continuous analog** $CA(p)$ of a point $p \in \mathbf{Z}^3$ is the closed unit cube centered at this point with faces parallel to the coordinate planes. The **continuous analog** of a digital set X (i.e., $X \subseteq \mathbf{Z}^3$) is defined as $CA(X) = \bigcup \{CA(x) : x \in X\}$ (see Figure 5.1(a)). Formally, CA is a function $CA : \mathcal{P}(\mathbf{Z}^3) \to \mathcal{P}(\mathbb{R}^3)$. In particular, we have $\mathcal{C} = \{CA(p) : p \in \mathbf{Z}^3\}$.

We also define a dual function $Dig_\in$ to CA which we call **subset (or element) digi-tization**: $Dig_\in : \mathcal{P}(\mathbb{R}^3) \to \mathcal{P}(\mathbf{Z}^3)$ is given by $Dig_\in(Y) = \{p \in \mathbf{Z}^3 : p \in Y\}$. Clearly, we have $Dig_{\in}(CA(X)) = X$ for every $X \subseteq \mathbf{Z}^3$. The equation $CA(Dig_{\in}(Y)) = Y$ holds only if $Y \subseteq \mathbb{R}^3$ is a union of some cubes in $\mathcal{C}$.

We will define a 3D digital picture as well-composed if the boundary surface of its continuous analog is a 2D manifold (i.e., it "looks" locally like a planar open set). This definition implies a simple correspondence between a 3D digital image and the boundary surface of its continuous analog when digital objects are identified with unions of cubes centered at their points. Thus, we can use well-known properties of continuous boundary surfaces, like the Jordan-Brouwer separation theorem, to determine and analyze properties of these digital images. Additionally, since we will study boundary surfaces, some of our results also apply to surfaces spanned on boundary points of digital pictures. For example, conditions given in Theorem 5.4 also apply to the simple closed surfaces in the Morgenthaler and Rosenfeld sense.

The adjacency relations between points in $\mathbf{Z}^3$ that we will use in this chapter are defined in Section 2.1.

A common **face** of two cubes centered at points $p, q \in \mathbf{Z}^3$ (i.e., a unit square parallel to one of the coordinate planes) can be identified with the pair (p, q). Such pairs are called "surface elements" in Herman [64], since they are constituent parts of object surfaces. We can extend CA to apply also to pairs of points by defining $CA((p,q)) = CA(p) \cap CA(q)$ for $p, q \in \mathbf{Z}^3$, and $CA(B) = \bigcup\{CA(x) : x \in B\}$, where B is a set of pairs of points in $\mathbf{Z}^3$. In particular, we have $\mathcal{F} = \{CA((p,q)) : p, q \in \mathbf{Z}^3$ and p is 6 adjacent to $q\}$.

The **(face) boundary** of a continuous analog $CA(X)$ of a digital set $X \subseteq \mathbf{Z}^3$ is defined as the union of the set of closed faces each of which is the common face of a cube in $CA(X)$ and a cube not in $CA(X)$. Observe that the face boundary of $CA(X)$ is just the topological boundary $bdCA(X)$ in $\mathbb{R}^3$. The face boundary $bdCA(X)$ can also be defined using only cubes of the set $CA(X)$ as the union of the set of closed faces each of which is a face of exactly one cube in $CA(X)$. We have $bdCA(X) = bdCA(X^c)$, where $X^c = \mathbf{Z}^3 \setminus X$ is the complement of X. The **(6-) boundary** of a digital set $X \subseteq \mathbf{Z}^3$ can be defined as the set of pairs

$$bd_6 X = \{(p,q) : p \in X \text{ and } q \notin X \text{ and } p \text{ is 6 adjacent to } q\}.$$

We have $bdCA(X) = CA(bd_6 X) = CA(bd_6(X^c))$.

Two distinct faces $f_1, f_2 \in \mathcal{F}$ are **edge-adjacent** if they share an edge, i.e., if $f_1 \cap f_2$ is a line segment in $\mathbb{R}^3$. Two distinct faces f_1, f_2 are **corner-adjacent** if they share a vertex but not an edge, i.e., if $f_1 \cap f_2$ is a single point in $\mathbb{R}^3$.

In Chapter 3 a special class of subsets of 2D binary and multicolor (i.e., segmented) digital pictures called "well-composed pictures" is defined (Latecki et al. [98] and Latecki [94]). The idea is not to allow the "critical configuration" shown in Figure 5.2 to occur in a digital picture. Note that this critical configuration can be detected locally.

Figure 5.2: Critical configuration for non-well-composed 2D pictures.

An important motivation for 2D well-composed pictures were connectivity paradoxes which occur if only one adjacency relation (e.g., 4-adjacency) is used in the whole picture (see Section 1.1). Such paradoxes are pointed out in Rosenfeld and Pfaltz [132] (see also Kong and Rosenfeld [82]). The most popular solution was the idea of using different adjacency relations for the foreground and the background: 8-adjacency for black points and 4-adjacency for white points, or vice versa (first recommended in Duda et al. [35]). Rosenfeld [129] developed the foundations of digital topology based on this idea, and showed that the Jordan curve theorem is then satisfied. However, the solution with two different adjacency relations does not work if one wants to distinguish more than two colors, i.e., to distinguish among different objects in a segmented image, as shown in Section 3.8. The same paradoxes appear in 3D multicolor images. In the following we will define and analyze 3D "well-composed pictures" in which the connectivity paradoxes do not occur.

5.2 Definition of 3D Well-Composed Pictures

We will interpret $\mathbf{Z}^3$ as the set of points with integer coordinates in 3D space $\mathbb{R}^3$. We denote by $(\mathbf{Z}^3, X)$, where $X \subseteq \mathbf{Z}^3$, a **binary digital picture** $(\mathbf{Z}^3, \lambda)$, where $\lambda : \mathbf{Z}^3 \to \{0,1\}$ is given by $\lambda(p) = 1$ iff $p \in X$. We assume that either X or its complement X^c is finite and nonempty.

A binary digital picture is obtained from a segmented multicolor picture if some set of points X is distinguished (e.g., points of the same color), which is treated as the **foreground**, and all the other points are lumped together to form the **background**. Usually, each point in X is assigned value 1 (i.e., black) and each point in X^c is assigned value 0 (i.e., white). Therefore, we will sometimes denote X by X_1 and X^c by X_0.

Let $\alpha-adjacency$ denote the ordinary adjacency relation, where $\alpha \in \{6, 18, 26\}$. We could also use other adjacency relations, e.g., 14-adjacency, which is defined for 3D binary pictures in Gordon and Udupa [52]. We say that two points $p, q \in \mathbf{Z}^3$ are $\alpha-$**adjacent** in digital picture $(\mathbf{Z}^3, \lambda)$ if p and q are $\alpha-$adjacent and p and q have the same color, i.e., $\lambda(p) = \lambda(q)$. Similarly, we can define $\alpha-$**paths** and $\alpha-$**components** (see Section 2.1).

Recall that a subset X of $\mathbb{R}^3$ is a **2D manifold** if each point in X has a neighborhood homeomorphic to $\mathbb{R}^2$.

Definition: We will call a 3D digital picture $(\mathbf{Z}^3, X)$ **well-composed** if $bdCA(X)$ is a 2D manifold.

Since $bdCA(X) = bdCA(X^c)$, $(\mathbf{Z}^3, X)$ is well-composed iff $(\mathbf{Z}^3, X^c)$ is well-composed. This definition can be visualized by Proposition 5.1, which shows the equivalence of this definition to two simple local conditions on cubes in the continuous analog.

Proposition 5.1 *A digital picture* $(\mathbf{Z}^3, X)$ *is well-composed iff the following critical configurations of cubes (1) and (2) (modulo reflections and rotations) do not occur in* $CA(X_\kappa)$ *for* $\kappa = 0, 1$ *(see Figure 5.3), where* $X_1 = X$ *and* $X_0 = X^c$:

(1) *Four cubes share an edge and exactly two of them which do not share a face are contained in* $CA(X_\kappa)$ *while the other two are not.*

(2) *Eight cubes share a corner point and exactly two of them which are corner-adjacent are contained in $CA(X_\kappa)$ while the other six are not.*

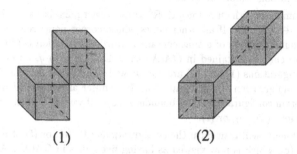

(1)   (2)

Figure 5.3: A digital picture $(\mathbf{Z}^3, X)$ is well-composed iff the critical configurations of cubes (1) and (2) (modulo reflections and rotations) do not occur in $CA(X_\kappa)$ for $\kappa = 0, 1$.

Proof:

"$\Rightarrow$" Evidently, if $(\mathbf{Z}^3, X)$ is well-composed, then configurations (1) and (2) do not occur in $CA(X_\kappa)$, since any interior point of the common edge of the two cubes in $CA(X_\kappa)$ in (1) and the common vertex of the two cubes in (2) do not have neighborhoods homeomorphic to $\mathbb{R}^2$ for $\kappa = 0, 1$ (see Figure 5.3).

"$\Leftarrow$" Assume now that configurations (1) and (2) do not occur in $CA(X)$ where $X = X_\kappa$ for $\kappa = 0, 1$. We recall that the face boundary $bdCA(X)$ is the union of the set of closed faces each of which is the common face of a cube in $CA(X)$ and a cube in $CA(X^c)$. Clearly, if a point $x \in bdCA(X)$ lies in the interior of some square contained in the boundary $bdCA(X)$, than x has a neighborhood homeomorphic to $\mathbb{R}^2$.

Now we consider the case in which $x \in bdCA(X)$ lies in the interior of some line segment that is an edge contained in the boundary $bdCA(X)$. Since configuration (1) does not occur in $CA(X)$, boundary faces of $CA(X)$ that contain point x can have only one of the two configurations shown in Figure 5.4 (modulo rotations and reflections). Thus, x has a neighborhood homeomorphic to $\mathbb{R}^2$.

Figure 5.4: In the continuous analog of a 3D well-composed picture, exactly two boundary faces can have a common edge.

It remains to consider the case in which $x \in bdCA(X)$ is a corner point of $bdCA(X)$. In this case eight cubes share x as their common corner point; some of them are contained in $CA(X)$ and some are not. By simple analysis of all possible configurations of the eight cubes, we will obtain that boundary faces of $CA(X)$ that contain point x can have only the configurations shown in Figure 5.5 (modulo rotations and reflections). This implies that x has a neighborhood homeomorphic to $\mathbb{R}^2$.

We start this analysis with one cube $q \subset \mathbb{R}^3$ whose corner point is x such that $q = CA(p)$ for some point $p \in X \subset \mathbb{Z}^3$. If all other cubes whose corner point is x are contained in $CA(X^c)$, then boundary faces of q that contain x form configuration (a) in Figure 5.5. If there is one more cube r contained in $CA(X)$ that shares x with q, r must share a face with q, since configurations (1) and (2) are not allowed. Thus, boundary faces of $q \cup r$ that contain x form configuration (b) in Figure 5.5. By similar arguments, if we add a third cube, we only obtain configuration (c) of boundary faces. If we add a forth cube, we obtain one of configurations (d), (e), or (f).

Adding a fifth cube will transform the configurations (d), (e), or (f) of boundary faces to configuration (c), which is now viewed as having five cubes in $CA(X)$. Adding a sixth cube will transform configuration (c) of boundary faces (of five cubes) to configuration (b), which is now viewed as having six cubes in $CA(X)$. Adding a seventh cube will yield configuration (a) of boundary faces of seven cubes in $CA(X)$. Thus, we have shown that boundary faces of $CA(X)$ that contain point x can only have the six configurations in Figure 5.5 (modulo rotations and reflections).   ∎

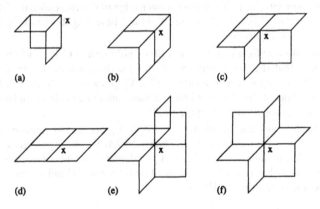

Figure 5.5: In the continuous analog of a 3D well-composed picture, only these configurations of boundary faces can occur around a corner point of the object boundary.

Observe that the six face neighborhoods of a corner point shown in Figure 5.5 are exactly the same as shown in Chen and Zhang [29] and in Francon [43]. In Artzy et al., [12] the digital 3D sets that do not contain configuration (1) in Figure 5.3 (modulo reflections and rotations) are defined to be solid. However, configuration (2) can occur in a solid set. As a simple consequence of Proposition 5.1, we obtain the following equivalent definition of well-composedness:

Proposition 5.2 *A digital picture* $(\mathbf{Z}^3, X)$ *is well-composed iff for any corner point* $x \in$ *bdCA(X), the boundary faces of* $CA(X)$ *that contain* x *have one of the six configurations shown in Figure 5.5 (modulo reflections and rotations).*

Proof:

"⇒" If $(\mathbf{Z}^3, X)$ is well-composed, the configurations (1) and (2) in Figure 5.3 (modulo reflections and rotations) do not occur in $CA(X_\kappa)$ for $\kappa = 0, 1$, by Proposition 5.1. By the second part of the proof of Proposition 5.1, we obtain that if configurations (1) and (2) do not occur in $CA(X_\kappa)$, then the boundary faces of $CA(X)$ that contain point x can have only the configurations shown in Figure 5.5.

"⇐" Since every point $y \in bdCA(X_\kappa)$ is an interior point (in the 2D sense) of one of the configurations of faces shown in Figure 5.5, y has a neighborhood homeomorphic to $\mathbb{R}^2$. Thus, $(\mathbf{Z}^3, X)$ is well-composed. ∎

Observe that there is only one connectedness relation on faces contained in the boundary of the continuous analog $CA(X)$ of a well-composed picture $(\mathbf{Z}^3, X)$: A set of boundary faces S is a corner-connected component of $bdCA(X)$ iff S is an edge-connected component of $bdCA(X)$.

Since every boundary $bdCA(X)$ is a finite union of some set of closed faces S, i.e., $bdCA(X) = \bigcup S$, the statement that $bdCA(X)$ is a **simple closed surface** means here that $bdCA(X)$ is a connected 2D manifold in $\mathbb{R}^3$. Hence, we obtain the following proposition as a direct consequence of the definition of a well-composed picture.

Proposition 5.3 *A digital picture* $(\mathbf{Z}^3, X)$ *is well-composed iff every component of bdCA(X) is a simple closed surface.* ∎

Observe also that a set $X \subseteq \mathbf{Z}^3$ is well-composed iff $CA(X)$ is a bordered 3D manifold, where a closed set $A \subseteq \mathbb{R}^3$ is a **bordered 3D manifold** if every point in A has a neighborhood homeomorphic to a relatively open subset of a closed half-space in $\mathbb{R}^3$. Now we give a "digital characterization" (using only points in $\mathbf{Z}^3$) of well-composed pictures.

Proposition 5.4 *A 3D digital picture* $(\mathbf{Z}^3, X)$ *is well-composed iff the following conditions hold for* $\kappa = 0, 1$ *(where* $X_1 = X$ *and* $X_0 = X^c$*):*

(C1) for every two 18-adjacent points x, y *in* X_κ*, there is a 6-path joining* x *to* y *in* $\mathcal{N}_{18}(x) \cap \mathcal{N}_{18}(y) \cap X_\kappa$ *and*

(C2) for every two 26-adjacent points x, y *in* X_κ*, there is a 6-path joining* x *to* y *in* $\mathcal{N}(x) \cap \mathcal{N}(y) \cap X_\kappa$*.*

Proof: Let $X = X_\kappa$, where $\kappa = 0, 1$. We show first that the negation of condition (C1) is equivalent to the fact that configuration (1) in Figure 5.3 occurs in $CA(X)$.

If configuration (1) occurs in $CA(X)$, then there exists four distinct points $x, y \in X$ and $a, b \notin X$ such that $CA(x), CA(y), CA(a), CA(b)$ share an edge. Then $x, y \in X$ are 18- but not 6-adjacent in X. Figure 5.6(a) shows the intersection $\mathcal{N}_{18}(x) \cap \mathcal{N}_{18}(y)$ of two 18- but not 6-adjacent points x and y. It is easily seen that there is no 6-path joining x to y in $\mathcal{N}_{18}(x) \cap \mathcal{N}_{18}(y) \cap X$.

Conversely, if there exists two 18-adjacent points x, y in X such that there is no 6-path joining x to y in $\mathcal{N}_{18}(x) \cap \mathcal{N}_{18}(y) \cap X$, then x and y are 18- but not 6-adjacent. Hence cubes $CA(x)$ and $CA(y)$ share an edge, and the other two cubes that share the same edge are not contained in $CA(X)$. Therefore, the configuration (1) (Figure 5.3) occurs in $CA(X)$, and by Proposition 5.1, $(\mathbf{Z}^3, X)$ is not well-composed.

Now we show that if configuration (2) in Figure 5.3 occurs in $CA(X)$, then condition (C2) does not hold. Let $x, y \in X$ be such that $CA(x)$ and $CA(y)$ form configuration (2). Then $x, y \in X$ are 26- but not 18-adjacent in X. Figure 5.6(b) shows the intersection $\mathcal{N}(x) \cap \mathcal{N}(y)$ of two 26- but not 18-adjacent points x and y. It is easily seen that the other six points in $\mathcal{N}(x) \cap \mathcal{N}(y)$ do not belong to X. Therefore, there is no 6-path joining x to y in $\mathcal{N}(x) \cap \mathcal{N}(y) \cap X_\kappa$.

Finally, we assume the negation of condition (C2). Let x, y in X be two 26-adjacent points such that there is no 6-path joining x to y in $\mathcal{N}(x) \cap \mathcal{N}(y) \cap X$. This implies that configuration (2) or configuration (1) occurs in $CA(X)$.   ∎

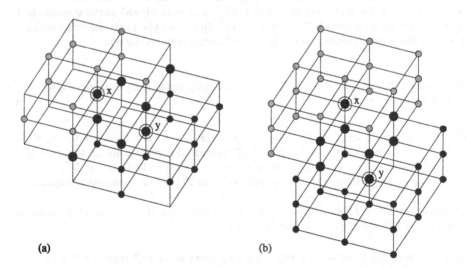

(a)   (b)

Figure 5.6: The slightly larger black balls illustrate in (a) the intersection $\mathcal{N}_{18}(x) \cap \mathcal{N}_{18}(y)$ of two 18- but not 6-adjacent points x and y, and in (b) the intersection $\mathcal{N}(x) \cap \mathcal{N}(y)$ of two 26- but not 18-adjacent points x and y.

The following proposition implies that there is only one kind of connected components in a well-composed picture, since 26-, 18-, and 6-connected components are equal.

Proposition 5.5 *Let* $(\mathbf{Z}^3, X)$ *be a well-composed picture. Then each 26-component of* X_κ *is a 6-component of* X_κ *and each 18-component of* X_κ *is a 6-component of* X_κ, *where* $\kappa = 0, 1$.

Proof: Let $x = x_1, x_2, ..., x_n = y$ be a 26–path joining x to y in X_κ. By condition (C2) in Proposition 5.4, for any two 26–neighbors x_i, x_{i+1}, $i = 1, ..., n-1$, there is a 6–path joining x_i to x_{i+1} in X_κ. Thus, there exists a 6–path joining x to y in X_κ. The argument for 18–components is similar. ∎

5.3 Jordan-Brouwer Separation Theorem

An important motivation for introducing 3D well-composed pictures is the following digital version of the Jordan-Brouwer Separation Theorem. We recall that in a digital picture $(\mathbf{Z}^3, X)$ either $X_1 = X$ or its complement $X_0 = X^c$ is finite and nonempty.

Theorem 5.1 *If a 3D digital picture* $(\mathbf{Z}^3, X)$ *is well-composed, then for every connected component* S *of* $bdCA(X)$, $\mathbb{R}^3 \setminus S$ *has precisely two connected components of which* S *is the common boundary.*

Proof: The proof of this theorem follows directly from Theorem 5.2, which is stated at the end of this section. It is sufficient to observe that by Proposition 5.2, a connected component of $bdCA(X)$ is a strongly connected polyhedral surface without boundary, which we define below. ∎

Note that if a digital picture is not well-composed, Theorem 5.1 does not hold, for example, if X is a two-point digital set such that $CA(X)$ is as shown in Figure 5.3.

Now we define polyhedral surfaces in $\mathbb{R}^3$. They were used in Kong and Roscoe [80] to prove 3D digital analogs of the Jordan Curve Theorem. Let $n \geq 0$ and let $\{T_i : 0 \leq i \leq n\}$ be a set of closed triangles in $\mathbb{R}^3$. The set $\bigcup\{T_i : 0 \leq i \leq n\}$ is called a **polyhedral surface** if the following conditions both hold:

(i) If $i \neq j$, then $T_i \cap T_j$ is either a side of both T_i and T_j or a corner of both T_i and T_j or the empty set.

(ii) Each side of a triangle T_i is a side of at most one other triangle.

The (1D) **boundary of a polyhedral surface** $S = \bigcup\{T_i : 0 \leq i \leq n\}$ is defined as $\bigcup\{s : s$ is a side of exactly one $T_i\}$. Observe that this definition produces the same boundary of S for every dissection of S into triangles fulfilling (i) and (ii). We say that S is a **polyhedral surface without boundary** if the boundary of S is the empty set. A polyhedral surface S is **strongly connected** if for any finite set of points $F \subseteq S$, the set $S \setminus F$ is polygonally connected, where the definition of a polygonally connected set is the following:

If u and v are two distinct points in $\mathbb{R}^3$, then uv denotes the straight line segment joining u to v. Suppose $n \geq 0$ and $\{x_i : 0 \leq i \leq n\}$ is a set of distinct points in $\mathbb{R}^3$ such that whenever $i \neq j$, $x_i x_{i+1} \cap x_j x_{j+1} = \{x_i, x_{i+1}\} \cap \{x_j, x_{j+1}\}$, then $arc(x_0, x_n) = \{x_i x_{i+1} : 0 \leq i < n\}$ is a **simple polygonal arc** joining x_0 to x_n. We call a subset S of $\mathbb{R}^3$ **polygonally connected** if any two points in S can be joined by a simple polygonal arc contained in S.

Now we can state the Jordan-Brouwer separation theorem for a strongly connected polyhedral surface without boundary. This theorem is a very important result of combinatorial topology (e.g., see Aleksandrov [8]). It was applied in Kong and Roscoe [80] to establish separation theorems for digital surfaces:

Theorem 5.2 *If S is a strongly connected polyhedral surface without boundary then $\mathbb{R}^3 \setminus S$ has precisely two components, and one of the components is bounded. S is the boundary of each component.*   ∎

Our proof of Theorem 5.1 is based on the Jordan-Brouwer separation theorem stated in Theorem 5.2, which is a powerful tool of combinatorial topology. Therefore, it seems to be an interesting question whether it is possible to derive a simple proof of Theorem 5.1 directly in discrete topology.

5.4   Properties of Boundary Faces

Recall that we interpret $\mathbf{Z}^3$ as a set of points with integer coordinates in the space $\mathbb{R}^3$, $\mathcal{C}$ is a set of closed unit upright cubes which are centered at points of $\mathbf{Z}^3$, and $\mathcal{F}$ is a set of closed faces of cubes in $\mathcal{C}$, i.e., each $f \in \mathcal{F}$ is a unit closed square in $\mathbb{R}^3$ parallel to one of the coordinate planes. Note that $\mathcal{C} = \{CA(p) : p \in \mathbf{Z}^3\}$ and $\mathcal{F} = \{CA((p,q)) : p, q \in \mathbf{Z}^3$ and p is 6 − adjacent to $q\}$. We also recall that the function $Dig_\in : \mathcal{P}(\mathbb{R}^3) \to \mathcal{P}(\mathbf{Z}^3)$ is defined by $Dig_\in(Y) = \{p \in \mathbf{Z}^3 : p \in Y\}$. We begin this section with a theorem relating well-composed pictures to simple closed surfaces composed of faces in $\mathcal{F}$.

Theorem 5.3 *Let $S \subset \mathcal{F}$ be a finite and nonempty set of faces in $\mathbb{R}^3$.*
$\bigcup S$ is a simple closed surface (i.e. $\bigcup S$ is a connected and compact 2D manifold in $\mathbb{R}^3$) iff $\mathbb{R}^3 \setminus \bigcup S$ has precisely two components X_1 and X_2, $\bigcup S$ is the common boundary of X_1 and X_2, and the binary digital picture $(\mathbf{Z}^3, Dig_\in(X_1))$ is well-composed.

The proof of this theorem will be given below. Observe that the implication "⇐" in Theorem 5.3 would not be true if the set $Dig_\in(X_1)$ were not well-composed. Let $S = bdCA(D)$, where D is a digital set of 1's in the following $2 \times 2 \times 2$ configuration (on a background of 0's):

$$
\begin{array}{cccc}
1 & 0 & \quad 1 & 1 \\
1 & 1 & \quad 0 & 1
\end{array}
$$

Then $\mathbb{R}^3 \setminus S$ has precisely two components, but S is not a simple closed surface, since the common corner of the six black (i.e., 1-) voxels does not have a neighborhood homeomorphic to $\mathbb{R}^2$.

To better understand the equivalence in Theorem 5.3, we consider again the six simple local configuration of faces shown in Figure 5.5.

Theorem 5.4 *If* $S \subset \mathcal{F}$ *is a finite and nonempty set of faces in* $\mathbb{R}^3$, *then the following conditions are equivalent:*

(i) $\bigcup S$ *is a simple closed surface (i.e.* $\bigcup S$ *is a connected and compact 2D manifold in* $\mathbb{R}^3$)

(ii) S *is corner-connected and for every corner point* $x \in \bigcup S$, *the boundary faces of* S *that contain* x *as their corner point have one of the six configurations shown in Figure 5.5 (modulo reflections and rotations).*

Proof:

"(i) $\Rightarrow$ (ii)" Since $\bigcup S$ is a simple closed surface, each point $s \in \bigcup S$ has a neighborhood homeomorphic to $\mathbb{R}^2$. Thus, in particular, each corner point x of a face in S has a neighborhood homeomorphic to $\mathbb{R}^2$. By simple case checking (similar to one in the second part of the proof of Proposition 5.1), it can be shown that Figure 5.5 shows all possible configurations (modulo rotations and reflections) of faces in $\mathcal{F}$ that share a common corner point x such that x has a neighborhood homeomorphic to $\mathbb{R}^2$. Now since $\bigcup S$ is connected, the set of faces S must be corner-connected. Thus, we obtain (i) $\Rightarrow$ (ii).

"(ii) $\Rightarrow$ (i)" We assume (ii). Then every point in the 2D interior of a face in S, clearly has a neighborhood homeomorphic to $\mathbb{R}^2$. Since every edge belongs to exactly two faces in S, every point of an edge (except the two corner points) has a neighborhood homeomorphic to $\mathbb{R}^2$. Since for every corner point x of a face in S, the set of faces sharing x has one of the six configuration of faces shown in Figure 5.5, x has a neighborhood homeomorphic to $\mathbb{R}^2$. Thus, $\bigcup S$ is a 2D manifold. $\bigcup S$ is a connected subset of $\mathbb{R}^3$, since S is corner-connected. Since $\bigcup S$ is a finite union of closed squares in $\mathbb{R}^3$, $\bigcup S$ is compact. Therefore, $\bigcup S$ is a simple closed surface. ∎

Now we are ready to prove Theorem 5.3.

Proof of Theorem 5.3:

"$\Rightarrow$" Let $\bigcup S$ be a simple closed surface. Then S satisfies condition (ii) of Theorem 5.4. Consequently, $\bigcup S$ is a strongly connected polyhedral surface without boundary. By Theorem 5.2, $\mathbb{R}^3 \setminus \bigcup S$ has precisely two components X_1 and X_2, and $\bigcup S$ is the common boundary of X_1 and X_2. It remains to show that the digital picture $(\mathbf{Z}^3, Dig_\in(X_1))$ is well-composed.

Note that $Dig_\in(X_1)$ is the set of black points and $Dig_\in(X_2)$ is the set of white points in $(\mathbf{Z}^3, Dig_\in(X_1))$. Since $X_i \cup \bigcup S = CA(Dig_\in(X_i))$, we have $\bigcup S = bd(CA(Dig_\in(X_i)))$ for $i = 1, 2$. Thus, the boundaries of the sets of black and white points are 2D manifolds. We obtain that $(\mathbf{Z}^3, Dig_\in(X_1))$ is well-composed.

"$\Leftarrow$" Since $(\mathbf{Z}^3, Dig_\in(X_1))$ is well-composed, $bd(CA(Dig_\in(X_1)))$ is a 2D manifold. Since the closed set $X_1 \cup \bigcup S$ is a union of some cubes in $\mathcal{C}$, we obtain $X_1 \cup \bigcup S = CA(Dig_\in(X_1))$. Hence $\bigcup S = bd(CA(Dig_\in(X_1)))$, which means that $\bigcup S$ is a 2D manifold in $\mathbb{R}^3$.

Since $\bigcup S$ is a finite union of closed squares in $\mathbb{R}^3$, it is compact. It remains to show that $\bigcup S$ is connected. If $\bigcup S$ were not connected, then there would be more than two components of $\mathbb{R}^3 \setminus \bigcup S$, since every connected component of $\bigcup S$ would be a strongly connected polyhedral surface without boundary, and therefore, it would satisfy Theorem 5.2. ∎

5.5   Surfaces in the Sense of Morgenthaler and Rosenfeld

In our approach we treat the surface of a digital object $X \subseteq Z^3$ as described in Herman [64], i.e., as the set of pairs of 6-adjacent points (p, q), where $p \in X$ and $q \in X^c$. In this way, these pairs correspond to faces of cubes in $CA(X)$ that are contained in $bdCA(X)$. In computer vision literature, a surface of a 3D digital object is also interpreted as being composed of image points. This approach is taken in Morgenthaler and Rosenfeld [116], where digital simple closed surfaces are defined with a goal that they have the Jordan separability property, i.e., if $S \subseteq \mathbf{Z}^3$ is a simple closed surface, then $\mathbf{Z}^3 \setminus S$ has precisely two components. We will call a digital simple closed surface in the sense of Morgenthaler and Rosenfeld [116] as M-R surface, where a 6-connected digital set $S \subseteq \mathbf{Z}^3$ in a digital picture $(\mathbf{Z}^3, S, 6, 26)$ is defined to be a **M-R surface** if the following three conditions hold for ever point $p \in S$ (recall that in a digital picture $(\mathbf{Z}^3, S, 6, 26)$, 6-adjacency is considered for points in X and 26-adjacency for points in X^c):

1. $S \cap \mathcal{N}(p)$ has exactly one 6-component 6-adjacent to p

2. $S^c \cap \mathcal{N}(p)$ has exactly two 26-components $C_1(p), C_2(p)$ 26-adjacent to p

3. If $q \in S$ and q is 6-adjacent to p, then q is 26-adjacent to both $C_1(p)$ and $C_2(p)$.

We will interpret the points of a digital picture $(\mathbf{Z}^3, X, 6, 26)$ as points of the following subset of the space $\mathbb{R}^3$:

$$\mathbf{Z}^3 + \frac{1}{2} = \{(k + \frac{1}{2}, l + \frac{1}{2}, m + \frac{1}{2}) : k, l, m \in \mathbf{Z}\}.$$

To avoid confusions, we will denote $(\mathbf{Z}^3, X, 6, 26)$ by $(\mathbf{Z}^3 + \frac{1}{2}, X, 6, 26)$ in the subsequent considerations. In this way, the points of the digital picture $(\mathbf{Z}^3 + \frac{1}{2}, X, 6, 26)$ are the corner points of cubes in $\mathcal{C}$ (that are centered at points of $\mathbf{Z}^3$) and also the corner points of faces in $\mathcal{F}$. Hence the boundary faces of pictures $(\mathbf{Z}^3 + \frac{1}{2}, X, 6, 26)$ and pictures $(\mathbf{Z}^3, X)$ are the same. The continuous analog of surfaces made of image points is defined in Kong and Roscoe [80]. Based on this definition, a **Kong's continuous analog** $KA(S)$ of a M-R surface $S \subseteq \mathbf{Z}^3$ (treated as a digital picture $(\mathbf{Z}^3 + \frac{1}{2}, S, 6, 26)$) is the union of all faces

$f \in \mathcal{F}$ such that all four corner points of f are in S. By the results in Chen and Zhang [29] (Theorems 2.1 and 4.1), for every point x in a M-R surface $S \subseteq \mathbf{Z}^3 + \frac{1}{2}$, the faces in $KA(S)$ that contain x (as their corner point) have one of the six configurations shown in Figure 5.5 (modulo reflections and rotations). By Theorem 5.4 ((ii) $\Rightarrow$ (i)), we obtain that $KA(S)$ of a M-R surface S is a simple closed surface in $\mathbb{R}^3$.

From Theorem 5.3, it follows that $\mathbb{R}^3 \setminus KA(S)$ has precisely two components X_1 and X_2, $KA(S)$ is the common boundary of X_1 and X_2, and the binary digital picture $(\mathbf{Z}^3, Dig_\in(X_1))$ is well-composed. Consequently, we obtain $KA(S) = bdCA(Dig_\in(X_1))$. Thus, every M-R surface $(\mathbf{Z}^3, S, 6, 26)$ can be interpreted as the boundary surface of the well-composed digital picture $(\mathbf{Z}^3, Dig_\in(X_1))$.

However, it is not the case that for every boundary surface $S = bdCA(X)$ in a binary well-composed digital picture $(\mathbf{Z}^3, X)$, the digital set $(\mathbf{Z}^3 + \frac{1}{2}, Dig_\in(S), 6, 26)$ is a M-R surface. The reason is that, although $S \subset \mathbb{R}^3$ is simple closed surface, the region surrounded by $Dig_\in(S)$ can contain none of the points in $\mathbf{Z}^3 + \frac{1}{2}$. For example, the digital image $(\mathbf{Z}^3, p)$ with a single black point p is well-composed and $S = bdCA(p)$ is the boundary of a unit cube centered at p. However, the digital set $Dig_\in(S) \subset \mathbf{Z}^3 + \frac{1}{2}$, which consists of the eight corner points of the cube $CA(p)$, does not surround any point in $\mathbf{Z}^3 + \frac{1}{2}$.

5.6 Components in 3D Well-Composed Pictures

For a 2D digital binary picture $(\mathbf{Z}^2, X)$, a set of black points X can be identified with the union of closed unit squares centered at points of X, which we denote $CA(X)$ (e.g., see Figure 1.8). We assume that either X or its complement X^c is finite and nonempty. The **boundary** $bdCA(X)$ of a 2D set X is the union of the set of unit line segments each of which is the common edge of a square in $CA(X)$ and a square in $CA(X^c)$. Observe that there is only one kind of adjacency for line segments contained in $bdCA(X)$: two segments are adjacent if they have an endpoint in common. Hence, there is only one kind of connectedness for $bdCA(X)$. The unit line segments contained in $bdCA(X)$ correspond to pairs of 4-adjacent points (p, q) such that $p \in X$ and $q \notin X$.

We recall that a 2D binary digital picture $(\mathbf{Z}^2, X)$ is well-composed iff the critical configuration shown in Figure 5.7 (and its 90° rotation) do not occur in $CA(X)$ and $CA(X^c)$. For 2D well-composed pictures, the following theorem can be easily proven:

Theorem 5.5 *A digital picture $(\mathbf{Z}^2, X)$ is well-composed iff $bdCA(X)$ is a compact 1D manifold (each point in bdX has a neighborhood homeomorphic to $\mathbb{R}$).* ∎

Figure 5.7: The continuous analog of a 2D well-composed picture does not contain this critical configuration and its 90° rotation.

Rosenfeld and Kong [135] proved the following theorem for 2D digital pictures:

Theorem 5.6 *For every finite and nonempty set $X \subset \mathbf{Z}^2$, the boundary $bdCA(X)$ is a simple closed curve (i.e., $bdCA(X)$ is connected and each line segment in $bdCA(X)$ is adjacent to exactly two others) iff X and X^c are both 4-connected.* ∎

As it is shown in [135], an analogous theorem does not hold in 3D: Let X be a set of 1's in the following $2 \times 2 \times 2$ configuration (on a background of 0's):

$$
\begin{array}{cc}
1 \ 1 \qquad 0 \ 1 \\
1 \ 1 \qquad 1 \ 0
\end{array}
$$

Then X and X^c are both 6-connected, but $bdCA(X)$ is not a simple closed surface. However, the inverse implication is proved in [135], Proposition 9:

Theorem 5.7 *If the boundary $bdCA(X)$ of a set $X \subset \mathbf{Z}^3$ is a simple closed surface, then X and X^c are both 6-connected.* ∎

Using the concept of well-composedness, we can generalize Theorem 5.6 to three dimensions:

Theorem 5.8 *For every finite and nonempty set $X \subset \mathbf{Z}^3$, the boundary $bdCA(X)$ is a simple closed surface iff X and X^c are both 6-connected and $(\mathbf{Z}^3, X)$ is well-composed.*

Proof:
"$\Rightarrow$:" By Theorem 5.7, we obtain that X and X^c are both 6-connected. Since a simple closed surface is in particular a 2D manifold, we obtain that $(\mathbf{Z}^3, X)$ is well-composed.

"$\Leftarrow$:" Since X and X^c are 6-connected, $CA(X)$ and $CA(X^c)$ are connected subsets of $\mathbb{R}^3$ and $bdCA(X)$ is their common boundary. Therefore, $bdCA(X)$ is also a connected subset of $\mathbb{R}^3$. Since $X \subset \mathbf{Z}^3$ is finite, $bdCA(X)$ is compact. By definition, the fact that $(\mathbf{Z}^3, X)$ is well-composed implies that $bdCA(X)$ is a 2D manifold. Consequently, $bdCA(X)$ is a simple closed surface. ∎

Chapter 6

Continuous Representations of Real Objects

Any continuous model of some class of real objects should on the one hand be able to reflect relevant shape properties as exactly as possible, and on the other hand should be mathematically tractable, in the sense that it should allow for precise, formal description of the relevant properties. For example, it does not make much sense to model the boundaries of 2D projections of real objects as all possible curves in $\mathbb{R}^2$. This class is too general to allow us to formally describe any shape properties of sets in this class and there are curves with very unnatural properties (e.g., plane filling curves). Therefore, some restrictions must be added.

It was not necessary to explicitly characterize continuous representations of real objects for the graph-based, axiomatic, and embedding approaches, since these characterizations were implicitly given by the nature of these approaches. In the graph-based approach, the representations of real objects were specified by particular properties of interest, e.g., we dealt with separability properties of simple closed curves in the digital plane which are specified for the plane $\mathbb{R}^2$ by the classical Jordan curve theorem. In the axiomatic approach, the continuous representations were characterized by a set of axioms, which should be satisfied by a continuous as well as by a discrete representation. In the embedding approach, we concentrated on continuous sets (subsets of the plane and 3D space) that are assigned to discrete sets, e.g., we dealt with finite unions of closed unit squares and cubes.

For the digitization approach, which we will treat in the next chapter, it is necessary to explicitly characterize continuous representations of real objects, since these representations will be mapped to discrete representations by functions modeling real digitization processes. Thus, continuous representations of real objects are the starting point for this approach. Therefore, in this chapter we describe the classes of continuous representations of real objects that will be used in Chapter 7 as input to digitization functions.

We first define parallel regular sets in Section 6.1, which model real objects and their 2D projections in the way commonly accepted in computer vision as subsets of $\mathbb{R}^3$ and $\mathbb{R}^2$ with "smooth" boundaries. However, we will not use the classical tools of differential geometry to define this class of sets. Differential geometry is based on the concept of derivative, which requires the calculation of limits of infinite sequences of numbers. Since this calculation cannot be transfered into discrete spaces, no analog of the concept of derivative in discrete spaces exists that has similar properties.

In Section 6.2 (Latecki et al. [99]) we define a property of CP_3 ("collinear P_3") convexity that characterizes (parts of) the boundaries of convex sets. We prove that a closed curve is the boundary of a convex set, and a simple arc is part of the boundary of a convex set, iff they have property CP_3. This result appears to be the first simple characterization of parts of the boundaries of convex sets; it solves a problem studied over 30 years ago by Menger [112] and Valentine [155].

The CP_3 property will be a useful tool in Section 6.3, where we introduce *supported sets*. As stated in Latecki and Rosenfeld [104], requiring the object boundaries to be differentiable is too restrictive, since this excludes polygons, which are not differentiable at their vertices. A somewhat better idea is to require differentiability at all but a finite number of points; but this is not restrictive enough, because it allows arcs that can oscillate infinitely often (e.g., the graph of function $x \sin(1/x)$) or turn infinitely often (e.g., the inward-turning spiral illustrated in Figure 1.13).

Based on Latecki and Rosenfeld [104] we define in Section 6.3 classes of continuous planar arcs and curves that exclude all these pathological cases. Our definitions are based on the concept of a *line of support* of a set — a line l through a point of the set S such that S lies in one of the closed halfplanes bounded by l. We do not have to assume (piecewise) differentiability, but our definitions imply it.

We call a set S *supported* if there is at least one line of support through every point of S. We show that a closed, bounded, connected S is supported iff S is (an arc of) the boundary of a convex set. In Sections 6.3.2 and 6.3.3 we prove that a supported arc A has left and right derivatives at every point, and that A is differentiable at a point if it has a unique line of support at that point. (Here and in what follows, "arc" is short for "arc or simple closed curve.")

We call an arc A *uniquely supported* if it has a unique line of support at every non-endpoint. In Section 6.3.4 we show that a uniquely supported arc has a well-defined curvature at every nonend point, and that its curvature has the same sign at every point.

We call an arc *tame* if it can be subdivided into a finite number of uniquely supported subarcs. It can be verified that the pathological examples described above are not tame. The subdivision points of a tame arc are called its *joints*. As we shall see in Section 6.3.5, joints can be classified as *cusps*, "optional" joints, and *inflections*, according to whether in a neighborhood of the joint, the arc has more than one, exactly one, or no line of support.

In Section 6.3.6 we show how the total turn of a tame arc can be defined in terms of lines of support In Section 7.7 of the next chapter we extend our theory of supported arcs to supported digital arcs. This can allow us, for example, to extend the definition of the total turn to digital arcs, which can become a useful tool in digital picture processing.

6.1   Parallel Regular Sets

In this section, we define 2D prallel regural sets. The definitions and properties of 3D prallel regural sets can be stated in an analogous way.

Let A be a planar set. We denote by A^c the complement of A, by bdA the topological boundary of A, by $intA$ the topological interior of A and by clA the topological closure of A in the usual topology of the plane determined by the Euclidean metric. The connected components of the boundary bdA are called **contours**.

We denote by $d(x, y)$ the Euclidean distance of points x, y and by $B(c, r)$ a closed ball of radius r centered at a point c. The definition of parallel regular sets is based on the classical concepts in differential geometry of osculating balls and normal vectors, which we define below without using derivatives and limit points.

6.1.1 Osculating Balls

Definition: We will say that a closed ball $B(c, r)$ is **tangent** to bdA at point $x \in bdA$ if $bdA \cap bd(B(c, r)) = \{x\}$. We will say that a closed ball $iob(x, r)$ of radius r is an **inside osculating ball** of radius r to bdA at point $x \in bdA$ if $bdA \cap bd(iob(x, r)) = \{x\}$ and $iob(x, r) \subseteq intA \cup \{x\}$ (see Figure 6.1). We will say that a closed ball $oob(x, r)$ of radius r is an **outside osculating ball** of radius r to bdA at point $x \in bdA$ if $bdA \cap bd(oob(x, r)) = \{x\}$ and $oob(x, r) \subseteq A^c \cup \{x\}$ (see Figure 6.1).

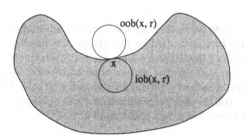

Figure 6.1: The inside and outside osculating balls of radius r to the boundary of the set A at point x.

Note that x is a boundary point, not the center, of both $iob(x, r)$ and $oob(x, r)$. According to this definition, for every boundary point of a given ball $B(c, s)$ of radius s, there exist inside osculating balls of radii r, where $0 < r < s$. However, $B(c, s)$ itself is not an inside osculating ball for any of its boundary points.

Now we define parallel regular subsets of the plane:

Definition: We assume that A is a closed subset of the plane such that its boundary bdA is compact.

A set A will be called **par(r,+)-regular** if there exists an outside osculating ball $oob(x, r)$ of radius r at every point $x \in bdA$.

A set A will be called **par(r,-)-regular** if there exists an inside osculating ball $iob(x, r)$ of radius r at every point $x \in bdA$.

A set A will be called **par(r)-regular** (or **r parallel regular**) if it is par(r,+)-regular and par(r,-)-regular. A set A will be called **parallel regular** if there exists a constant r such that A is par(r)-regular. We will sometimes call parallel regular sets (**spatial**) **objects**.

In Figure 6.2 the set A is par(r)-regular while the set B is not par(r)-regular, where r is the radius of the depicted circles. Note that a parallel regular set, as well as its boundary, does not have to be connected.

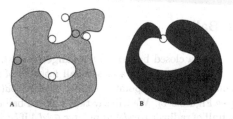

Figure 6.2: The set A is par(r)-regular while the set B is not par(r)-regular, where r is the radius of the depicted circles.

Definition: Let an outside osculating ball $oob(x, r)$ and an inside osculating ball $iob(x, r)$ exist at some point $x \in bdA$. Let $nl(x)$ be the straight line passing through the centers of balls $oob(x, r)$ and $iob(x, r)$ (see Figure 6.3.a). From Proposition 6.1 (3) below, it follows that $x \in nl(x)$ and $nl(x)$ contains the centers of all balls $oob(x, s)$ and $iob(x, s)$ for every $0 < s \leq r$. Since $nl(x)$ is uniquely determined, we call $nl(x)$ the **normal line** to bdA at point $x \in bdA$. The straight line perpendicular to $nl(x)$ passing through x, we call the **tangent line** to bdA at point $x \in bdA$ and denote it $t(x)$.

In the remaining part of this section, we state some basic properties of parallel regular sets. We first show that outside and inside osculating balls and normal lines are uniquely defined.

Proposition 6.1 *Let an outside osculating ball $oob(x, r)$ and an inside osculating ball $iob(x, r)$ exist at some point $x \in bdA$.*

(1) If OB is an outside osculating ball at $x \in bdA$ of radius s, where $0 < s \leq r$, we obtain $OB = oob(x, r)$ if $s = r$, and $OB \subseteq oob(x, r)$ and $bd(OB) \cap bd(oob(x, r)) = \{x\}$ if $s < r$.

(2) If IB is an inside osculating ball at $x \in bdA$ of radius s, where $0 < s \leq r$, we obtain $IB = iob(x, r)$ if $s = r$, and $IB \subseteq iob(x, r)$ and $bd(IB) \cap bd(iob(x, r)) = \{x\}$ if $s < r$.

(3) Let $nl(x)$ be the straight line passing through the center points of balls $oob(x, r)$ and $iob(x, r)$ (see Figure 6.3.a). Then x and the centers of $oob(x, s)$ and $iob(x, s)$ lie on $nl(x)$ for $0 < s \leq r$.

Proof: We prove (1) and (3), the proof of (2) is analogous to the proof of (1). Since $iob(x,r) \subseteq intA \cup \{x\}$, $oob(x,r) \subseteq A^c \cup \{x\}$, and $bdA \cap bd(iob(x,r)) \cap bd(oob(x,r)) = \{x\}$, we obtain $iob(x,r) \cap oob(x,r) = \{x\}$.

We now show that $x \in nl(x)$. Let c_i be the center of $iob(x,r)$ and let c_o be the center of $oob(x,r)$. Then

$$d(c_i, c_o) \le d(c_i, x) + d(x, c_o) = 2r.$$

Suppose $x \notin nl(x)$. Let y_i be the closest point to x in $bd(iob(x,r)) \cap nl(x)$ and let y_o be the closest point to x in $bd(oob(x,r)) \cap nl(x)$. Then $y_i \ne y_o$, and

$$d(c_i, c_o) = d(c_i, y_i) + d(y_i, y_o) + d(y_o, c_o) > 2r.$$

This is a contradiction. Therefore, we must have $x \in nl(x)$.

Let $t(x)$ be the straight line perpendicular to $nl(x)$ passing through x. Then $oob(x,r) \cap t(x) = \{x\}$ and $iob(x,r) \cap t(x) = \{x\}$.

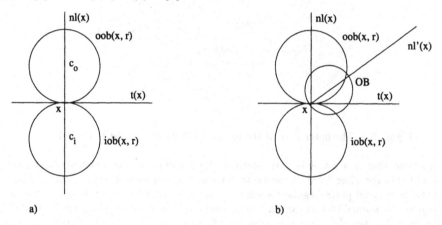

a)   b)

Figure 6.3:

Let OB be an outside osculating ball at $x \in bdA$ of radius s, where $0 < s \le r$, i.e., $bdA \cap bdOB = \{x\}$ and $OB \subseteq A^c \cup \{x\}$. We show that if $nl'(x)$ is the straight line passing through the center point of ball OB and point x, then $nl'(x) = nl(x)$. Assume that $nl'(x) \ne nl(x)$, then $int(OB) \cap int(iob(x,r)) \ne \emptyset$ (see Figure 6.3.b). However, $int(OB) \subseteq A^c$ and $int(iob(x,r)) \subseteq A$. It follows that $OB \subseteq oob(x,r)$ and $bd(OB) \cap bd(oob(x,r)) = \{x\}$ if $s < r$. ∎

As a simple consequence of Proposition 6.1 we obtain:

Corollary 6.1 *(1) If an outside osculating ball $oob(x,r)$ and an inside osculating ball $iob(x,r)$ exist at some point $x \in bdA$, then there exist exactly one outside osculating ball $oob(x,s)$ and exactly one inside osculating ball $iob(x,s)$ at $x \in bdA$ for every $0 < s \le r$.*
(2) If a set A is par(r)-regular, then A is par(s)-regular for every $0 < s \le r$. ∎

6.1.2   Normal Vectors

Definition: Let $x \in bdA$. Let an outside osculating ball $oob(x, r)$ and an inside osculating ball $iob(x, r)$ of radius r exist at x for some $r > 0$.

The **outer normal vector** $n(x, s)$ of length s to bdA at $x \in bdA$ is a line segment emanating from x of length s such that $n(x, s) \subseteq nl(x)$ and $n(x, s) \cap int[oob(x, r)] \neq \emptyset$ (see Figure 6.4).

The **inner normal vector** $-n(x, s)$ of length s to bdA at $x \in bdA$ is a line segment emanating from x of length s such that $-n(x, s) \subseteq nl(x)$ and $-n(x, s) \cap int[iob(x, r)] \neq \emptyset$.

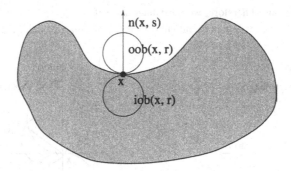

Figure 6.4: The outer normal vector $n(x, s)$ of length s to bdA at $x \in bdA$.

Observe that if a set A is par(r)-regular, then normal vectors exist at every point $x \in bdA$. On the other hand, it can be that normal vectors exist at every point $x \in bdA$, but the set A is not par(r)-regular for some $r > 0$, since the radius of osculating balls which determine the normal vectors can vary form point to point. For example, it can be that the outer normal vector $n(x, r)$ at some point $x \in bdA$ exists, but there exists no outside normal ball of radius r at x. In this case, since the tangent line $nl(x)$ is well-defined, there must exist an outside normal ball $oob(x, s)$ and an inside normal ball $iob(x, s)$ at $x \in bdA$ for some $s < r$. The relationship between the concepts of osculating balls and normal vectors is exactly described in Theorem 6.1, below. First we state the following propositions, which are simple consequences of the definition of normal vectors.

Proposition 6.2 *Let A be a par(r)-regular set and $x \in bdA$. Then, for every $c \in n(x, r)$, $x \in bdA$ is the closest point to c on bdA.*   ∎

Proposition 6.3 *Let A be a par(r)-regular set and $c \notin A$. Let $x \in bdA$ be a point with the closest distance to c on bdA. Then $c \in n(x, s)$ for every $s \geq d(x, c)$.*

Proof: Let $0 < t < d(c, x)$. Let OB be a closed ball of radius t such that $OB \subseteq B(c, d(c, x))$ and $bd(OB) \cap bd(B(c, d(c, x))) = \{x\}$ (see Figure 6.5). Since $B(c, d(c, x)) \cap intA = \emptyset$, we obtain that $OB \subseteq A^c \cup \{x\}$ and $bd(OB) \cap bdA = \{x\}$. Therefore, OB is an outer osculating

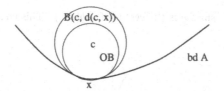

Figure 6.5: $x \in bdA$ is a point with the closest distance to c on bdA.

ball at x. Thus, the straight line passing through the center of OB and point x is the normal line $nl(x)$. Since $c \in nl(x)$, we obtain that $c \in n(x, s)$ for every $s \geq d(x, c)$. ∎

We have the following equivalence:

Theorem 6.1 *A set A is par(r)-regular iff, for every two distinct points $x, y \in bdA$, the outer normal vectors $n(x, r)$ and $n(y, r)$ exist and they do not intersect, and the inner normal vectors $-n(x, r)$ and $-n(y, r)$ exist and they do not intersect.*

For example, in Figure 6.6, set X is not par(r)-regular while set Y is par(r)-regular, where r is the length of the depicted vectors.

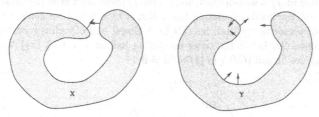

Figure 6.6: X is not par(r)-regular, but Y is par(r)-regular.

Proof: "⇒" Since A is par(r)-regular, we obtain for every point $x \in bdA$ that the outer normal vector $n(x, r)$ and the inner normal vector $-n(x, r)$ exist. We show that $n(x, r)$ and $n(y, r)$ do not intersect for every two distinct points $x, y \in bdA$. The proof of the same fact for inner normal vectors is similar. We know that $n(x, r)$ begins at point x and ends at the center of $oob(x, r)$ for every $x \in bdA$.

Assume that there exists two distinct points $x, y \in bdA$ such that $n(x, r)$ and $n(y, r)$ intersect. We show that this contradicts the fact that A is par(r)-regular.

Let $c \in n(x, r) \cap n(y, r)$. If $c = x$, then $x \in n(y, r) \subseteq oob(y, r)$. This contradicts the fact that $oob(y, r) \subseteq A^c \cup \{y\}$. Therefore, $c \neq x$, as well as $c \neq y$.

Let e be the endpoint of $n(x, r)$ and v the endpoint of $n(y, r)$ (see Figure 6.7). Let $p \in bdA$ be a closest point to c on bdA. Since $p \neq x$ or $p \neq y$, we can assume that $p \neq x$. Since $d(p, c) \leq d(x, c)$, we obtain

$$d(p, e) \leq d(p, c) + d(c, e) \leq d(x, c) + d(c, e) = r.$$

Therefore, $p \in oob(x, r)$, since e is the center of $oob(x, r)$. This contradicts the fact that $oob(x, r) \subseteq A^c \cup \{x\}$.

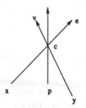

Figure 6.7:

"$\Leftarrow$" We show that if A is not par(r)-regular and, for every point $p \in bdA$, the outer normal vector $n(p, r)$ and the inner normal vector $-n(p, r)$ exist, then there exists two distinct points $x, y \in bdA$ such that either $n(x, r)$ and $n(y, r)$ intersect or $-n(x, r)$ and $-n(y, r)$ intersect.

Since A is not par(r)-regular, we may assume that there does not exist the outside normal ball of radius r at some point $x \in bdA$. Since there exists the outer normal vector $n(x, r)$ at x, the normal line $nl(x)$ is well-defined, and therefore there must exist the outside osculating ball $oob(x, s)$ and the inside osculating ball $iob(x, s)$ at $x \in bdA$ for some $s < r$. Let e be the endpoint of vector $n(x, r)$ and let OB be a closed ball of radius r centered at e (see Figure 6.8). Since OB is not the outer osculating ball at x, $(OB \setminus \{x\}) \cap A \neq \emptyset$. Since $oob(x, s) \subseteq OB$, we obtain $(OB \setminus \{x\}) \cap bdA \neq \emptyset$.

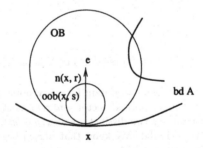

Figure 6.8:

If $e \in A$, then there exists a point $y \neq x$ such that $y \in bdA \cap n(x, r)$, since $((oob(x, s) \cap n(x, r)) \setminus \{x\}) \subseteq A^c$. Then $n(x, r)$ and $n(y, r)$ intersect.

Therefore, we can assume that $e \notin A$. If $int(OB) \cap A = \emptyset$, then there exists $y \in (bd(OB) \setminus \{x\}) \cap bdA$. In this case, y is a closest point to e on bdA and $d(e, y) = r$.

If $int(OB) \cap A \neq \emptyset$, then let $y \in bdA \cap OB$ be a closest point to e on bdA. Clearly, $d(y, e) < r$, and consequently $y \neq x$.

Thus, in both cases $y \in bdA$ is a closest point to e, $d(y,e) \leq r$, and $y \neq x$. By Proposition 6.3, $e \in n(y,r)$. Hence $e \in n(x,r) \cap n(y,r)$. ∎

Definition: $B(x,r)$ denotes the closed ball of radius r centered at a point x. The **parallel set** of set $A \subset \mathbb{R}^2$ with distance r is given by

$$Par(A,r) = A \cup \bigcup \{B(x,r) : x \in bdA\}.$$

This set is also called a **dilation** of A with radius r. We define

$$Par(A,-r) = cl(A \setminus \bigcup \{B(x,r) : x \in bdA\}).$$

For illustration, see Figure 6.9. The boundaries of Par(A, r) and Par(A, -r) sets are often called offset curves.

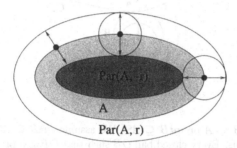

Figure 6.9: The set A and its parallel sets $Par(A,r)$ and $Par(A,-r)$.

It can be shown that $A = Par(Par(A,r),-r) = Par(Par(A,-r),r)$ for a par(r)-regular set A. Thus, a par(r)-regular set A is invariant with respect to morphological operations of opening and closing with a closed ball of radius r as a structuring element (see Serra [140] for definitions). The following proposition motivates the name of parallel regular sets.

Proposition 6.4 *Let A be a par(r)-regular set. Then (see Figure 6.9)*

$$Par(A,r) = A \cup \bigcup \{n(a,r) : a \in bdA\} \quad and \quad Par(A,-r) = cl(A \setminus \bigcup \{-n(a,r) : a \in bdA\}).$$

Proof: We show only the first equation; the proof of the second is analogous. It is easy to see that $A \cup \bigcup \{n(a,r) : a \in bdA\} \subseteq Par(A,r)$; simply observe that $n(s,r)$ is contained in the dilation ball $B(s,r)$ for every $s \in bdA$.

It is clear that $A \subseteq Par(A,r)$. So, let $x \in Par(A,r)$ and $x \notin A$. Let $s \in bdA$ be a point having the shortest distance d from x to bdA. Such a point exists, since bdA is compact. Of course, $d \leq r$. By Proposition 6.3, $x \in n(s,r)$. Thus, $x \in \bigcup \{n(a,r) : a \in bdA\}$. ∎

Proposition 6.5 *Let A be a par(r)-regular set. If x and y belong to two different components of bdA, then $d(x,y) > 2r$.*

Proof: Let $C_1, ..., C_n$ be all connected components of bdA (there is only a finite number of them, since bdA is compact), where $n \geq 2$. For every $i \neq j$, $i, j \in \{1, ..., n\}$, let $d_{ij} : C_i \times C_j \to \mathbb{R}$ be the Euclidean distance d restricted to $C_i \times C_j$. Since d_{ij} is a continuous function on a compact set, there exists $(c_i, c_j) \in C_i \times C_j$ such that $d_{ij}(c_i, c_j) > 0$ is the minimal value of d_{ij}. Let a pair (c_k, c_m), $k \neq m$, be such that $d_{km}(c_k, c_m) \leq d_{ij}(c_i, c_j)$ for all $i, j \in \{1, ..., n\}$ with $i \neq j$.

We obtain that $d(x, y) \geq d(c_k, c_m) = d_{km}(c_k, c_m)$ for every x and y belonging to two different components of bdA. We now show that $d(c_k, c_m) \geq 2r$.

Assume that $d(c_k, c_m) \leq 2r$. Consider the closed ball B such that $c_k, c_m \in bdB$ and the line segment $c_k c_m$ is the diagonal of B (see Figure 6.10). Clearly, the radius of B is not greater than r and $B \cap bdA = \{c_k, c_m\}$.

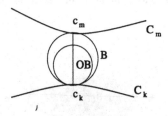

Figure 6.10:

Therefore, either $B \subseteq A$ or $intB \subseteq A^c$. We assume $intB \subseteq A^c$. The proof in the second case is analogous. Every closed ball OB such that OB is a proper subset of B and $OB \cap B = \{c_k\}$ is an outside osculating ball of A at c_k. Since the radius of B is not greater than r and the center of B is collinear with all centers of balls OB, we obtain that B is an outside osculating ball of A at c_k. Yet, this contradicts the fact that $B \cap bdA = \{c_k, c_m\}$. Therefore, $d(c_k, c_m) > 2r$, and consequently $d(x, y) > 2r$ for every x and y belonging to two different components of bdA.   ∎

Definition: The **Hausdorff distance** d_H of sets $A, B \subseteq \mathbb{R}^2$ is given by

$$d_H(A, B) = \inf\{r \geq 0 : A \subseteq Par(B, r) \text{ and } B \subseteq Par(A, r)\}.$$

6.2 Generalized Convexity and Boundaries of Convex Sets

A set S is *convex* if for every pair of points $P, Q \in S$, the line segment PQ is contained in S. This definition can be generalized in various ways. For example in Rosenfeld and Kak [133], S is called *starshaped from* $P_0 \in S$ if P_0Q is contained in S for all $Q \in S$; thus S is convex iff it is starshaped from all of its points. As another example (Rawlins and Wood [124]), S is called *orthoconvex* if PQ is contained in S for all $P, Q \in S$ such that PQ is horizontal or vertical.

One class of generalizations of convexity, due to Valentine [154], makes use of triples (or k-tuples), rather than pairs, of points. A set satisfies Valentine's property P_3 if for every triple of points P, Q, R of S, at least one of the line segments PQ, QR, or RP is contained in S. For example, a polygonal arc consisting of two non-collinear line segments (Figure 6.11.a) is not convex, but is easily seen to have property P_3. It can be shown that if a set has property P_3, it is a union of at most three convex sets. Note, however, that the three-segment polygonal arc in Figure 6.11.b does not have property P_3.

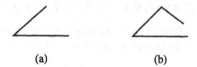

(a)   (b)

Figure 6.11: The polygonal arc in (a) is not convex, but is easily seen to have property P_3. The three-segment polygonal arc in (b) does not have property P_3, but has property CP_3.

We study a property closely related to, but weaker than, P_3. We say that S has *property* CP_3 ("collinear P_3") if P_3 holds for all *collinear* triples of points of S. For example, the three-segment arc in Figure 6.11b has property CP_3. This property turns out to characterize (parts of) the boundaries of convex sets. For arcs and closed curves, convexity is a very strong property; in fact, a closed curve or a nonsimple arc cannot be convex, and a simple arc is convex iff it is a straight line segment. The weaker property CP_3, on the other hand, will be shown to define very useful classes of arcs and curves.

In Section 6.2.1 we describe the partial characterizations of boundaries of convex sets given by Menger and by Valentine. In Section 6.2.2 we define property CP_3. In Section 6.2.3 we prove that: A simple closed curve has property CP_3 iff it is the boundary of a convex set, and an arc has property CP_3 iff it is a connected subset of such a boundary. Finally, in Section 6.2.4 we establish some additional results about property CP_3: an arc has property CP_3 iff there is at least one supporting line (= line such that the arc lies on one side of it) through each of its points; and a path having property CP_3 is a simple closed curve, provided it does not have infinitely many multiple points. Definitions and properties of basic geometric concepts can be found in Section 2.2.2.

6.2.1   Characterizations of Boundaries of Convex Sets

Menger [112] gave a rather complicated characterization of the boundary of a convex set which was simplified by Valentine [155] (p. 106, T8.1) essentially as follows:

Let S be a compact set in the plane containing at least three points. Suppose that for each triple of non-collinear points $x_i (i = 1, 2, 3)$ of S we have

$$S \cap \text{int}\Delta = \emptyset$$
$$V_i \cap S = \emptyset \quad i = 1, 2, 3$$
$$W_{jk} \cap S \neq \emptyset \quad j, k = 1, 2, 3; j \neq k$$

where (see Figure 6.12) Δ is the closed triangle determined by x_1, x_2, x_3; intΔ is the interior of Δ; V_i is the open V-shaped unbounded region abutting Δ at vertex x_i; and W_{ij} is an unbounded three-sided set abutting the edge $x_i x_j$. We define W_{ij} to contain the open line segment $x_i x_j$, and to be disjoint from the lines $x_i x_k$, $x_j x_k$ ($k \neq i, j$), so that it is neither open nor closed. Also if x_1, x_2, x_3 are three distinct collinear points of S suppose that

$$S \cap \text{intv} x_i x_j \neq \emptyset \qquad i, j = 1, 2, 3; i \neq j$$

where intv$x_i x_j$ is the interior of the interval $x_i x_j$. If all of these conditions are satisfied, S is the boundary of a convex set. The converse is also true for compact sets.

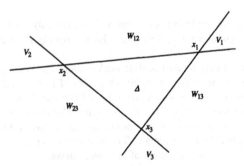

Figure 6.12: Illustration for Menger's characterization of the boundary of a convex set.

Valentine [155] (p. 108, T8.3) stated a condition slightly stronger than our property CP_3, and tried to relate it to the property of being a **convex curve**, i.e., a (proper or improper) subset of the boundary of a convex set:

Let S be a closed connected set in the plane. Suppose that for each triple of distinct collinear points in S, the minimal line segment containing them belongs to S. Then the set S satisfies at least one of the following four statements:

- S is closed convex set.

- S is a convex curve.
- S is the union of two linear elements $R_i (i = 1, 2)$ with $R_1 \cap R_2 \neq \emptyset$, where a linear element is either a closed line segment, a closed half line (ray), or a line.
- S is the union of three linear elements R_1, R_2, R_3 having a common endpoint x such that $x \in$ int conv $(R_1 \cup R_2 \cup R_3)$, where int conv(A) means the interior of the convex hull of the set A. (Hence, S is a kind of three-legged star.)

Note that Valentine's condition does not imply that S is a convex curve. Conversely, Figure 6.13 shows a convex curve which does not fulfill Valentine's condition (consider the triple of collinear points x, y and z).[1] We will show that a slightly weaker property, which we call CP_3, does completely characterize convex curves.

Figure 6.13: This convex curve does not fulfill Valentine's condition.

6.2.2 CP_3-Convexity

Definition: A set $S \subseteq R^2$ will be said to have property CP_3 if for every three collinear points in S, at least two of them are joined by a line segment contained in S.

The main result of this section is that property CP_3 characterizes convex curves. We first need to establish some properties of CP_3-convex sets.

Definition: A set S will be said to have property C_3 if for each triple of collinear points in S, the minimal line segment containing them belongs to S.

Note that this is the condition given by Valentine (see Section 6.2.1). It is clear that property C_3 implies property CP_3.

Proposition 6.6 The boundary of a bounded convex set has property C_3.

Proof: Let S be the boundary of a bounded convex set C, and let L be any straight line. If L contains an interior point of C, then L intersects S in exactly two points (Theorem 2.1), so it cannot contain three collinear points of S. If L does not contain any interior point of C and $L \cap (C \cup S) \neq \emptyset$, then $L \cap (C \cup S) = L \cap S$. But $L \cap (C \cup S)$ is a convex

---

[1]This example was suggested by Prof. David Mount, University of Maryland at College Park.

subset of L, since $C \cup S$ is convex (Proposition 2.13). Hence $L \cap (C \cup S)$ is a line segment, so that if L contains three collinear points of S, the minimal line segment containing them belongs to $L \cap S \subseteq S$, which proves that S has property C_3. ∎

Corollary 6.2 *The boundary of a bounded convex set has property CP_3.*

Lemma 6.1 *Let S be an arc with endpoints a and b such that $S \neq ab$. Let $L(a,b)$ be the straight line passing through points a and b. If S has property CP_3, then $S \cap L(a,b)$ has exactly two connected components, one containing a and the other containing b, and when these components are deleted, S lies in one of the open half planes into which $L(a,b)$ divides $\mathbb{R}^2$.*

Proof: The assumption that $S \neq ab$ implies that ab cannot be contained in S; otherwise ab would be a proper subarc of S with the same endpoints, which is impossible (Proposition 2.9). Hence $S \cap L(a,b)$ has at least two connected components, since the connected components $C(a)$ and $C(b)$ containing a and b cannot be the same. On the other hand if $S \cap L(a,b)$ had a third component, S could not have property CP_3.

$C(a)$ and $C(b)$ are subarcs of S (Proposition 2.1), and so must be the images of initial and final subintervals $[f^{-1}(a), u]$ and $[v, f^{-1}(b)]$ of I, respectively, where $u < v$. Let x, y be distinct points of S that do not lie on $L(a,b)$, where (say) $f^{-1}(x) < f^{-1}(y)$; then we must have $u < f^{-1}(x) < f^{-1}(y) < v$. Let A be the subarc of S joining x and y; then $A = f([f^{-1}(x), f^{-1}(y)])$, i.e., A is the image of a subinterval of I that is disjoint from $[f^{-1}(a), u]$ and $[v, f^{-1}(b)]$. Thus A cannot intersect $L(a,b)$; but this means that x and y must lie in the same open half plane defined by $L(a,b)$. ∎

Lemma 6.2 *Let S be an arc or a simple closed curve. Let $x, z, y \in S$ be three different points, and let $L(x,z) = L$ be the straight line containing x and z (Figure 6.14a). Let the subarcs $\mathrm{arc}(x,z)$ and $\mathrm{arc}(z,y)$ of S be such that $\mathrm{arc}(x,z) \cap \mathrm{arc}(z,y) = \{z\}$ and $\mathrm{arc}(z,y) \not\subseteq xz$. If there exists a point $p \in \mathrm{arc}(x,z)$ with nonzero distance to L such that p and y lie in one of the closed half planes into which L divides $\mathbb{R}^2$, then S does not have property CP_3.*

Proof: Let M be any straight line intersecting line segments xp, pz and zy but not passing through points x, z, p or y. Such a line exists, since x and z are different points of line L, p and y are two different points in one of the closed half planes into which L divides R^2, and p is at nonzero distance from L. (The cases in which y is also at a positive distance from L, and y lies on L, are illustrated in Figures 6.14b and 6.14c.) By Proposition 2.14, M intersects S in at least three points lying on the following subarcs of S: $\mathrm{arc}(x,p)$, $\mathrm{arc}(p,z)$, and $\mathrm{arc}(z,y)$. One of these points, say q, lies between the other two on M. Let J and K be two straight lines different from M and from each other which pass through q and satisfy the same conditions as M (see Figure 6.14d); the lines J and K can evidently be obtained by slightly rotating line M around point q so that the rotated lines still intersect lines segments xp and zy. Each of the lines M, J and K intersects S in at least two

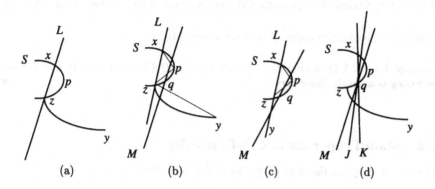

Figure 6.14:

points different from q in such a way that q lies between these two points (on M, J and K, respectively).

We now have six rays emanating from q and intersecting S. By Proposition 2.5, initial segments of at most two of these rays can be contained in S. Therefore, for at least one of the three lines, neither of its two intersection points with S different from q can be joined with q by a line segment contained in S. This implies that S does not have property CP_3. ∎

Proposition 6.7 *Let S be an arc with endpoints x and y. If S has property CP_3 and $S \neq xy$, then $S \cap xy = \{x, y\}$.*

Proof: Let $z \in S \cap xy$ be different from x and y. Since S has property CP_3, at least one of xz and zy, say zy, is contained in S. Then xz cannot be contained in S. Indeed if xz were contained in S, then xy would be contained in S, so that xy would be a proper subarc of S with the same endpoints as S, which is impossible (Proposition 2.9). Since S is arc-connected, there exists an arc $\text{arc}(x, z) \subseteq S$ joining x and z. Let L be the straight line containing x and z and let $p \in \text{arc}(x, z)$ be any point whose distance to L is greater than 0. Such a point exists, since $\text{arc}(x, z) \neq xz$. (See Figure 6.15.)

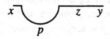

Figure 6.15:

Then the assumptions of Lemma 6.2 are fulfilled for x, z, y, and p: x and z lie on L; $\text{arc}(x, z)$ and $\text{arc}(z, y) = zy$ are subarcs of S such that $\text{arc}(x, z) \cap \text{arc}(z, y) = \{z\}$ (Proposition 2.7). The assumption that $z \in S \cap xy$ implies that $\text{arc}(z, y) \nsubseteq xz$. Points p and y lie in one of the closed half planes into which L divides $\mathbb{R}^2$, since y lies on L. Hence by Lemma 6.2, S cannot have property CP_3, contradiction; it follows that $S \cap xy = \{x, y\}$.∎

The following corollary makes use of Proposition 2.10.

Corollary 6.3 *Let S be an arc with endpoints x and y. If S has property CP_3 and $S \neq xy$, then $S \cup xy$ is a simple closed curve.*   ∎

6.2.3   Main Properties of CP_3-Convexity

In this section we prove the main properties of CP_3-convexity:

Theorem 6.2 *A simple closed curve has property CP_3 iff it is the boundary of a convex set.*

Theorem 6.3 *An arc has property CP_3 iff it is a connected subset of the boundary of a convex set.*

By Theorems 6.2 and 2.3, a set is a simple closed curve and has property CP_3 iff it is the boundary of a bounded convex set with nonempty interior. Similarly, a set is an arc and has property CP_3 iff it is a closed, connected subset of the boundary of a convex set.

Proof of Theorem 6.2.
"$\Leftarrow$": This follows from the Corollary to Proposition 6.6.

"$\Rightarrow$": Let S be a simple closed curve. By the Jordan curve theorem, S separates $\mathbb{R}^2$ into exactly two components, one bounded and the other unbounded, and S is the boundary of each of these two components. Let C be the bounded component together with S. Then S is the boundary of C, and C is closed.

We will show that if C is not convex, then S does not have property CP_3. Let L be a straight line passing through an interior point of C and intersecting S (the boundary of C) in at least three distinct points, say x, z and y (Theorem 2.1). We can assume that z is between x and y on L, and that the interior point is between x and z. Therefore, xz cannot be contained in S. If zy is also not contained in S, then S does not have property CP_3; so, it remains only to consider the case where zy is contained in S. Since $(S \backslash zy) \cup \{z, y\}$ is an arc containing z, y and x, there exists an arc joining x and z: $\text{arc}(x, z) \subseteq (S \backslash zy) \cup \{z, y\} \subseteq S$. Therefore, $\text{arc}(x, z) \cap zy = \{z\}$. Let $p \in \text{arc}(x, z)$ be any point with nonzero distance to L; such a point exists, since $\text{arc}(x, z) \neq xz$, because xz is not contained in S.

Hence the assumptions of Lemma 6.2 are satisfied for x, z, y, and p: x and z lie on L; $\text{arc}(x, z)$ and $\text{arc}(z, y) = zy$ are subarcs of S such that $\text{arc}(x, z) \cap \text{arc}(z, y) = \{z\}$; $\text{arc}(x, z) \neq xz$; and points p and y lie in one of the closed half planes into which L divides R^2, since y lies on L. Thus by Lemma 6.2, S does not have property CP_3.   ∎

Remark: Theorem 6.2 can also be proved along the same lines as the proof of Theorem 2.1 given in Yaglom and Boltyanskii [164], p. 114–116, Solutions 1-4 and 1-5.

From Theorem 2.1 we have also

Corollary 6.4 *A simple closed curve S has property CP_3 iff every straight line passing through an arbitrary interior point of C (the set bounded by S) intersects S in exactly two points.* ∎

Corollary 6.5 *A simple closed curve has property CP_3 iff it is C_3-convex.*

Proof: This follows from Theorem 6.2 and from the Corollary to Proposition 6.6. ∎

In order to prove Theorem 6.3, we first prove

Theorem 6.4 Let S be an arc with a and y as endpoints. If S has property CP_3, so has $S \cup ay$.

Proof: If $S = ay$, the theorem is trivially true; therefore we assume that $S \neq ay$. Note that in this case ay cannot be completely contained in S (Proposition 2.9). Let L be the straight line containing ay. By Lemma 6.1, S lies in one of the closed half planes into which L divides R^2.

Suppose $S \cup ay$ did not have property CP_3, and let M be a straight line intersecting $S \cup ay$ in three different points x, z and d in such a way that no line segment joining two of them is contained in $S \cup ay$. It is easy to see that two of these points must belong to $S \setminus ay$ and the third one to ay, say $x, z \in S \setminus ay$ and $d \in ay$. Furthermore d cannot be between x and z on M, since then x and z could not lie in the same closed half plane defined by L (see Figure 6.16a). We will now show that this situation contradicts the assumption that S has property CP_3.

Since x and z lie on the same side of d on line M, the distances from x and z to d cannot be equal. Let x be farther from d than z. Since xz is not contained in S, the subarc $\mathrm{arc}(x, z) \subseteq S$ joining x and z is not contained in M (see Figure 6.16a). Therefore, there exists a point $p \in \mathrm{arc}(x, z)$ with nonzero distance to M. Since d is on ay, either a or y must lie in the same closed half plane defined by M as point p does; suppose, as shown in Figure 6.16a, y and p lie in the same closed half plane. There exists a subarc $\mathrm{arc}(z, y) \subseteq S$ joining z and y (see Figures 6.16b and 6.16c). By Proposition 2.8, either $\mathrm{arc}(x, z) \subseteq \mathrm{arc}(z, y)$ or $\mathrm{arc}(x, z) \cap \mathrm{arc}(z, y) = \{z\}$. If $\mathrm{arc}(x, z) \subseteq \mathrm{arc}(z, y)$ (Figure 6.16c), then the set $\mathrm{arc}(x, y) = (\mathrm{arc}(z, y) \setminus \mathrm{arc}(z, x)) \cup \{x\}$ is evidently an arc joining x and y with the property $\mathrm{arc}(x, y) \cap \mathrm{arc}(z, x) = \{x\}$. Therefore we know that there is an arc joining either x or z to y (Figures 6.16c and 6.16b, respectively) such that $\mathrm{arc}(x, y) \cap \mathrm{arc}(z, x) = \{x\}$ or $\mathrm{arc}(x, y) \cap \mathrm{arc}(z, x) = \{z\}$, respectively. In either case, the assumptions of L2 are fulfilled: Points x and z lie on a straight line M; $\mathrm{arc}(z, x)$ and $\mathrm{arc}(z, y)$ (or $\mathrm{arc}(x, y)$) are subarcs of S such that $\mathrm{arc}(z, y) \cap \mathrm{arc}(z, x) = \{z\}$ (or $\mathrm{arc}(x, y) \cap \mathrm{arc}(z, x) = \{x\}$) and $\mathrm{arc}(z, x) \neq zx$;

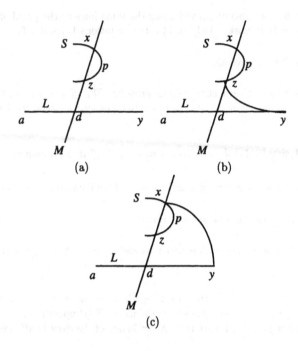

Figure 6.16:

$p \in \text{arc}(z, x)$ has nonzero distance to M; and p and y lie in one of the closed half planes defined by M. Hence by Lemma 6.2, S cannot have property CP_3, contradiction.   ∎

Proof of Theorem 6.3:
"⇒": Let S be an arc with a and b as endpoints. If $S = ab$, the theorem is trivially true. If $S \neq ab$, then by Proposition 6.7, $S \cap ab = \{a, b\}$; hence $S \cup ab$ is a simple closed curve (Proposition 2.10). Since S has property CP_3, Theorem 6.4 implies that $S \cup ab$ also has property CP_3. Thus Theorem 6.2 implies that $S \cup ab$ is a boundary of a convex set. Therefore, S is a connected subset of the boundary of a convex set.

"⇐": Let S be the boundary of a convex set C. We prove this part of the theorem for every connected bounded proper subset of S, and therefore for every arc. Let T be a connected bounded proper subset of S. If the interior of C is empty, then T is a line segment, and the theorem is trivially true. If the interior of C is nonempty, then S is a simple closed curve (Theorem 2.3). Let $a, b, c \in T$ be three collinear points with b between a and c. By Proposition 6.6, S has property C_3; therefore the minimal line segment ac containing a, b, c belongs to S. Since T is a connected subset of a simple closed curve containing a, b, c, at least one of line segments ab and bc must be contained in T; indeed, if neither of them were contained in T, then T would not be connected (Proposition 2.11). ∎

While proving Theorem 6.3, we have also proved

Theorem 6.5 *Let S be an arc with endpoints a and b. S has property CP_3 iff $S \cup ab$ is the boundary of a convex set.*   ∎

Corollary 6.6 *If a simple arc or curve S has property CP_3, so has any arc-connected subset of S.*

Proof: This follows from Theorems 6.2 and 6.3 and Propositions 2.1 and 2.2.   ∎

6.2.4   Supporting Lines and Simplicity

Theorem 6.6 *An arc S has property CP_3 iff through each of its points there passes at least one supporting line.*

Proof:

"⇒": If S has property CP_3, by Theorem 6.3 it is part of the boundary of a convex set. Hence Theorem 2.2 implies that through each point of S there passes at least one supporting line.

"⇐": Let S be an arc such that through each of its points there passes at least one supporting line. Let S' be the intersection of all closed half planes containing S. Then S' is convex. Since through each point of S there passes at least one supporting line, every point of S is a boundary point of S'. Since S is an arc that is contained in the boundary of a convex set S', it follows from Theorem 6.3 that S has property CP_3.   ∎

Note that when $f(I)$ is a simple closed curve, only the endpoints of I are mapped into a multiple point, which is the only such point; and that $f(I)$ is an arc iff f has no multiple points.

Theorem 6.7 *Let $f(I)$ be a path defined by $f : I \to \mathbb{R}^2$ such that the preimage of the set of multiple points of f is a finite nonempty subset of I. If $f(I)$ has property CP_3, then $f(I)$ is a simple closed curve.*

Proof: Let $J \subseteq I$ be the preimage of the set of multiple points of f. Let $x, y \in J$, where $x < y$, be points of I such that $f(x) = f(y)$ and such that there exists no pair of points of J strictly between x and y with the same property, i.e., there do not exist $a, b \in J$, where $x < a < b < y$, such that $f(a) = f(b)$. Such points x, y must exist, because otherwise J would be infinite. The restriction $f|_{(x,y)}$ of f to the open interval (x, y) is an injection and f is continuous. Therefore, $S = f([x, y])$ is a simple closed curve. If x and y are the endpoints of I, we are done; hence we can assume that at least one of them is not an endpoint. We show that this assumption leads to inconsistency with property CP_3 of $f(I)$.

By the Jordan curve theorem, S separates $\mathbb{R}^2$ into exactly two components, one bounded and the other unbounded, and S is the boundary of each of these components. Let C be the bounded component together with S; then S is the boundary of C. Since at least one of x and y is not an endpoint, there exists a point $z \in I \setminus [x, y]$ such that $z \notin J$.

Let L be a straight line passing through $f(z)$ and through an interior point of C, but not intersection $f(J)$, i.e., L does not contain any multiple point of f (see Figure 6.17a–b); such a line exists since J, hence $f(J)$, is finite. Then L intersects S in at least two distinct points $f(u), f(v)$ such that the line segment $f(u)f(v)$ contains an interior point c of C. Therefore, $f(u)f(v)$ is not contained in S. By Lemma 6.3, $f(u)f(v)$ cannot be contained in $f(I)$.

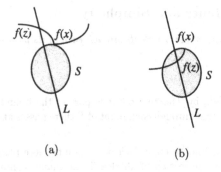

(a)   (b)

Figure 6.17:

Evidently $f(u)f(z)$ is not contained in S, since $f(z) \notin S$. Hence by Lemma 6.3, $f(u)f(z)$ cannot be contained in $f(I)$. In exactly the same way, we can show that $f(v)f(z)$ cannot be contained in $f(I)$. Since the line segment joining any two of the three collinear points $f(z), f(u)$, and $f(v)$ in $f(I)$ cannot be contained in $f(I)$, $f(I)$ does not have property CP_3. This contradiction proves the theorem.   ∎

Lemma 6.3 *Let $f(I)$ be a path defined by $f : I \to \mathbb{R}^2$, and suppose $f(x) = f(y)$ for some $x, y \in I$, where $x < y$. Let $f([x, y]) = S$, and let K be a line segment in $\mathbb{R}^2$ which does not contain any multiple point of f. If K intersects S and is not contained in S, then K is not contained in $f(I)$.*

Proof: Since K does not contain any multiple point of f and $f(x) = f(y)$ is a multiple point of f, we have $K \cap S \subseteq f((x, y))$, where (x, y) is an open interval. We show that the assumption $K \subseteq f(I)$ leads to inconsistency.

Let I be the unit interval $[0, 1]$. If $K \subseteq f([0, 1])$, then $K \setminus S \neq \emptyset$ and $K \setminus S \subseteq f([0, x] \cup [y, 1])$. Since $[0, x] \cup [y, 1]$ is a compact set, $f([0, x] \cup [y, 1])$ is also compact, and therefore closed. Hence $\mathrm{cl}(K \setminus S) \subseteq f([0, x] \cup [y, 1])$, where cl is the usual closure operator in R^2. Since S is closed (as an image of a compact set) and K is a line segment (and therefore closed), $K \setminus S$ is not closed. Therefore, there exists $p \in \mathrm{cl}(K \setminus S)$ such that $p \notin (K \setminus S)$. Now $p \in \mathrm{cl}(K \setminus S)$ implies that $p \in f([0, x] \cup [y, 1])$. On the other hand $p \in K \cap S$, since $p \in \mathrm{cl}(K \setminus S) \subseteq K$ and $p \notin K \setminus S$. Hence $p \in f((x, y))$, because $K \cap S \subseteq f((x, y))$. Thus p is in the image (under f) of both (x, y) and its complement, and so is a multiple point; but $p \in K$, contradiction. ∎

6.3   Differentialless Geometry of Plane Curves

6.3.1   Lines of Support; Supported Sets

Definition: Let S be a subset of the plane, and p a point of S. A straight line $l_S(p)$ through p is called a **line of support** of S at p if S is contained in one of the closed half-planes into which $l_S(p)$ divides $\mathbb{R}^2$. This closed half-plane is called a **half-plane of support**.

Definition: A subset S of the plane is **supported** if, for every $p \in S$, there exists at least one line of support of S at p.

Note that if S has a line of support at p, then p must be a boundary point of S (i.e., any neighborhood of p contains points of the complement of S). Note also that lines of support need not be unique. For example, if S is a single point, every line through that point is a line of support of S; if S is a segment of a straight line l, the same is true for its endpoints, but at its interior points, l is the only line of support of S.

Theorem 6.8 *A closed, bounded, connected planar set S is supported iff S is a planar arc (not necessarily proper) of the boundary of a convex set (the convex hull of S).*

Proof:

"$\Rightarrow$:" We recall [155, 164] that the closed convex hull $H(S)$ of a set S is the intersection of all the closed half-planes that contain S. If S has a line of support l at p, we have $p \in S \subseteq H(S)$, and l must also be a line of support of $H(S)$, so that p must be on the boundary of $H(S)$. Hence if a set S is supported, it is contained in the boundary of its closed convex hull $H(S)$.

If the interior of $H(S)$ is empty, then since $H(S)$ is a closed, bounded connected, and convex subset of the plane, it must be a single point or a line segment, and thus $S \subseteq H(S)$ must be all of $H(S)$. Otherwise, $H(S)$ is a closed, bounded convex set with nonempty interior, so its boundary is a simple closed curve (Theorem 32 in [99]). If S is all of the boundary of $H(S)$, then S is a simple closed curve. If S is a proper, nontrivial, closed, connected subset of the boundary of $H(S)$, then S is an arc.

"$\Leftarrow$:" Conversely, we show that if a point $p \in X$ is on the boundary of a convex set X, X must have a line of support at p. If the lines joining p to all the other points of X did not lie in a sector of angle $\leq 180^o$, p would lie in the interior of the triangle spanned by three points of X; since X is convex, this entire triangle is in X, so that p is an interior point of X, contradiction.   ∎

In particular, from the proof of Theorem 6.8 we obtain

Corollary 6.7 *A set S is supported iff it is contained in the boundary of its closed convex hull.*   ∎

Let C be a simple closed curve. By the Jordan curve theorem, the complement of C has two nonempty connected components, one of which is bounded and surrounded by C. Let C^* be the closure of of the bounded component. By the Jordan curve theorem, C is the boundary of C^*, and the interior of C^* is nonempty. For any point p of C^*, since C surrounds p, any ray emanating from p must meet C; hence p lies on many line segments whose endpoints are in C so that C^* is contained in the closed convex hull $H(C)$ of C. Thus $H(C)$ is a closed, bounded convex set with nonempty interior, so its boundary is a simple closed curve, call it B. If C is supported, C must be contained in B by Theorem 6.8. Since B and C are both simple closed curves, this implies that $C = B$, so that $C^* = H(C)$.

Conversely, if C^* is convex, by the first part of the proof of Theorem 6.8, it has lines of support at just the points of C, so that C is supported. We have thus proved

Corollary 6.8 *Let C be a simple closed curve and let C^* be the closed bounded region surrounded by C. Then C is supported iff C^* is convex.* ∎

This result is a special case of a theorem which was proved by a number of prominent mathematicians, including Caratheodory [23], Brunn [18], and Minkowski [113], and which can also be found in a more general version in Valentine [155] (Theorem 4.1, p. 47).

The characterization of supported arcs can similarly be derived from the concept of CP_3 convexity introduced in Section 6.2. It is shown in Theorem 6.6 that an arc A is supported iff it has property CP_3, and that this in turn is equivalent to $A \cup ab$ being the boundary of a convex set (Theorem 6.5). If $A \neq ab$, $A \cup ab$ is a simple closed curve (Corollary 6.3); thus either a supported arc is a line segment, or joining its endpoints yields a supported simple closed curve. We thus have

Corollary 6.9 *Let A be an arc with endpoints a and b; then A is supported iff $A \cup ab$ is the boundary of a convex set.* ∎

The following simple but general characterization of lines of support will be a useful tool in proving several of our later results.

Proposition 6.8 *Let S be a planar set. There exists a line of support of S at $p \in S$ iff there do not exist three points $q, r, s \in S$ such that p lies in the interior of the triangle spanned by points q, r, and s.*

Proof:
"⇒:" If p is in the interior of such a triangle, any line l through p must intersect an interior point of at least one side if the triangle, so that the endpoints of that side cannot lie in the same closed half-plane defined by l (see Figure 6.18(a)).

"⇐:" Conversely, the set of rays joining p to all the other points of S is contained in some closed angular sector with vertex p, possibly with vertex angle 360°. The intersection of all such sectors is also a closed angular sector with vertex p, say with vertex angle α.

If $\alpha \leq 180°$, there is a line of support of S at p. If $\alpha > 180°$ (see Figure 6.18(b)), then there exist three points $q, r, s \in S$ such that p is in the interior of the triangle spanned by q, r, and s. ∎

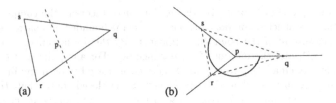

Figure 6.18:

6.3.2   Sectors of Support

Definition: Let p be a point of a set S such that at least one line of support of S at p exists. The **sector of support** $\sigma_S(p)$ is defined as the intersection of all the closed half-planes of support of S at p.

Clearly $\sigma_S(p)$ is a closed and convex subset of the plane. We assume from now on that S is not a subset of a line (the contrary case was discussed in Section 6.3.1). If there is a unique line of support l of S at p, then $\sigma_S(p)$ is the closed half-plane determined by l that contains S (see Figure 6.19(a)). If there is more than one line of support of S at p, then $\sigma_S(p)$ is a closed angular sector with angle $\alpha_S(p)$ less than $180°$ (see Figure 6.19(b)). Note that a line through p is a line of support of S at p iff it is contained in the closure of the complement of $\sigma_S(p)$.

If S has a unique line of support at p, we define the **turn angle** of S at p as $0°$. If S has more than one line of support at p, we define the **turn angle** of S at p as $180° - \alpha_S(p)$.

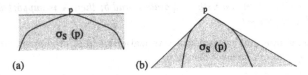

Figure 6.19: $\sigma_S(p)$ is the sector of support of S at point p.

We now assume that the set A is an arc. The sector of support $\sigma_A(p)$ of an arc A is bounded by two rays emanating from p that make an angle $\alpha_A(p) \le 180°$. We will call these rays the left and right rays of support of A at p depending on the direction in which we traverse A; these concepts will now be defined.

Let $p = A(x)$ for some point $x \in (a,b)$. Let $r < \min\{d(A(x), A(a)), d(A(x), A(b))\}$, where d is Euclidean distance in the plane. Then the circle $C(p,r)$ with the center p and radius r intersects arc A in at least two points (see Figure 6.20(a)). This follows from the fact that a circle is a Jordan curve and p is inside the bounded region enclosed by $C(p,r)$ while the arc endpoints $A(a)$ and $A(b)$ are outside of this region. Let $x_- \in (a,x)$ be a point such that $A(x_-) \in C(p,r) \cap A$ and $A((x_-, x)) \cap C(p,r) = \emptyset$ (i.e., $x_- = \sup\{y \in (a,x) : A(y) \in C(p,r) \cap A\}$; since the set $C(p,r) \cap A$ is compact, we have $A(x_-) \in C(p,r) \cap A\}$). Similarly, let $x_+ \in (x,b)$ be a point such that $A(x_+) \in C(p,r) \cap A$ and $A(x,x_+) \cap C(p,r) = \emptyset$.

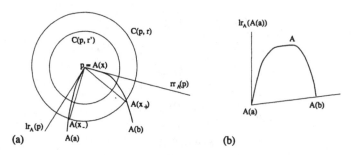

Figure 6.20:

Since $A([x_-, x_+])$ is a subarc of A, it is contained in the sector $\sigma_A(p)$. In particular, the points $A(x_-)$ and $A(x_+)$ lie on $C(p, r) \cap \sigma_A(p)$.

The ray bounding $\sigma_A(p)$ that can be reached from point $A(x_-)$ while traversing $C(p, r) \cap \sigma_A(p)$ without going through $A(x_+)$ will be denoted by $lr_A(p)$ and called the **left ray of support** of A at p (see Figure 6.20(a)). Similarly, the ray bounding $\sigma_A(p)$ that can be reached from point $A(x_+)$ while traversing $C(p, r) \cap \sigma_A(p)$ without going through $A(x_-)$ will be denoted by $rr_A(p)$ and called the **right ray of support** of A at p.

We next show that if A is supported, $lr_A(p)$ and $rr_A(p)$ do not depend on the radius of the circle $C(p, r)$. To see this, note that the subarc $A([x_-, x])$ is contained in the sector determined by the ray $lr_A(p)$ and the line segment $A(x)A(x_-)$ (see Figure 6.20(a)), since the interior of triangle $A(x_-)A(x)A(x_+)$ cannot contain any points of arc A (Theorem 6.8). If $r' < r$, the point $A(x'_-)$ determined with respect to circle $C(p, r')$ must thus be contained in this sector; therefore, the ray $lr_A(p)$ can be reached from $A(x'_-)$ along $C(p, r')$ without going through point $A(x'_+)$. A similar argument applies for $rr_A(p)$.

It remains to define the left and right rays of support at the endpoints of arc A. This can be done even if A is equal to the line segment $A(a)A(b)$ (where $a \neq b$); the angle $\alpha_A(p)$ is $0°$ if $p = A(a)$ or $A(b)$, and $180°$ otherwise. In the latter case, $\sigma_A(p)$ cuts off a semicircle on $C(p, r)$, and the subarcs $A(x)A(x_-)$, $A(x)A(x+)$ coincide respectively with rays $lr_A(p)$, $rr_A(p)$. In the former cases, $\sigma_A(p)$ is a ray, and it coincides with $lr_A(p) = rr_A(p)$ if $p = A(a)$ or $p = A(b)$.

Now suppose that A is different from line segment $A(a)A(b)$. As we see in Figure 6.20(b), at $A(a)$ one of the bounding rays of $\sigma_A(S(a))$ is just the line segment $A(a)A(b)$; see Corollary 6.9. We define this ray to be $lr_A(A(a))$, and the other bounding ray of the sector $\sigma_A(A(a))$ to be $rr_A(A(a))$; and vice versa at $A(b)$.

The foregoing discussion gives us

Proposition 6.9 *Let $A : [a, b] \to \mathbb{R}^2$ be a supported arc. Let A' be the subarc $A([p, c])$, where $a \leq p < c \leq b$. The subarc A' is contained in the sector defined by the right ray of support $rr_A(A(p))$ and the line segment $A(p)A(c)$ (see Figure 6.21). The analogous statement holds for the left ray of support.*

As a consequence of Proposition 6.9 we have

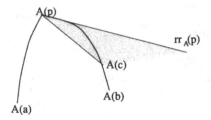

Figure 6.21:

Proposition 6.10 *Let A and A' be as in Proposition 6.9. Then* $rr_A(A(p)) = rr_{A'}(A(p))$. *The analogous statement holds for the left ray of support.*

Proof: Clearly, $A(p) = A'(p)$. Since A' is a subarc of A, sector of support $\sigma_{A'}(A(p))$ of A' is contained in $\sigma_A(A(p))$. Suppose $rr_A(A(p)) \neq rr_{A'}(A(p))$; then there would be a point $A(t)$ of A in $\sigma_A(A(p)) \setminus \sigma_{A'}(A(p))$ which lies between $rr_A(A(p))$ and $rr_{A'}(A(p))$. Consider the triangle $A(p)A(c)A(t)$ (see Figure 6.22). Since A is supported, no point of A can lie in the interior of this triangle (Theorem 6.8). But by Proposition 6.9, $A([p,c])$ is contained in the angular sector spanned by line segment $A(p)A(c)$ and $rr_A(A(p))$; hence there exist parts of A in the interior of the triangle, contradiction. ∎

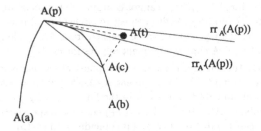

Figure 6.22:

Corollary 6.10 *Let A be a supported arc and A' a proper subarc of A. If p is not an endpoint of A', then* $\sigma_{A'}(p) = \sigma_A(p)$. *If p is an endpoint of A, then* $\sigma_{A'}(p)$ *is a proper subset of* $\sigma_A(p)$.

6.3.3   Differentiability

Any arc is continuous, but we have not assumed that our arcs are differentiable. In this section we show, using the results of Section 6.3.2, that a supported arc must have left and right derivatives at every point, and is differentiable at point p if it has a unique line of support at p.

Let $A : [a, b] \to \mathbb{R}^2$ be an arc and let $x, y \in (a, b)$. Consider the vector $\frac{A(x)-A(y)}{|x-y|}$. As y approaches x from the left (right), this vector may approach a finite, nonzero limit; if so, the limit is called the left (right) derivative of A at x and is denoted by $A'_-(x)$ $(A'_+(x))$. The right derivative of A at a, and the left derivative of A at b, are defined similarly.

The left (right) derivative exists at $x \in (a, b)$ and is a finite and non-zero vector $A'_-(x)$ $(A'_+(x))$ iff the limit of the lines through $A(x)$ and $A(t)$ as t approaches x from below, i.e., $t < x$ (above, i.e., $x < t$).

If the left and right derivatives $A'_-(x)$ and $A'_+(x)$ exist and are equal, then we say that the derivative of A at x exists and has value $A'(x) \equiv A'_-(x) = A'_+(x)$.

Theorem 6.9 *Let $A : [a, b] \to \mathbb{R}^2$ be a supported arc. Then the left and right derivatives $A'_-(x)$ and $A'_+(x)$ exist and are finite and non-zero at every point $x \in (a, b)$, and the same for $A'_-(a)$ and $A'_+(b)$.*

Proof: We give the proof only for $A'_+(x)$, where $x \in (a, b)$; the proofs in the other cases are analogous. Let $p = A(x)$. For every $y \in (x, b]$, we denote by $\sigma(p, A(y))$ the closed angular sector contained in $\sigma(p)$ and spanned by the right ray of support $rr_A(p)$ and the line segment $pA(y)$ (see Figure 6.23). Let $\beta(p, A(y))$ denote the angle of this sector.

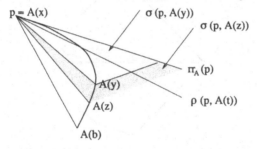

Figure 6.23:

Let $y, z \in [a, b)$ be such that $x < y < z$. Since arc A is supported, its subarc $A' = A([x, z])$ is also supported. By Corollary 6.9, the closed curve $A([x, z]) \cup pA(z)$ is the boundary of a convex set, which we denote by B. Since $A(y) \in B$ and B is convex, the line segment $pA(y)$ is contained in B. Thus $\sigma(p, A(y)) \subseteq \sigma(p, A(z))$ and $\beta(p, A(y)) \leq \beta(p, A(z))$ (see Figure 6.23). Hence the function $y \to \beta(p, A(y))$ is non-increasing as y approaches x from above, and therefore $\beta(p, A(y))$ converges to a finite value β as y approaches x from above.

We show that $\beta = 0^\circ$, which means that the rays emanating from $p = A(x)$ and passing through the points $A(z)$ have $rr_A(p)$ as their limit as z approaches x from above, which implies the existence of $A'_+(x)$. It is enough to show that for every $z \in (x, b]$ and every angle $\alpha > 0$, there exists $t \in (x, z]$ such that $\beta(p, A(t)) < \alpha$. If this were not the case, then there would exist $z \in (x, b]$ and $\alpha > 0$ such that for every $t \in (x, z]$, we have $\beta(p, A(t)) \geq \alpha$. This would imply that $rr_A(p)$ is not the right ray of support of the subarc $A' = A([x, z])$, which contradicts Proposition 6.10.   ∎

If the line of support at a point x of A is unique, the left and right rays of support at x are collinear, which implies that the left and right derivatives at x are equal. We thus have

Corollary 6.11 *Let $A : [a, b] \to \mathbb{R}^2$ be a supported arc, and let $x \in (a, b)$. Then the derivative $A'(x)$ exists (i.e., $A'(x) = A'_-(x) = A'_+(x)$) iff the line of support at x is unique.*

Definition: We define a non-endpoint p of a supported arc A to be a **cusp** if there is more than one line of support of A at p.

By Corollary 6.11, the arc A is not differentiable at a cusp. Note that a supported arc can have infinitely many cusps, as illustrated in Figure 6.24. It is not hard to see that at the accumulation point of the cusps in Figure 6.24, the arc is differentiable.

Note that differentiability does not imply supportedness (i.e., the converse of Corollary 6.11 is not true); at a point of inflection of an arc (see Section 6.3.5), its derivative may exist, but it has no line of support.

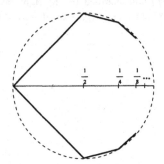

Figure 6.24: A supported arc can have infinitely many cusps.

6.3.4   Uniquely Supported Arcs; Curvature

Definition: An arc A is **uniquely supported** if at every non-endpoint $p \in A$ there exists a unique line of support $l_A(p)$.

Clearly, if an arc is uniquely supported, it is supported. However, the converse is not true; for example, a convex simple polygonal arc is supported but does not have unique lines of support at its vertices.

In this section, we will show that a supported arc can curve in only one direction. In order to be able to talk about curvature of arcs, we consider arcs that belong to class C^2, where an arc $A : [a, b] \to \mathbb{R}^2$ belongs to class C^2 if its first and second derivatives exist and are non-zero vectors for every point t in the open interval (a, b). (Note that we require that a C^2 arc is an immersion as defined in Spivak [144], p. 1-1.) For a simple closed curve $A : [a, b] \to \mathbb{R}^2$ to belong to class C^2, we additionally require that $A(a) = A(b)$, $A'(a) = A'(b)$, and $A''(a) = A''(b)$. Clearly, a supported C^2 arc (or curve) is uniquely supported.

We recall that the curvature of an arc can be defined as rate of change of slope (as a function of arc length). The definition can be found in standard textbooks and will not be given here. The magnitude of the curvature depends on how the arc is parameterized (which need not be by arc length), but its sign does not depend on the parameterization. We can now restate Theorem 8, p. 1-26, from Spivak [144] (Spivak calls supported simple closed C^2 curves *convex*, p. 1-16):

Theorem 6.10 *A simple closed C^2 curve $C : [a, b] \to \mathbb{R}^2$ is supported iff, for every $p \in [a, b]$, the curvature $\kappa(p)$ exists and satisfies $\kappa(p) \geq 0$ or $\kappa(p) \leq 0$ for every $p \in [a, b]$ (depending on the direction in which C is traversed).* ∎

The following theorem is a simple consequence of Theorem 6.10.

Theorem 6.11 *If a C^2 arc A is supported, then for every non-endpoint $p \in A$, the curvature $\kappa(p)$ exists and satisfies $\kappa(p) \geq 0$ or $\kappa(p) \leq 0$ (depending on the direction in which A is traversed).*

Proof: We can extend arc A to a supported simple closed C^2 curve C, and then apply Theorem 6.10 to C. We need only construct a supported arc B, lying in the half-plane determined by the line segment $A(a)A(b)$ that does not contain arc A, such that the endpoints and first and second derivatives at the endpoints of B coincide with those of A. ∎

The converse of Theorem 6.11 is not true. Consider a spiral S such that for all non-endpoints $p \in S$ the curvature $\kappa(p)$ exists and has the same sign; see Figure 6.25. Evidently, for any point $p \in S$ such that the total turn of the part of the spiral from p to one of the endpoints is greater than $360°$, there is no line of support of S at p. (In Section 6.3.6 we will define the total turn of a supported arc and show that it is at most $360°$.)

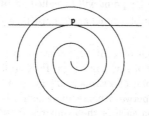

Figure 6.25: A differentiable arc may not be supported.

6.3.5   Tame Arcs

The class of supported arcs is quite restricted; they cannot turn by more than $360°$, and they can only turn in one direction, so they cannot have inflections. In this section we study a class of arcs which we call "tame"; a tame arc consists of a finite number of subarcs each of which is supported.

Definition: An arc $T : [a, b] \to \mathbb{R}^2$ will be called **tame** if there exist points $x_1, ..., x_n \in [a, b]$ with $x_1 = a$ and $x_n = b$ such that $T([x_i, x_{i+1}])$ is supported for $i = 0, ..., n - 1$. The points $x_2, ..., x_{n-1}$ will be called the **joints** of T.

Note that there are many choices for the joints; as we shall see below, only inflections are mandatory joints, but it may also be necessary to introduce additional "optional" joints to ensure that the subarcs are supported (e.g., see Figure 6.25).

Trivially, a supported arc is tame. In general, a tame arc T can be described as "piecewise" supported. Note that even at its joints, a tame arc has one-sided derivatives. If they are unequal, so that the union of the left and right rays of support is not a straight line, we shall call the joint a **cusp**.

The class of tame arcs seems to be general enough to describe (arcs of) the boundaries of planar objects. On the other hand, this class is restrictive enough to rule out the pathological examples of arcs and curves discussed in Section 1.5. For example, the spiral shown in Figure 1.13, which turns inward infinitely often, is an arc, but is not tame, since no matter how we divide it into a finite number of subarcs, the first or last arc still turns infinitely often, and so does not have a line of support at every point. Note also that a tame arc can only have finitely many inflections, since its curvature cannot change sign except possibly at the x_i's. Thus, for example, the graph of $x\sin(1/x)$ is not tame, since it oscillates infinitely often as x approaches 0. Sierpinski's "snowflake" curve and Peano's "space-filling" curves are not tame for the same reason.

A polygonal arc (or polygon) is piecewise straight, so that in particular it is tame. The term "tame" is used in knot theory to describe knots that are equivalent to polygonal knots [68]; in our case too, tameness is a generalization of polygonality.

Definition: A point x of a tame arc T will be called a **regular point** if there exists a supported subarc T' of T such that x is interior to T', i.e., $x \in T'$ and x is not an endpoint of T'. A point that is not a regular point will be called an **inflection point**.

Evidently, an inflection point of a tame arc T must be a joint of T. The other joints of T, if any, are "optional" joints.

Classically, an inflection point of a differentiable arc A (e.g., Figure 6.26(a)) is a non-endpoint at which the curvature of A changes sign. By Corollary 5 and Theorem 6.11, such a point cannot be an interior point of a supported subarc of A; hence, if A is differentiable and tame, each of its subarcs between consecutive joints is uniquely supported, and its curvature has a constant sign on each of these subarcs. However, a tame arc not need be differentiable; it can have both regular and inflection points that are cusps. For example, the cusps in Figures 6.26(b), (c) and (d) are inflection points. In Section 6.3.7 we will use total turn concepts to classify inflection cusps.

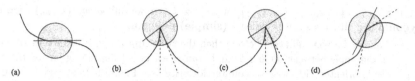

Figure 6.26: Inflection points.

As we have already seen, a tame arc that contains only regular points is not necessarily supported, e.g., the spiral in Figure 1.13(b). A polygonal arc also has no inflection points, but as shown in Figure 6.27(a), it need not be supported. More generally, an arc that has a straight subarc (Figure 6.27(b)) may have no inflection points, but may not be supported. In both of the cases in Figure 6.27, at least one of the points in the subarc uv must be a joint.

Definition: A maximal straight subarc S of a tame arc T will be called an **inflection segment** if there does not exist a supported subarc T' of T such that S is interior to T', i.e., $S \subseteq T'$ and S does not contain an endpoint of T'.

Evidently, at least one point of an inflection segment must be a joint.

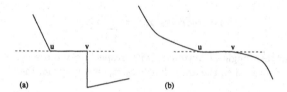

Figure 6.27: Inflection segments.

6.3.6 The Total Turn of a Tame Arc

In differential geometry, the total curvature of an arc is defined by integrating the curvature. Similarly, the "total turn" of a polygonal arc is defined by summing the turns of its vertices. In Section 6.3.2, we defined the turn angle at a point of a supported arc. In this section we will define the (total) turn of a tame arc. Our definition will be based on associating a polygonal arc with the tame arc. The associated polygonal arc is not unique, but as we shall see, the turn of every polygonal arc associated with a given tame arc is the same. Therefore, we can define the total turn of a tame arc as the total turn of any associated polygonal arc.

Simple Polygonal Arcs

Let $\{x_i : 0 \leq i \leq n-1\}$ be distinct points in the plane. The ordered sequence of vectors $(x_i x_{i+1})_{i=0,...,n-1}$ defines a polygonal arc $polyarc(x_0, x_n)$ joining x_0 to x_n. If

$x_i x_{i+1} \cap x_j x_{j+1} = \{x_i, x_{i+1}\} \cap \{x_j, x_{j+1}\}$ for $0 \leq i \neq j \leq n$, we call $polyarc(x_0, x_n)$ a **simple polygonal arc**. If $x_0 = x_n$, it is called a **(simple) polygon**.

Let ab and bc be non-collinear vectors; then the **turn angle** $\tau(b)$ is defined as $sign * \alpha$, where α is the angle between ab and bc and $sign = +1$ or -1 depending on whether the triangle abc is oriented clockwise or counterclockwise (see Figure 6.28(a) and (b)). If ab and bc are collinear, then $\tau(b) = 0$ if ab and bc point in the same direction (see Figure 6.28(c)). (The case where ab and bc are collinear but point in opposite directions will be discussed later.)

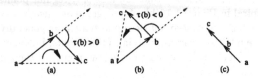

Figure 6.28: The turn angle $\tau(b)$ at a vertex b with respect to two vectors ab and bc: (a) $\tau(b) > 0$, (b) $\tau(b) < 0$, and (c) $\tau(b) = 0$.

Definition: If $x_0 \neq x_n$, we define the **turn** of a simple polygonal arc $polyarc(x_0, x_n)$ as

$$\tau(polyarc(x_0, x_n)) = \sum_{i=1}^{n-1} \tau(x_i),$$

where $\tau(x_i)$ is the turn angle at vertex x_i with respect to vectors $x_{i-1} x_i$ and $x_i x_{i+1}$ for $i = 1, ..., n-1$. If $x_0 = x_n$, i.e., the arc $polyarc(x_0, x_n)$ is a polygon, then we define its turn as

$$\tau(polyarc(x_0, x_n)) = \sum_{i=0}^{n-1} \tau(x_i),$$

where the turn angle at vertex x_0 is defined with respect to vectors $x_{n-1} x_0$ and $x_0 x_1$. For example, the turn of $polyarc(x_0, x_5)$ in Figure 6.29(b) is given by $\tau(polyarc(x_0, x_5)) = \tau(x_1) + \cdots + \tau(x_4)$, and the turn of $polyarc(x_0, x_6)$ with $x_0 = x_6$ in Figure 6.29(a) is given by $\tau(polyarc(x_0, x_5)) = \tau(x_0) + \cdots + \tau(x_5)$.

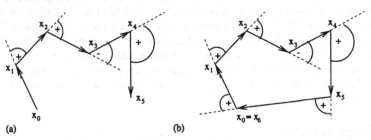

Figure 6.29: The turn of the polygonal arc in (a) is $\tau(x_1) + \cdots + \tau(x_4)$. The turn of the closed polygonal arc in (b) is $\tau(x_0) + \cdots + \tau(x_5)$.

If $polyarc(x_0, x_n) = (x_i x_{i+1})_{i=0,...,n-1}$ is a simple polygon, the bounded region surrounded by $polyarc(x_0, x_n)$ is called its **interior**. If the interior of the polygon is to the right of each vector $x_i x_{i+1}$, then the turn angle $\tau(x_i)$ at each vertex x_i is equal to 180° minus the interior angle of the simple polygon at x_i. A positive value of the turn at a vertex x_i indicates that x_i is a convex vertex of the polygon (e.g., $\tau(x_2) > 0$ in Figure 6.29(b)), and a negative value of the turn at a vertex x_i indicates that x_i is a concave vertex of the polygon (e.g., $\tau(x_3) < 0$ in Figure 6.29(b)).

It is well known that if $polyarc(x_0, x_n)$ is a simple polygon, then $|\tau(polyarc(x_0, x_n))| = 360°$ (see, e.g., Klein [76]). Note that the sign of the turn depends on the direction in which we traverse the polygonal arc, i.e., $\tau(polyarc(x_0, x_n)) = -\tau(polyarc(x_n, x_0))$, where $polyarc(x_n, x_0) = (x_{k+1} x_k)_{i=n-1,...,0}$. We thus have

Proposition 6.11 *The turn of a simple polygon C is $\tau(C) = \pm 360°$.* ∎

Supported Arcs

We will now show how to associate a polygonal arc $P(A)$ with any supported arc A. We will then define the turn of A as the turn of $P(A)$, and show that this turn is the same for any $P(A)$ associated with A.

Definition: Let $A : [a, b] \to \mathbb{R}^2$ be a supported arc. We will show below that there exists a set of points $\{a_i \in A : 0 \le i \le k\}$ such that $A(a) = a_0$, $A(b) = a_k$, and

$$\bigcap \{\sigma_A(a_i) : 0 \le i \le k\}$$

is a bounded region whose boundary is a simple polygon (see Figure 6.30(a)). Let $\{x_i : 0 \le i \le n\}$ be the set of vertices of this polygon ordered such that $a_0 = x_0$ and $a_k = x_n$, and such that the interior of the polygon is either to the right of each vector $x_i x_{i+1}$ or to the left of each vector $x_i x_{i+1}$ (see Figure 6.30(b)). We associate the simple polygonal arc $P(A) = (x_i x_{i+1})_{i=0,...,n-1}$ with the supported arc A, and define the turn of A as $\tau(A) = \tau(P(A))$.

We now show that for any supported arc A, there always exists such a set of points $\{a_i \in A : 0 \le i \le k\}$. In fact, in addition to the endpoints $A(a) = a_0$ and $A(b) = a_k$, it is sufficient to take a point of A with maximal positive x-coordinate, one with maximal negative x-coordinate, one with maximal positive y-coordinate, and one with maximal negative y-coordinate; thus four points (besides the endpoints) always suffice. We emphasize that the a's are not unique; a different set of a's is shown in Figure 6.31.

Note that if a point v of the supported arc A coincides with a vertex of an associated $P(A)$, which is the case for $a_2 = x_3$ in Figure 6.30, then $|\tau(v)| = 180° - \alpha_A(v)$, where $\alpha_A(v)$ is the angle of the sector of support $\sigma_A(v)$ of A at $v \in A$, i.e., $|\tau(v)|$ (with respect to $P(A)$) is the turn angle of A at v.

We now show that the turn of arc A defined in this way does not depend on the choice of the points $\{a_i \in A : 0 \le i \le k\}$. Observe first that $\bigcap \{\sigma_A(a_i) : 0 \le i \le k\}$ is convex (it is a finite intersection of half-planes of support of A). Consequently, the polygonal arc $P(A)$ is part of the boundary of a convex set.

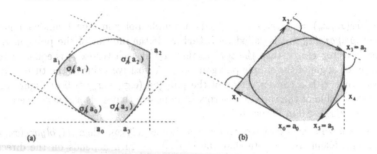

Figure 6.30: (b) shows an associated polygonal arc of the supported arc in (a).

Suppose first that $a_0 = a_k$ (i.e., A is a simple closed curve). Then $P(A)$ is a simple polygon, and $\tau(P(A)) = \pm 360^\circ$ by Proposition 6.11. Since $\tau(P(A)) = \pm 360^\circ$ for every simple polygon, this result does not depend on the choice of the $a's$. Thus we have

Proposition 6.12 *The turn of a supported simple closed curve A is $\tau(A) = \pm 360^\circ$.*   ∎

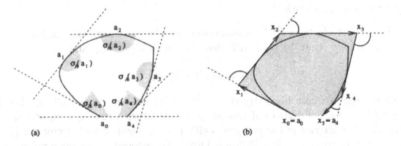

Figure 6.31: (b) shows a different associated polygonal arc of the supported arc in (a).

We now assume that $a_0 \neq a_k$. Consider the polygonal arc $P'(A) = P(A) \circ x_n x_0$, where "$\circ$" represents concatenation, so that $P'(A)$ is $P(A)$ followed by $x_n x_0$. Evidently, $P'(A)$ is a simple polygon; thus $|\tau(P'(A))| = 360^\circ$ (Proposition 6.11). The turn of $P(A)$ is equal to the turn of $P'(A)$ minus the turn angles at vertices $a_0 = x_0$ and $a_k = x_n$. These turn angles are $|\tau(a_0)| = 180^\circ - \alpha_A(a_0)$ and $|\tau(a_k)| = 180^\circ - \alpha_A(a_k)$. Therefore

$$\begin{aligned}
|\tau(A)| &= |\tau(P(A))| = |\tau(P'(A)) - (\tau(a_0) + \tau(a_k))| \\
&= |360^\circ - (180^\circ - \alpha_A(a_0) + 180^\circ - \alpha_A(a_k))| \\
&= \alpha_A(a_0) + \alpha_A(a_k).
\end{aligned}$$

Consequently, the absolute value of the turn of a supported arc A does not depend on the choice of $a_0, ..., a_k$. We also have

Proposition 6.13 *The absolute turn of a supported arc A with endpoints $A(a) \neq A(b)$ is given by*

$$|\tau(A)| = \alpha_A(A(a)) + \alpha_A(A(b)).$$

Since a supported arc A is contained in one of the closed half-planes determined by its endpoints $A(a) \neq A(b)$, the angle of the sector of support $\alpha_A(p)$ is less than or equal to $180°$, where $p = A(a)$ or $p = A(b)$. Consequently, we obtain

Proposition 6.14 *The absolute turn of a supported arc A is $|\tau(A)| \leq 360°$.* ∎

Proposition 6.15 *Let $A : [a, b] \to \mathbb{R}^2$ be a supported arc. Then A is contained in the convex hull of an associated polygonal arc $P(A)$.*

Proof: We showed above that there exists a set of points $\{a_i \in A : 0 \leq i \leq k\}$ such that $A(a) = a_0$, $A(b) = a_k$, and

$$C(A) = \bigcap \{\sigma_A(a_i) : 0 \leq i \leq k\}$$

is a bounded region whose boundary is a simple polygon which contains $P(A)$. The statement of the proposition follows from the facts that $C(A)$ is the convex hull of $P(A)$ and A is contained in $C(A)$. ∎

Proposition 6.16 *Let $A : [a, b] \to \mathbb{R}^2$ be a supported arc. For every $\epsilon > 0$, there exists a subarc A' of A such that $A(a) \in A'$ and $|\tau(A')| < \epsilon$.*

Proof: Let $a_0, \ldots, a_k$ be as in the proof of Proposition 6.15. Since the sectors of support at the a's intersect in a bounded region, in particular $lr_A(a_0)$ intersects $rr_A(a_1)$ (see Figure 6.32(a)). Let B be the subarc of A between a_0 and a_1. The angle α between $lr_A(a_0)$ and $rr_A(a_1)$ shown in Figure 6.32(a) is equal to $|\tau(B)|$, and $|\tau(B)| < 180°$.

It is not hard to see that there exists a point $p_1 \in B$ distinct from a_0 and a_1 such that the line l parallel to line segment $a_0 a_1$ is a line of support of B at p_1 (see Figure 6.32(b)). [Proof: Consider the function d which associates with each point of B its perpendicular distance to line segment $a_0 a_1$. Since d is a continuous function, and B is a compact set, there is a point of B at which d attains its maximum value. Evidently the line through any such point p_1 parallel to $a_0 a_1$ must be a line of support of B.]

The angle β between $lr_A(a_0)$ and l is equal to $\alpha_B(a_0)$, the angle of the sector of support $\sigma_B(a_0)$. Let B_1 be the subarc of A with endpoints a_0 and p_1. Then β is the turn of B_1.

Let $a_1 = b_1, b_2, \ldots$ be a sequence of points of B that converge to a_0 (in the standard Euclidean distance on the plane). Let p_i be determined for each b_i, $i > 1$, in the same way that p_1 was determined for $b_1 = a_1$, and let B_i be the subarc of B with endpoints a_0 and p_i. Then $\tau(B_i) = \alpha_{B_i}(a_0)$.

In the proof of Theorem 6.9, we showed that $\alpha_{B_i}(a_0)$ goes to 0 if b_i approaches a_0. Therefore, for every $\epsilon > 0$, there exists an i such that $|\tau(B_i)| < \epsilon$. ∎

Tame Arcs

Let $T : [a, b] \to \mathbb{R}^2$ be a tame arc (or in particular a tame simple closed curve). Then T can be divided into a finite number of supported arcs, i.e., there exist points

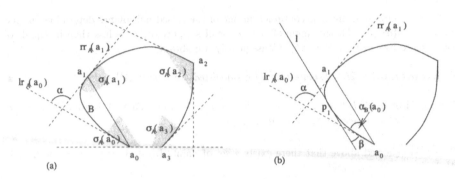

Figure 6.32: Steps in the proof of Proposition 6.16.

$t_0 < ... < t_m \in [a, b]$ with $t_1 = a$ and $t_m = b$ such that $T_i = T([t_i, t_{i+1}])$ is supported for $i = 0, ..., m - 1$. Let $\bigcirc$ denote concatenation of polygonal arcs. With every T_i we can associate a simple polygonal arc $P(T_i)$ such that $\bigcirc_{i=0}^{m-1} P(T_i)$ is also a polygonal arc (not necessarily simple). This means that all the $P(T_i)$ have a consistent order, i.e., we can traverse them from $T(a)$ to $T(b)$ following the directions of their vectors. This associates a polygonal arc

$$P(T) = \bigcirc_{i=0}^{m-1} P(T_i)$$

with T. An example is given in Figure 6.33; here T is divided into two supported arcs $T = T_1 \cup T_2$ at the joint a_3. $P(T_1)$ has vertices $x_0, ..., x_5$, and $P(T_2)$ has vertices x_5, x_6, x_7. The two polygonal arcs $P(T_1)$ and $P(T_2)$ have a consistent order in the sense that we can traverse them from x_0 to x_7 by following their vectors. The resulting polygonal arc associated with T is $P(T) = P(T_1) \circ P(T_2)$.

Definition: We define the absolute turn of the tame arc T as

$$\tau(T) = |\tau(P(T))|,$$

where $P(T)$ is a polygonal arc associated with T.

This definition is easy to apply if the right ray of support of T_{i-1} and the left ray of support of T_i do not coincide at their common endpoint x. When the rays are collinear, however, as shown in Figures 6.34(a) and (b), then vectors v and w of $P(T)$ that are contained in these rays and that have x as their common vertex are collinear and point in opposite directions. In this case, neither of the rules shown in Figure 6.28 applies to x as a vertex of $P(T)$. It is clear that the absolute value of the turn $\tau(x)$ with respect to $P(T)$ is $180°$, but it is not immediately clear how to determine the sign of $\tau(x)$.

We shall now define the sign of $\tau(x)$ with respect to $P(T)$. Let v be the last vector of $P(T_{i-1})$ and w the first vector of $P(T_i)$. Clearly $x \in v \cap w$ and $\tau(x)$ (in $P(T)$) is the angle between v and w.

At least one of the arcs T_{i-1} and T_i is not a line segment, since otherwise T would not be a simple arc (we would have $v = T_{i-1}$, $w = T_i$, and v and w would coincide near x).

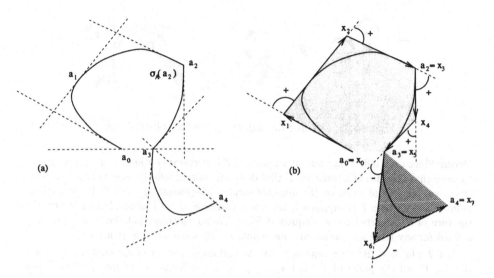

Figure 6.33: A polygonal arc associated with a tame arc.

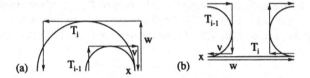

Figure 6.34: For illustration purposes, the associated polygonal arcs are slightly translated.

If one of T_{i-1} and T_i is a line segment, say T_{i-1}, then $\tau(x)$ is defined to have the opposite sign to the sign of $\tau(T_i)$ (see Figure 6.35(a)).

Suppose now that both T_{i-1} and T_i are not line segments. Let l be the straight line containing v and w. Since l contains the right ray of support of T_{i-1} and the left ray of support of T_i, both T_{i-1} and T_i are contained in closed half-planes determined by l. If T_{i-1} and T_i are contained in two different closed half-planes of l, then T_{i-1} and T_i must have the same sign of turn (see Figure 6.35(b)). In this case, $\tau(x)$ is defined to have the opposite sign to the sign of $\tau(T_i)$.

It remains only to consider the case in which T_{i-1} and T_i are contained in the same closed half-plane of l. In this case $\tau(T_{i-1})$ and $\tau(T_i)$ have opposite signs. If the convex hull of T_{i-1} contains a subarc T_i beginning at x, then $\tau(x)$ is defined to have the same sign as the sign of $\tau(T_{i-1})$; otherwise, $\tau(x)$ is defined to have the same sign as $\tau(T_i)$ (see Figure 6.35(c)).

Proposition 6.17 *The turn $\tau(T)$ of a tame arc T is uniquely defined, i.e., $\tau(T)$ does not depend on the subdivision of T into supported subarcs T_i.*

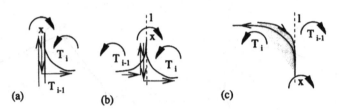

Figure 6.35: Defining the sign of $\tau(x)$ in the collinear case.

Proof: Since each inflection point of a tame arc T is necessarily a joint of T, it is sufficient to show that the turn of a tame arc T that does not contain inflections is uniquely defined. We prove this by induction on the minimal number of optional joints of T. If the minimal number is zero, then T is supported, and the uniqueness of $\tau(T)$ follows from the fact that the turn of a supported arc is uniquely defined. We now assume that the turn is uniquely defined for any tame arc whose minimal number of optional joints is at most $n-1$.

Let $T : [a, b] \rightarrow \mathbb{R}^2$ be a tame arc with the minimal number of optional joints n. Let $t_1, ..., t_n$ be all the joints of T. Let $s_1, ..., s_m$ be any different set of joints of T. There exists an i such that the subarc $T_i = T([t_i, t_{i+1})$ contains some of the joints $s_1, ..., s_m$, say $s_k, ..., s_l$. Since T_i is supported, the turn of T_i determined with respect to joints $s_k, ..., s_l$ is equal to $\tau(T_i)$. By the induction assumption, the turn of $T([a, t_i)$ determined with respect to $s_1, ..., s_{k-1}$ is equal to the turn of $T([a, t_i)$ determined with respect to $t_1, ..., t_{i-1}$, and the same applies to the turn of $T([t_{i+1}, b)$. Consequently, the turn $\tau(T)$ is uniquely defined. ∎

6.3.7 Classification of Points of a Tame Arc

In this section we use total turn concepts to classify inflection points and cusps of a tame arc T. When we classify a given point $x \in T$, we can always assume that x is a joint of T, and is a vertex of an associated polygonal arc $P(T)$. We will characterize x using the turn angle $\tau(x)$ in $P(T)$ and the signs of the turns of the supported subarcs T_{i-1} and T_i (determined with respect to $P(T)$) such that x is the endpoint of T_{i-1} and the beginning point of T_i.

We recall that x is a cusp if the union of the left ray of support of T_{i-1} at x, $lr_{T_{i-1}}(x)$, and the right ray of support of T_i at x, $rr_{T_i}(x)$, is not a straight line, i.e., either $lr_{T_{i-1}}(x)$ and $rr_{T_i}(x)$ are not collinear or $lr_{T_{i-1}}(x) = rr_{T_i}(x)$. We will show that $x \in T$ is a cusp of a tame arc T iff $\tau(x) \neq 0$. Then we will show that $x \in T$ is a regular point of a tame arc T iff $\tau(T_{i-1})$, $\tau(T_i)$, and $\tau(x)$ (in $P(T)$) have the same sign. For example, this is the case for x in Figure 6.36(b), while x in Figures 6.36(a), (c), or (d) is an inflection point.

Theorem 6.12 *$x \in T$ is a cusp of a tame arc T iff $\tau(x) \neq 0$.*

Proof: Let $P(T)$ be a polygonal arc associated with T. Let v be the vector of $P(T)$ whose endpoint is x and w be the vector of $P(T)$ whose beginning point is x. Then clearly

Figure 6.36: A regular point (b) and three inflection points (a), (c), and (d).

$x \in v \cap w$ and $\tau(x)$ (in $P(T)$) is the angle between v and w. The theorem follows from the fact that v is contained in the left ray of support at x and w is contained in the right ray of support at x. ∎

Theorem 6.13 $x \in T$ *is a regular point of a tame arc* T *iff there exist supported subarcs* T_{i-1} *and* T_i *of* T *such that* x *is the endpoint of* T_{i-1} *and the beginning point of* T_i, *and* $\tau(T_{i-1})$, $\tau(T_i)$, *and* $\tau(x)$ *(in* $P(T)$*) have the same sign[2] (see Figure 6.36(b)).*

Proof:

"⇒": There exists a supported subarc $A \subseteq T$ such that x is interior to A. Let T_{i-1} and T_i be two subarcs of A such that x is the endpoint of T_{i-1} and the beginning point of T_i and $A = T_{i-1} \cup T_i$. Since T_{i-1} and T_i are supported (non-degenerate) subarcs of A, $\tau(T_{i-1})$, $\tau(T_i)$, and $\tau(x)$ have the same sign as $\tau(A)$.

"⇐": If $|\tau(x)| = 180°$, it follows from the definition of $\tau(x)$ in Section 6.3.6 that $\tau(T_{i-1})$, $\tau(T_i)$, and $\tau(x)$ cannot have the same sign. Therefore, we can assume that $|\tau(x)| < 180°$.

By Proposition 6.16, there exists a subarc T'_{i-1} of T_{i-1} containing x whose absolute turn is arbitrarily small, and the same holds for T_i. Therefore, we can assume that $|\tau(T_{i-1}) + \tau(T_i) + \tau(x)| < 180°$.

We show that the arc $R = T_{i-1} \circ T_i$ is supported. i.e. that there is a line of support of R at any point y of R. Without loss of generality, we can assume that $y \in T_{i-1}$.

Let $P(T_{i-1})$ and $P(T_i)$ be polygonal arcs associated with T_{i-1} and T_i such that $y \in P(T_{i-1})$. Then $P(R) = P(T_{i-1}) \circ P(T_i)$ is associated with R. We know that $|\tau(P(R))| < 180°$ and that $P(R)$ turns in one direction. Therefore, $P(R)$ is a convex (i.e., supported) polygonal arc.

Let CH denote the convex hull operator. From Proposition 6.15 it follows that $T_{i-1} \subseteq CH(P(T_{i-1}))$ and $T_i \subseteq CH(P(T_i))$. Since $CH(P(T_{i-1})) \subseteq CH(P(R))$ and $CH(P(T_i)) \subseteq CH(P(R))$, we obtain $R = (T_{i-1} \circ T_i) \subseteq CH(P(R))$. Since $y \in P(R)$, there is a line of support of $CH(P(R))$ at y, and therefore there is a line of support of R at y. ∎

---

[2] Here we consider the sign of a turn of 0 as both positive and negative.

Chapter 7

Digitization Approach

In this Chapter we relate topological and geometric properties of digital objects to their continuous originals by digitization and embedding approaches. A digitization is modeled as a mapping from the real plane or space to a discrete graph structure. Based on technical properties of sampling devices which are the main source of spatial information for artificial systems, the graph structure is usually assumed to form a square grid and is modeled as a finite subset of $\mathbf{Z}^2$ (or $\mathbf{Z}^3$ for computer tomography scanners) with some adjacency relations. For example, digital images obtained by a CCD camera are represented as finite rectangular subsets of $\mathbf{Z}^2$. We characterize a digitization as a function that maps subset of the real plane to discrete objects represented in a graph structure. Our starting point is a digitization and segmentation scheme defined in Pavlidis [120] and in Gross and Latecki [55], in which the sensor value depends on the area of the object in the square at which the sensor is centered.

We derive conditions relating properties of real objects to the grid size of the square grid which guarantee that a real object and its digital image are topologically equivalent (Section 7.2). These conditions also imply that any two digital images of a given object are topologically equivalent. Thus, the topological properties are invariant with respect to the camera or object transformations like translations, rotations, and reflections by the digitization process. Another consequence of this approach is the fact that an output digital image must be well-composed if the resolution of the digitization process is fine enough to ensure topology preservation (Section 7.3).

Moreover, these conditions imply that only a few digital patterns can occur as neighborhoods of boundary points in the digital image. We give a complete list of such patterns for the intersection digitization, which is equivalent to setting a very low threshold value on the sensor output for segmentation purposes (Section 7.4). Since each of these patterns has a well-defined tangent span, we classify the patterns into convex, concave, and linear. Then we show that if the resolution is fine enough, the digitization of an object A will not change the convexity properties of the boundary of A, i.e., a boundary point which is locally convex cannot be digitized to a locally concave pixel and a boundary point which is locally concave cannot be digitized to a locally convex pixel. Thus, using the set of realizable boundary patterns, we can safely recover geometric properties of the boundary of a digital object, such as convexity and inflection. We also construct an adjacency graph

147

of the boundary patterns, which can be used to recursively generate the set of all possible digital boundary curves. In addition, since all the realizable patterns are known, any other pattern can be labeled as either noise or a critical part of the boundary if the real object was only partially parallel regular. In Section 7.5 we show how to determine a scaling factor such that the scaled projected image and the original image are topologically equivalent.

In Sections 7.7 and 7.8 we define object boundary quantization and relate it to intersection digitization. We show that a digital image of a supported arc by object boundary quantization is a supported digital arc. This result allows us to extend our theory of supported arcs (presented in Section 6.3) to supported digital arcs. Since in Section 7.8 we show that intersection digitization of a half-plane completely determines object boundary quantization and vice versa, all results obtained for recovering straight lines resulting from the digitization based on the object boundary quantization can be used to recover straight lines in digital images even if the threshold v used to segment the object boundary is unknown.

In Section 7.9, we extend the digitization schemes to real objects with blurred boundaries as it is the case for real sampling devices like CCD camera. We obtain a much more realistic model of the real sensor digitization process that handles both blurring and arbitrary thresholding. Moreover, we present experimental results which justify the accuracy of the extended model (Section 7.12). We show that recovering the slope of a blurred half-plane given its digital image obtained by an unknown threshold reduces to recovering the slope under object boundary quantization of a perfectly focused half-plane. Thus, we show that a blurred image of a half-plane contains the same slope information as an ideal image with perfectly focused edges. Therefore, the previous results and algorithms for recovery of straight lines are also valid if we assume this more realistic digitization model (e.g. Debled and Reveilles [32], Dorst and Smeulders [34], [143], Freeman [45], Koplowitz and Sundar Raj [87], Koplowitz and Bruckstein [88], Rosenfeld and Kim [134], and Veelaert [156]). Our results allow us to extend the definition of linearity to practically relevant digital images.

In Section 7.9 we formally define the digitization scheme called v-digitization for intensity images. Based on results in Section 7.10, we show in Section 7.11 that a digital image of a blurred half-plane obtained by v-digitization for some unknown threshold value v is equal to the image of some translation of the half-plane obtained by intersection digitization.

Since for most digital objects the boundary is locally indistinguishable from a digital linear boundary, we can assume that the digital boundary is piecewise linear so that, in effect, the boundary can be locally modeled by a digital line. Therefore, we can regard the model of a digital sensor half-plane under blurring and arbitrary digitization threshold as a model of a real sensor edge. Based on this mathematical model, it is possible to develop an algorithm for edge detection in which our edge characterization helps to preserve the connectivity of the recovered edge boundary (Section 7.12).

We begin with Section 7.1, where digitization and segmentation processes are defined for binary images.

7.1 Digitization and Segmentation

Definition: Let $\mathcal{Q}$ be a cover of the plane with closed squares of diameter r such that if two squares intersect, then their intersection is either their common side or a corner point. Such a cover is called a **square grid** with diameter r. A **digital image** can be described a set of points that are located at the centers of the squares of a grid $\mathcal{Q}$ and that are assigned some value in a gray level or color scale. By a **digitization process** we understand a function mapping a planar set X to a digital image. By a **segmentation process** we understand a process grouping digital points to a set representing a digital object. Therefore, the output of a segmentation process can be interpreted as a binary digital image, where each point is either black or white. We assume that digital objects are represented as sets of black points. Thus, the input of a digitization and segmentation process is a planar set X and the output is a binary digital image, which will be called a **digitization** of X with diameter r and denoted $Dig(X, r)$.

We will interpret a black point $p \in Dig(X, r)$ as a closed (black) square of cover $\mathcal{Q}$ centered at p and the digitization $Dig(X, r)$ as the union of closed squares centered at black points, i.e., $Dig(X, r)$ will denote a closed subset of the plane.

We will treat digitization and segmentation processes satisfying the following conditions relating a planar par(r)-regular set X to its digital image $Dig(X, r)$:

ds1 If a square $q \in \mathcal{Q}$ is contained in X, then $q \in Dig(X, r)$ (i.e., q is black).

ds2 If a square $q \in \mathcal{Q}$ is disjoint from X, then $q \notin Dig(X, r)$ (i.e., q is white).

ds3 If a square q is black and $area(X \cap q) \leq area(X \cap p)$ for some square $p \in \mathcal{Q}$, then square p is black.

These conditions describe a standard model of the digitization and segmentation process for CCD cameras if we exclude digitization errors. In the following, we define some important digitization and segmentation processes satisfying the conditions ds1, ds2, and ds3 above.

Definition: Let X be any set in the plane. A square $p \in \mathcal{Q}$ is black (belongs to a digital object) iff $p \cap X \neq \emptyset$, and white otherwise. We will call such a digital image an **intersection digitization** with diameter r of set X, and denote it with $Dig_\cap(X, r)$, namely $Dig_\cap(X, r) = \bigcup\{p \in \mathcal{Q} : p \cap X \neq \emptyset\}$. See Figure 7.1 (a), for example, where the union of all depicted squares represents the intersection digitization of an ellipse. With respect to real camera digitization and segmentation, the intersection digitization corresponds to the procedure of coloring a pixel black iff there is part of the object A in the field "seen" by the corresponding sensor. When digital straight line models were first studied by Freeman and Rosenfeld, the digitization models that were assumed were based on the intersection digitization, which is called square-box quantization by Freeman [45].

Now we consider digitizations corresponding to the procedure of coloring a pixel black iff the object X fills the whole field "seen" by the corresponding sensor. For such digitizations, a square p is black iff $p \subseteq X$ and white otherwise. We will refer to such a digital image of a set X as a **square subset digitization** and denote it by $Dig_C(X,r)$, where $Dig_C(X,r) = \bigcup\{p \in Q : p \subseteq X\}$. In Figure 7.1 (b), the two squares represent $Dig_C(X,r)$, where X is an ellipse.

Figure 7.1: a) The union of all squares represents the *intersection digitization* of the ellipse. b) The two squares represent the *square subset digitization* of the ellipse. c) The eight squares represent a *digitization* of an ellipse *with the area ratio equal to* $\frac{1}{5}$.

Next, let us consider a digitization and segmentation process in which a pixel is colored black iff the ratio of the area of the continuous object in a sensor square to the area of the square is greater than some constant threshold value v. An example is given in Figure 7.1 (c), where the squares represent a digitization of the ellipse with the ratio equal to $\frac{1}{5}$. A square $p \in Q$ is black iff $area(p \cap X)/area(p) > v$ and white otherwise, where $0 \leq v < 1$ is a constant. We will refer to such a digital image of a set X as a v-**digitization** of X with diameter r. We will denote such digitizations by $Dig_v(X,r)$. We recall that we identify the digitization of X with the union of black closed squares. Thus $Dig_v(X,r)$ denotes the digital picture which is the union of black closed squares. We will also denote $Dig_1(X,r)$ as the digitization in which the ratio of the area is equal to 1. This process models a segmentation by applying a threshold value to a gray-level digital image for all real devices in which the sensor values can be assumed to be monotonic with respect to the area of the object in the sensor square.

We have the following inclusions

$$Dig_C(X,r) \subseteq Dig_v(X,r) \subseteq Dig_\cap(X,r)$$

for every $v \in [0,1]$ and

$$Dig_v(X,r) \subseteq Dig_w(X,r) \quad \text{if} \quad w \leq v$$

for every $v, w \in [0,1]$.

We will hereafter use $Dig(X,r)$ without subscript to denote any digitization and segmentation process satisfying ds1, ds2, and ds3. Thus, in particular, $Dig(X,r)$ denotes $Dig_\cap(X,r)$, $Dig_C(X,r)$, and $Dig_v(X,r)$ for every $v \in [0,1]$.

7.2 Topology Preservation

In this section we prove our main theorems on topology preservation by digitization and segmentation processes.

Definition: We will say that a digitization $Dig(X, r)$ of some set X is **topology preserving** if X and $Dig(X, r)$ are homeomorphic.

The definition of homeomorphism is given in Chapter 2. Homeomorphism is the standard concept to describe the equivalence of sets in topology.

We now consider another topological concept that is a special case of homotopy equivalence called a strong deformation retraction. Intuitively, saying that there is a strong deformation retraction from a set X to a set $Y \subseteq X$ means that we can continuously shrink X to Y.

Definition: Let X and $Y \subseteq X$ be two topological spaces. A continuous function $H :$ $X \times [0, 1] \to X$, where $[0, 1]$ is the unit interval, is called a **strong deformation retraction** of X to Y if $H(x, 1) = x$ and $H(x, 0) \in Y$ for every $x \in X$, and $H(x, t) = x$ for every $x \in Y$ and $t \in [0, 1]$. Y is called a **strong deformation retract** of X.

Note that if Y is a strong deformation retract of X, then Y is homotopy equivalent to X. To see this, take $f : X \to Y$ to be $f(x) = H(x, 0)$ and $g : Y \to X$ to be inclusion.

Theorem 7.1 *Let A be a par(r)-regular set. Then $Par(A, -r)$ is a strong deformation retract of A.*

Proof: If $x \in (A \setminus Par(A, -r))$, then there exists a unique normal vector $-n(a, r)$, for some $a \in bdA$, such that $x \in -n(a, r)$ (see Figure 7.2). We define

$$\pi : (A \setminus Par(A, -r)) \to bdPar(A, -r)$$

by $\pi(x) =$ the end point of the vector $-n(a, r)$, where a is such that $x \in -n(a, r)$. Thus, $\pi(x)$ denotes the single point on $bdPar(A, -r)$ with the closest distance to x, and therefore, π is a metric projection onto $bdPar(A, -r)$.

Let H be a function defined as follows:

$H : A \times [0, 1] \to A$,

$H(x, t) = x$ for every $x \in Par(A, -r)$ and $t \in [0, 1]$,

$H(x, t) = (1 - t)\pi(x) + tx$ for every $x \in (A \setminus Par(A, -r))$ and $t \in [0, 1]$.

Note that $H(x, 1) = x$ for every $x \in A$ and that $H(x, t) = x$ for every $x \in Par(A, -r)$ and $t \in [0, 1]$. Note also that $H(x, 0) = \pi(x)$ for all $x \in (A \setminus Par(A, -r))$. Thus, $H(x, 0) \in Par(A, -r)$ for every $x \in A$.

To prove that H is a strong deformation retraction, it remains to show that H is a continuous function. Clearly, for a fixed x, $H(x, t)$ as a function of t is continuous. If t is fixed, the continuity of $H(x, t)$ as a function of x follows from the continuity of the metric projection π, since π is a point valued function. This implies that if x and y are close to each other, then $\pi(x)$ and $\pi(y)$ are close to each other, and consequently, the line segments

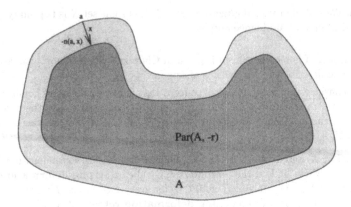

Figure 7.2: $Par(A, -r)$ is a strong deformation retract of A.

$x\pi(x)$ and $y\pi(y)$ are close to each other. Therefore, H is a strong deformation retraction of A to $Par(A, -r)$.   ∎

Theorem 7.2 *Let A be a par(r)-regular set. Then $Par(A, -r)$ is a strong deformation retract of $Dig(A, r)$ for every digital image $Dig(A, r)$ (which satisfies conditions ds1, ds2, and ds3), and $d_H(A, Dig(A, r)) \leq r$, where d_H is the Hausdorff distance of sets (see Figure 7.3 for an illustration).*

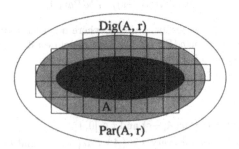

Figure 7.3: $Par(A, -r)$ is a strong deformation retract of $Dig(A, r)$.

Proof: Let p be a closed square with diameter r such that $p \cap A \neq \emptyset$. Since $p \subseteq B(x, r)$ for every closed ball $B(x, r)$ such that the center $x \in p$, we obtain that $p \subseteq Par(A, r)$. Therefore $Dig_\cap(A, r) \subseteq Par(A, r)$. For every closed square p with diameter r, it similarly holds that if $p \cap Par(A, -r) \neq \emptyset$, then $p \subseteq A$. Therefore $Dig_\cap(Par(A, -r), r) \subseteq Dig_\subset(A, r)$. Since it is clear that $Par(A, -r) \subseteq Dig_\cap(Par(A, -r), r)$, we obtain $Par(A, -r) \subseteq Dig_\subset(A, r)$. Thus we obtain the following inclusions: $Par(A, -r) \subseteq Dig_\subset(A, r) \subseteq Dig_\cap(A, r) \subseteq$

$Par(A, r)$. Since by the definition of $Dig(A, r)$ (conditions ds1, ds2), $Dig_\subset(A, r) \subseteq Dig(A, r) \subseteq Dig_\cap(A, r)$, we obtain that

$$Par(A, -r) \subseteq Dig(A, r) \subseteq Par(A, r).$$

These inclusion relations imply that $d_H(A, Dig(A, r)) \leq r$, since $Par(Par(A, -r), r) = A$.

Let $a \in bdPar(A, -r)$ and let $x \in bdA$ be such that a is the end point of the inner normal vector $-n(x, r)$ (see Figure 7.4). The outer normal vector at a to $bdPar(A, -r)$ of length $2r$ can be defined as $n(a, 2r) = -n(x, r) \cup n(x, r)$ oriented in the direction from a to x. Clearly, for every two distinct points $a, b \in bdPar(A, -r)$, $n(a, 2r)$ and $n(b, 2r)$ do not intersect.

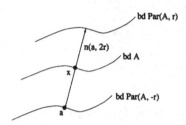

Figure 7.4: $n(a, 2r) = -n(x, r) \cup n(x, r)$.

We intend to construct a strong deformation retraction

$$D : Dig(A, r) \times [0, 1] \to Dig(A, r)$$

from $Dig(A, r)$ onto $Par(A, -r)$.

In the following, $x \in Dig(A, r) \setminus Par(A, -r)$. Let $p(x)$ be a point on $bdPar(A, -r)$ with the closest distance to x. Let $xp(x)$ be the line segment joining x with $p(x)$. Since $xp(x) \subseteq n(p(x), 2r)$ and the normal vectors $n(a, 2r)$ do not intersects for $a \in bdPar(A, -r)$, $p(x)$ is uniquely determined. The metric projection p is a continuous function from $Dig(A, r) \setminus Par(A, -r)$ to $bdPar(A, -r)$.

If $xp(x) \subseteq Dig(A, r)$, then we could define $D(x, t) = (1-t)p(x) + tx$ for every $t \in [0, 1]$. However, it can happen that $xp(x) \not\subseteq Dig(A, r)$ (see Figure 7.5). Therefore, for every line segment $xp(x)$, we must define a modified path $mp(x, p(x)) \subseteq Dig(A, r)$ from x to $p(x)$. If $xp(x) \subseteq Dig(A, r)$, then $mp(x, p(x)) = xp(x)$.

If $xp(x) \not\subseteq Dig(A, r)$, then there exists two different sides $s_1, s_2 \subseteq bdDig(A, r)$ of squares in grid Q such that $xp(x)$ intersects s_1 in point a_1, s_2 in point a_2, and $a_1a_2 \cap Dig(A, r) = \{a_1, a_2\}$, where a_1a_2 is the line segment joining a_1 and a_2. Since $xp(x) \subseteq n(p(x), 2r)$, we can apply Lemma 7.1, which is stated below. We obtain that the sides s_1, s_2 share a vertex and are perpendicular (see Figure 7.6). Let c be the common vertex of sides s_1, s_2. We define $mp(x, p(x)) = p(x)a_1 \cup a_1c \cup ca_2 \cup a_2x$ (see Figure 7.5). If $mp(x, p(x)) \not\subseteq Dig(A, r)$, then we can repeat this construction for $p(x)a_1$ or a_2x. We continue this process a finite number of iterations until the modified path $mp(x, p(x))$ is contained in $Dig(A, r)$.

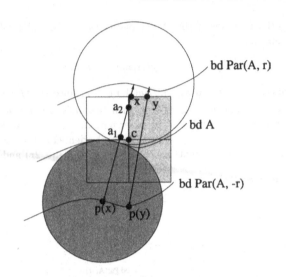

Figure 7.5: The construction of a modified path $mp(x, p(x)) \subseteq Dig(A, r)$.

Observe that if two points $x, y \in Dig(A, r)$ are close to each other, then the line segments $xp(x)$ and $yp(y)$ are close to each other, since $p(x)$ and $p(y)$ are close to each other by the continuity of the metric projection p. We now show that in this case, also the modified paths $mp(xp(x))$ and $mp(yp(y))$ are close to each other. If $n(p(x), 2r)$ and $n(p(y), 2r)$ intersect the same sides s_1, s_2, then $xp(x)$ and $yp(y)$ are clearly close to each other. If $n(p(y), 2r)$ does not intersect the sides s_1, s_2, then $a_1c \cup ca_2$ of $mp(xp(x))$ is contained in the strip region determined by $n(p(x), 2r)$ and $n(p(y), 2r)$ (see Figure 7.5).

For every $x \in Dig(A, r) \setminus Par(A, -r)$, we parameterize uniformly $mp(x, p(x))$ with a continuous function
$f_x : [0, 1] \to mp(x, p(x))$ such that $f_x(0) = p(x)$ and $f_x(1) = x$.
    Now we can define
$$D : Dig(A, r) \times [0, 1] \to Dig(A, r).$$
If $x \in Dig(A, r) \setminus Par(A, -r)$, then we define $D(x, t) = f_x(t)$.
If $x \in Par(A, -r)$, then $D(x, t) = x$ for every $t \in [0, 1]$.
    It is easy to observe that for a fixed x, $D(x, t)$ as a function of t is continuous. If t is fixed, the continuity of $D(x, t)$ as a function of x follows from the continuity of the metric projection p, which implies that if x and y are close to each other, then the modified paths $mp(xp(x))$ and $mp(yp(y))$ are close to each other, as shown above.
    Finally, we need to establish that D satisfies the other properties of a strong deformation retraction. By definition, $D(x, t) = x$ for every $x \in Par(A, -r)$ and $t \in [0, 1]$. Clearly, $D(x, 1) = x$ and $D(x, 0) \in Par(A, -r)$ for every $x \in Dig(A, r)$. Thus, D is a strong deformation retraction of $Dig(A, r)$ to $Par(A, -r)$.   ∎

In the proof of Theorem 7.2 we used the following lemma:

Lemma 7.1 *Let A be a par(r)-regular set and let $Dig(A,r)$ be a digital image of A (which satisfies conditions ds1, ds2, and ds3).*
Let s_1, s_2 be two different sides of some squares in grid Q such that $s_1, s_2 \subseteq bdDig(A,r)$. For every $x \in bdPar(A,-r)$, if $n(x,2r)$ intersects first s_1 in point a_1 and then s_2 in point a_2 such that $a_1 a_2 \cap Dig(A,r) = \{a_1, a_2\}$, where $a_1 a_2$ is the line segment joining a_1 and a_2, then the sides s_1, s_2 share a vertex and are perpendicular, and the square determined by s_1, s_2 is white (i.e., does not belong to $Dig(A,r)$). (see Figure 7.6).

Figure 7.6: The only possible situation in $Dig(A,r)$.

Proof: Let $x \in bdPar(A,-r)$ and let $v = n(x,2r)$. Since v has length $2r$, v can intersect at most three parallel horizontal grid lines or three parallel vertical grid lines.

If the distance of two sides s_1, s_2 is exactly $2r$, then the situation described in the assumption cannot happen, since the endpoint of v belongs to the side s_2. Yet, this implies that any square with side s_2 must be white, which contradicts the fact that $s_2 \subseteq bdDig(A,r)$.

These two facts imply that we have 15 cases (modulo reflection and $90°$ rotation) which satisfy the assumptions of this lemma. The 7 cases in which sides s_1, s_2 are parallel are shown in Figure 7.7 and the remaining 8 cases in which sides s_1, s_2 are perpendicular are shown in Figure 7.8. We show that only the case number 8 is possible.

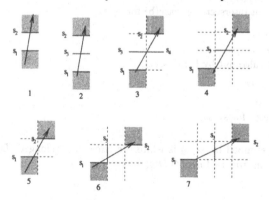

Figure 7.7: The 7 cases in which sides s_1, s_2 are parallel.

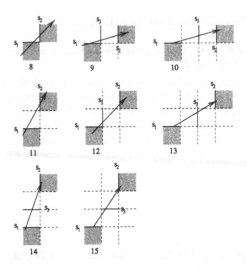

Figure 7.8: The 8 cases in which sides s_1, s_2 are perpendicular.

We show that cases 1-7 and 9-15 are not possible by applying Lemma 7.2 (which follows). In the following we indicate whether we apply case(a) or case(b) of Lemma 7.2 and to which sides (see Figures 7.7 and 7.8):

1. case(a) applied to sides s_1, s_2.

2. case(a) applied to sides s_3, s_2.

3. If v intersects side s_4, then we have case(a) applied to sides s_4, s_2. If v intersects side s_3, then we have case(b) for s_3, s_2.

4. In this case v must intersects s_3. case(b) for s_3, s_2.

5. case(b) for s_1, s_2.

6, 7. case(b) for s_3, s_2.

8. This case is not ruled out by Lemma 7.1.

9, 10. case(a) for s_3, s_2.

11. case(b) for s_1, s_2.

12, 13, 14, 15. case(b) for s_3, s_2.

The square determined by s_1, s_2 is white (i.e., does not belong to $Dig(A, r)$), since it contains line segment a_1a_2 and $a_1a_2 \cap Dig(A, r) = \{a_1, a_2\}$. ∎

Lemma 7.2 *Let A be a par(r)-regular set and let $Dig(A, r)$ be a digital image of A which satisfies conditions ds1, ds2, and ds3. Let $x \in bdPar(A, -r)$ and let $v = n(x, 2r)$ (v is oriented from x to its end point).*

case(a) *Let squares s_1, s_2 of $Dig(A,r)$ share the side $s = s_1 \cap s_2$ (see Figure 7.9.case(a)). Let v intersect first the side parallel and opposite to the side s and then the side s. If square s_2 is black (i.e., $s_2 \in Dig(A,r)$), then s_1 is black.*

case(b) *Let squares s_1, s_2 share a vertex c but not share a side (see Figure 7.9.case(b)). Let v intersect first a side of s_1 that does not contain c and then a side of s_2 that contains c. If square s_2 is black (i.e., $s_2 \in Dig(A,r)$), then s_1 is black.*

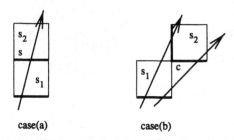

case(a)   case(b)

Figure 7.9: In both cases, if square s_2 is black, then s_1 is black.

Proof: Let m be the midpoint of vector v. Then $m \in bdA$. We show

$$area(A \cap s_1) \geq area(A \cap s_2). \tag{7.1}$$

Since (see Figure 7.10)

$$area(A \cap s_1) \geq area(iob(m,r) \cap s_1) \tag{7.2}$$

and

$$area((oob(m,r))^c \cap s_2) \geq area(A \cap s_2), \tag{7.3}$$

it is sufficient to show

$$area(iob(m,r) \cap s_1) \geq area((oob(m,r))^c \cap s_2), \tag{7.4}$$

as then (7.1) will follow from (7.4). The inequality (7.4) is proven in Section 7.6. ∎

Now we are ready to prove the main theorems of this chapter.

Theorem 7.3 *Let A be a par(r)-regular set. Then A and $Dig(A,r)$ are homotopy equivalent for every digital image $Dig(A,r)$, and $d_H(A, Dig(A,r)) \leq r$, where d_H is the Hausdorff distance of sets (which satisfies conditions ds1, ds2, and ds3).*

Proof: By Theorem 7.1, $Par(A,-r)$ is a strong deformation retract of A, and therefore A and $Par(A,-r)$ are homotopy equivalent. By Theorem 7.2, $Par(A,-r)$ and $Dig(A,r)$ are homotopy equivalent. Thus, A and $Dig(A,r)$ are homotopy equivalent. By Theorem 7.2,

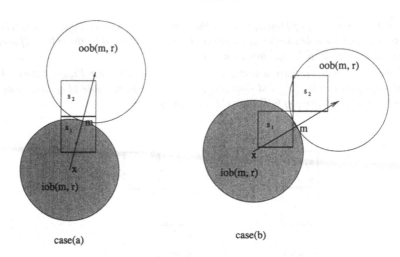

Figure 7.10: In both cases, $area(iob(m,r) \cap s_1) \geq area((oob(m,r))^c \cap s_2)$.

we also have that $d_H(A, Dig(A,r)) \leq r$.   ∎

For Theorem 7.4, we need the following concepts:

Definition: We call a closed set A a **bordered 2D manifold** if every point in A has a neighborhood homeomorphic to a relatively open subset of a closed half-plane. A connected component of a 2D bordered manifold is called a **bordered surface**.

Theorem 7.4 *Let A be a par(r)-regular bordered 2D manifold. Then A and $Dig(A,r)$ are homeomorphic for every digitization $Dig(A,r)$ (which satisfies conditions ds1, ds2, and ds3).*

Proof: We will base our proof on the following theorem[1] from Ahlfors and Sario [3], Section 42A, page 98:
"Two bordered surfaces are topologically equivalent (i.e., homeomorphic) if and only if they agree in character of orientability, number of contours, and Euler characteristic."

Since A and $Dig(A,r)$ are subsets of the plane, they agree in character of orientability. Without loss of generality, we can assume that set A is connected, since if A is not connected, we can apply the following proof to every connected component of A and we have a complete correspondence of components of A and $Dig(A,r)$, since A and $Dig(A,r)$ are homotopy equivalent by Theorem 7.3. We recall that a connected 2D bordered manifold is a bordered surface. Thus, A is a bordered surface.

---

[1]We would like to thank Prof. Yung Kong (Queens College, CUNY, New York) for pointing out to us both this theorem and its consequences.

By Theorem 7.3, A and $Dig(A, r)$ agree in Euler characteristic, and since A is connected, $Dig(A, r)$ is also connected. By Theorem 7.8 (given below), $Dig(A, r)$ is a bordered surface. It remains to show that A and $Dig(A, r)$ agree in number of contours.

For (connected) bordered surfaces in the plane, the Euler characteristic is equal to (2 - the number of contours). This follows, for example, from Theorem 1 of Chapter 13 (p. 91) in Moise [115].[2] Thus, we obtain that A and $Dig(A, r)$ agree in number of contours, since A and $Dig(A, r)$ agree in Euler characteristic. ∎

An important consequence of Theorem 7.4 is the fact that under sufficient digitization resolution any two digital images of a given spatial object A are topologically equivalent. This means, for example, that shifting or rotating an object or the camera cannot lead to topologically different images, i.e., topological properties of obtained digital images are invariant under shifting and rotation.

Theorem 7.5 *Let A be a par(r)-regular bordered manifold. Then any two digitizations $Dig^1(A, r)$ and $Dig^2(A, r)$ of A are homeomorphic.*

Proof: By Theorem 7.4, both $Dig^1(A, r)$ and $Dig^2(A, r)$ are homeomorphic to A. ∎

Theorem 7.6 *Let A be a C^2 subset of the plane (i.e., A is the closure of an open set whose boundary can be described as a disjoint finite union of twice continuously differentiable simple closed curves). Then there always exists a digitization resolution $r > 0$ such that every digitization $Dig(A, r)$ of A is topology preserving.*

Proof: First we show that there always exists $r > 0$ such that, for every $x, y \in bdA$, $n(x, r)$ and $n(y, r)$ do not intersect.

Step 1. Let k_{max} be the maximum of the absolute value of the principal curvature at every point on bdA (the existence follows from compactness of bdA).

Step 2. Let $t < \frac{1}{k_{max}}$ be fixed. By elementary arguments from differential geometry (see [24], for example), it follows that, for every $x \in bdA$, there exists $e(x) > 0$ such that, for all $y \in bdA$, $d_{bdA}(x, y) < e(x)$ implies that $n(x, t)$ and $n(y, t)$ do not intersect, where d_{bdA} is the intrinsic distance on bdA.

Step 3. Let $B_{bdA}(x, e(x))$ be an open ball in the intrinsic distance d_{bdA} on bdA. Since the collection $\{B_{bdA}(x, e(x)) : x \in bdA\}$ is an open covering of a compact set bdA, there exists a finite subcovering $\{B_{bdA}(x_1, e(x_1)), ..., B_{bdA}(x_n, e(x_n))\}$. Therefore, there exists $\epsilon > 0$ such that $\forall x \in bdA \ \exists i \in \{1, ..., n\} \ B_{bdA}(x, \epsilon) \subseteq B_{bdA}(x_i, e(x_i))$. Hence, for every $x, y \in bdA$, $d_{bdA}(x, y) < \epsilon$ implies that $n(x, t)$ and $n(y, t)$ do not intersect.

---

[2]This theorem implies that any k-annulus is homeomorphic to some simple standard k-annulus of our choice, for which we can easily relate the Euler characteristic and the number of contours and show that (Euler characteristic = 2− the number of contours).

Step 4. For every $x \in bdA$, let $A(x) = \{y \in bdA: d_{bdA}(x,y) \geq \epsilon\}$. Since $x \notin A(x)$ and the set $A(x)$ is compact, we obtain that $d(x, A(x)) > 0$, where d is the Euclidean distance in $\mathbb{R}^2$. By compactness of bdA, there exists $\delta > 0$ such that $\delta \leq d(x, A(x))$ for every $x \in bdA$.[3] Hence, for every $x, y \in bdA$, $d_{bdA}(x,y) \geq \epsilon$ implies $d(x,y) \geq \delta$.

Step 5. Let $0 < r < min\{\delta/2, t\}$. For every $x, y \in bdA$, $n(x,r)$ and $n(y,r)$ do not intersect: Let $x \in bdA$. From Step 3, it follows that, for every $y \in bdA$ such that $d_{bdA}(y,x) < \epsilon$, $n(x,r)$ and $n(y,r)$ do not intersect. From Step 4, it follows that, for every $y \in bdA$ such that $d_{bdA}(y,x) \geq \epsilon$, $n(x,r)$ and $n(y,r)$ do not intersect, since $d(x,y) \geq \delta > 2r$.

Applying these steps to clA^c, we obtain that there exists a constant $s > 0$ such that, for every $x, y \in bdA$, $-n(x,s)$ and $-n(y,s)$ do not intersect. Taking $t = min(r,s)$, we obtain that A is t parallel regular, by Theorem 6.1. The assertion follows from Theorem 7.4. ■

It is easy to give examples of non par(r)-regular sets which are not topologically equivalent to their digital images. For example, set A in Figure 7.11(a) is simply connected, but $Dig_\cap(A, r)$ represented by gray squares is not simply connected. Of course, one can always find a set X having some special shape which is not par(r)-regular, yet X and $Dig_\cap(X, r)$ are homotopy equivalent, like the set presented in Figure 7.11(b). Although topology was preserved in digitizing the set shown in Figure 7.11(b), it is clear that important local geometric properties were lost. In Section 7.4 we show that if a set A is par(r)-regular, then $Dig_\cap(A, r)$ will never significantly change its local geometric properties (Gross and Latecki [55]).

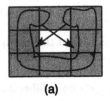   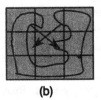

(a)   **(b)**

Figure 7.11: (a) A and $Dig_\cap(A, r)$ are not homotopy equivalent. (b) X and $Dig_\cap(X, r)$ are homotopy equivalent.

There are many important object classes used in computer vision that can be modeled as par(r)-regular sets for some r and for which the calculation of r is straightforward. One such class is that of planar generalized tubular surfaces, which are constructed by sweeping a planar curve around a planar axis. For objects in this class, it is shown in (Gross [53]) that the parameter curves are also lines of curvature, so that the calculation of r can follow

---

[3]We can obtain δ by similar arguments as for ϵ in Step 3 or by the continuity of function $x \longmapsto d(x, A(x))$.

the following scheme. For example, we show how to calculate r for a given torus T such that each $Dig(T, r)$ is topology preserving. By Theorem 7.6, it is sufficient to find the value of r such that T is par(r)-regular. We use the construction given in the proof of Theorem 7.6 to compute the maximal value of r such that T is par(r)-regular. We assume that T is parameterized as

$$T = (b + a\sin\phi)(\cos\theta)e_1 + (b + a\sin\phi)(\sin\theta)e_2 + (a\cos\phi)e_3,$$

where T is obtained by sweeping a circle of radius a around a circular axis of radius b, where $b > a$, and (e_1, e_2, e_3) form an orthonormal basis in $\mathbb{R}^3$ (see Figure 7.12).

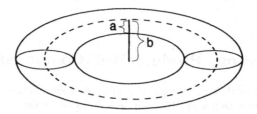

Figure 7.12: It is easy to calculate r for a torus T such that each $Dig(T, r)$ is topology preserving.

Following Step 1 of the proof of Theorem 7.6, we first calculate k_{max}. For a torus k_{max} is given by $k_{max} = \frac{1}{a}$ if $b - a \le a$, and by $k_{max} = \frac{1}{(b-a)}$ if $b - a > a$. Let $r < \frac{1}{k_{max}} = min\{a, b-a\}$. Observe that in the case of a torus, this not only guarantees us that locally in some neighborhood of every point $x \in T$ the normal vectors of the length r do not pairwise intersect, but also that globally these vectors do not pairwise intersect for all points in T. Thus, if $r < min\{a, b - a\}$, then $n(x, r) \cap n(y, r) = \emptyset$ and $-n(x, r) \cap -n(y, r) = \emptyset$ for all $x, y \in T$, which means that T is par(r)-regular so that any digitization $Dig(T, r)$ of the torus is topology preserving.

The digitization model we have proposed does not handle projection, yet in computer vision we generally have to deal with the digitization of the projection of an object. How can we use our digitization results in the general case of an image contour formed by digitizing the projection of the object boundary?

Let us assume a model of scaled orthographic projection. Under this model the viewing direction remains constant over the entire object. A well-known result (see Koenderink [72], p. 432–433), due to Blaschke more than half a century ago, relates the curvature of the contour under parallel projection to the principal curvatures on the object surface. This relationship, where k_c denotes the curvature of the contour, is given by:

$$\kappa_c^{-1}(\psi) = \kappa_1^{-1}\sin^2\psi + \kappa_2^{-1}\cos^2\psi,$$

where k_1 and k_2 are the principal curvatures on the surface and ψ denotes the angle of the visual ray with respect to the first principal direction. Since $\sin^2\psi + \cos^2\psi = 1$, it follows

from Blaschke's result that

$$|\kappa_c^{-1}| \geq min(|\kappa_1^{-1}|, |\kappa_2^{-1}|).$$

Since $r_c = |\kappa_c^{-1}|$ is the radius of the contour curvature, it follows from the definition of parallel regular sets that under orthography if the object is par(r)-regular then the image contour is locally par(r)-regular.

Assuming that the scaling factor s in the imaging process is either known or can be bounded *a priori*, then under scaled orthography the contour is locally par(rs)-regular. If there is no self-occlusion, then the object contour will be par(rs)-regular. Thus, we now have a way to determine either the camera resolution or the camera distance such that topology and geometry is preserved under projection and digitization.

7.3   Digitizations Produce Well-Composed Images

In this section, we show that if A is a par(r)-regular set, then some digital patterns cannot occur in its digitization $Dig(A, r)$. This can be very useful for the identification of noise-induced irregular patterns, since if these patterns occur, they can be identified by a simple local pattern matching. Consequently, if in a practical application the resolution r of the digitization is such that the parts of the object which have to be preserved under the digitization are compatible with the square sampling grid, then our results allow for efficient noise detection.

By the following theorem, $Dig(A, r)$ is well-composed. Well-composed sets have very nice digital topological properties, in particular, a digital version of the Jordan Curve Theorem holds for them and the Euler characteristic is locally computable. The property of well-composedness is presented in more details in Chapter 3.

Theorem 7.7 Let A be par(r)-regular. Then the pattern shown in Figure 7.13 and its 90° rotation cannot occur in any $Dig(A, r)$.

Figure 7.13: This pattern and its 90° rotation cannot occur in every $Dig(A, r)$.

Proof: Let c be the common vertex of all four closed squares. We first assume that $c \notin A$ and show that the pattern shown in Figure 7.13 and its 90° rotation cannot occur in the configuration of the four squares.

Let S_2 and S_4 be black, and S_1 and S_3 be white as shown in Figure 7.14.a, where $S_1, S_2, S_3,$ and S_4 are closed squares. We prove that this assumption leads to a contradiction. Since A is closed and $c \notin A$, there is an $e > 0$ such that $B(c, e) \cap A = \emptyset$, where $B(c, e)$ denotes (as always) a closed ball.

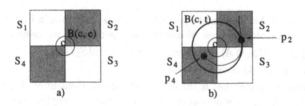

Figure 7.14: The small circle illustrates ball $B(c,e)$ and the big circle illustrates ball $B(c,t)$.

There must be points of A in both squares S_2 and S_4, since if $S_2 \cap A = \emptyset$, then S_2 would be white by **ds2**. Therefore, $S_2 \cap A \neq \emptyset$, and similarly $S_4 \cap A \neq \emptyset$.

Let p_2 be a point with the shortest distance t to c in $S_2 \cap A$.

Let p_4 be a point with the shortest distance d to c in $S_4 \cap A$.

Clearly, points p_2, p_4 belong to bdA and $t > 0$, $d > 0$, since $c \notin A$, $c \in S_2$, and $c \in S_4$. Without loss of generality, we assume that $t \geq d$. Consider the closed ball $B(c,t)$. We show that p_2 and p_4 belong to two different components of $B(c,t) \cap bdA$. Assume that this is not the case. Then, for some component C of bdA, it follows that $C = arc_1(p_2, p_4) \cup arc_2(p_2, p_4)$, $arc_1(p_2, p_4) \cap arc_2(p_2, p_4) = \{p_2, p_4\}$, and $arc_1(p_2, p_4) \subseteq B(c,t)$ or $arc_2(p_2, p_4) \subseteq B(c,t)$.

Assume $arc_1(p_2, p_4) \subseteq B(c,t)$ and, without loss of generality, assume that $arc_1(p_2, p_4)$ goes through S_3. Then

$$arc_1(p_2, p_4) \cap face(S_2, S_3) \cap (B(c,t) \setminus B(c,e)) \neq \emptyset$$

and

$$arc_1(p_2, p_4) \cap face(S_3, S_4) \cap (B(c,t) \setminus B(c,e)) \neq \emptyset,$$

where $face$ denotes the common face of two squares (see Figure 7.14.b). In this case,

$$arc_1(p_2, p_4) \cap S_3 \subseteq (B(c,t) \setminus B(c,e)) \cap S_3.$$

Since the diameter of square S_3 is r, no component other then C of bdA intersects S_3, by Proposition 6.5. Therefore, $A \cap S_3$ contains $(S_3 \setminus B(c,t))$ together with part of A between $arc_1(p_2, p_4)$ and $bdB(c,t)$ in S_3. We also have that $A \cap S_2 \subseteq (S_2 \setminus B(c,t))$, since no point in $S_2 \cap A$ is closer to c than distance t (by the definition of constant t). Consequently, $area(A \cap S_3) \geq area(A \cap S_2)$. Thus, square S_3 should be black.

This contradiction implies that $arc_i(p_2, p_4) \not\subseteq B(c,t)$ for $i = 1, 2$. Therefore, $bdA \cap B(c,t)$ has at least two components, one containing p_2 and the second containing p_4. In each of these components there is a point with the shortest distance $(\leq t)$ to c; call them x_2 and x_4. Then $c \in n(x_2, r) \cap n(x_4, r)$, a contradiction. We have thus shown for a par(r)-regular set A that

(∗)   if $c \notin A$, then the pattern shown in Figure 7.13 and its $90°$ rotation cannot occur in the four squares of $Dig(A, r)$ which have c as their common vertex.

The case in which $c \in A \setminus bdA$ follows directly from the result above applied to the digitization of the complement A^c of A (i.e., the roles of A^c and A are interchanged). For completeness, the proof is given below.

Let again S_2 and S_4 be black, and S_1 and S_3 be white, as shown in Figure 7.14.a, where S_1, S_2, S_3, and S_4 are closed squares. Without loss of generality, we assume that

$$area(S_2 \cap A) \geq area(S_4 \cap A) \text{ and } area(S_1 \cap A) \geq area(S_3 \cap A).$$

Then, by **ds3**, $area(S_4 \cap A) > area(S_1 \cap A)$.

We will digitize the set B that is the closure of the complement of A, i.e., $B = cl(A^c)$. Since A is par(r)-regular, B is also par(r)-regular. Clearly, $area(S_i \cap B) = area(S_i) - area(S_i \cap A)$ for $i = 1, 2, 3, 4$. Since $area(S_i \cap B) = -area(S_i \cap A) + area(S_i)$, where $area(S_i)$ is a constant value, we obtain that

$$area(S_4 \cap B) < area(S_1 \cap B) \text{ as well as}$$
$$area(S_2 \cap B) \leq area(S_4 \cap B) \text{ and } area(S_1 \cap B) \leq area(S_3 \cap B).$$

Thus, in $Dig(B, r)$ we have the pattern: S_2 and S_4 are white, and S_1 and S_3 are black. Since $c \notin B$, we obtain by the above result ($*$) applied to B that this pattern cannot occur in squares S_1, S_2, S_3, and S_4 which belong to $Dig(B, r)$. The obtained contradiction proves that if $c \in A \setminus bdA$, then the pattern shown in Figure 7.13 and its 90° rotation cannot occur in the four squares of $Dig(A, r)$ which have c as their common vertex.

It remains to consider the case in which $c \in bdA$. Let again S_2 and S_4 be black, and S_1 and S_3 be white in $Dig(A, r)$, as shown in Figure 7.14.a, where S_1, S_2, S_3, and S_4 are closed squares. This implies that

$$\epsilon = min\{area(S_2 \cap A), area(S_4 \cap A)\} - max\{area(S_1 \cap A), area(S_3 \cap A)\} > 0. \quad (7.5)$$

We denote by $X + v$ the translation of a set X by vector v and by $A \triangleleft B = (A - B) \cup (B - A)$. It is easy to observe that (see Figure 7.15)

$$|area(S \cap A) - area((S + v) \cap A)| \leq area(S \triangleleft (S + v)) \quad (7.6)$$

for every square $S \in \mathcal{Q}$ and every vector v, where $|r|$ denotes the absolute value of r.

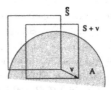

Figure 7.15: $|area(S \cap A) - area((S + v) \cap A)| \leq area(S \triangleleft (S + v))$.

Since $c \in bdA$, there are points of the complement A^c in every neighborhood of c. Therefore, there exists a vector v such that $c + v \notin A$ and $area(S \triangleleft S') < \epsilon/2$, where $S' = S + v$ for every square $S \in \mathcal{Q}$. As a consequence of this fact and inequalities (7.5) and (7.6), we obtain

$$min\{area(S_2' \cap A), area(S_4' \cap A)\} - max\{area(S_1' \cap A), area(S_3' \cap A)\} > 0. \quad (7.7)$$

Therefore, S_2' and S_4' are black, and S_1' and S_3' are white, in the digitization $Dig'(A, r)$ of A with respect to the square cover $\mathcal{Q}$ translated by v. This contradicts ($*$), since $c + v \notin A$

and $c+v$ is the common vertex of the four squares. The obtained contradiction proves that if $c \in bdA$, then the pattern shown in Figure 7.13 and its 90° rotation cannot occur in the four squares of $Dig(A, r)$ which have c as their common vertex. ∎

The following theorem that we used to prove Theorem 7.4 is a simple consequence of Theorem 7.7.

Theorem 7.8 *Let A be par(r)-regular. Then $Dig(A, r)$ is a bordered 2D manifold and the boundary of $Dig(A, r)$ is a 1D manifold.*

Proof: Since the configuration shown in Figure 7.13 (and its 90° rotation) cannot occur in $Dig(A, r)$ by Theorem 7.7, there exist only three 2×2 configurations of boundary squares in $Dig(A, r)$ shown in Figure 7.16 (modulo reflection and 90° rotation).

Figure 7.16: The only possible 2×2 configurations of boundary squares in $Dig(A, r)$ of a par(r)-regular set A (modulo reflection and 90° rotation).

Therefore, if we view $Dig(A, r)$ as a subset of $\mathbb{R}^2$, every point in $Dig(A, r)$ has a neighborhood homeomorphic to a relatively open subset of a closed half-plane. Hence $Dig(A, r)$ is a bordered 2D manifold and the boundary of $Dig(A, r)$ is a 1D manifold. ∎

The well-composedness of an output digital image by the intersection digitization, can also be guaranteed without the requirement that the input continuous image was parallel regular.

Theorem 7.9 *Let G be a set with the property that the intersection of G with every open ball with radius d is connected. Then the intersection digitization $Dig_\cap(G, d)$ of G with diameter d is well-composed.*

Proof: Let a, b, c and d be four closed squares of cover Q sharing a common corner point x which are arranged as follows:

a	b
c	d

Let $\mathcal{O}(x, d)$ be the open ball centered at x with radius d. We will show that the configurations $a \cap G \neq \emptyset$, $d \cap G \neq \emptyset$, and $c \cap G = b \cap G = \emptyset$ or $b \cap G \neq \emptyset$, $c \cap G \neq \emptyset$, and $a \cap G = d \cap G = \emptyset$, which lead to non-well-composedness of the digitization of G, are impossible. For example, if $a \cap G \neq \emptyset$, $d \cap G \neq \emptyset$, and $b \cap G = c \cap G = \emptyset$,

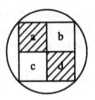

then $G \cap \mathcal{O}(x, d)$ is disconnected, since $G \cap \mathcal{O}(x, d) = G \cap (\mathcal{O}(x, d) \setminus (c \cup d))$, which is clearly a disconnected subset of $\mathcal{O}(x, d)$.   ∎

7.4   Digital Patterns in Digital Images

In this section, we show that if A is a par(r)-regular set, then only a few digital patterns can occur as neighborhoods of boundary points in its 2D digital image $Dig_\cap(A, r)$. This can be very useful for the identification of noise-induced irregular patterns, since if the neighborhood of a boundary point does not match one of these patters, it must be due to noise. Consequently, if in a practical application the resolution r of the digitization is such that the parts of the object which have to be preserved under the digitization form a par(r)-regular set, then our results allow for efficient noise detection.

We also show that the digitization $Dig_\cap(A, r)$ of a par(r)-regular set A will not change qualitative geometric properties of the boundary of A: a boundary point which is locally convex cannot be digitized to a locally concave pixel and a boundary point which is locally concave cannot be digitized to a locally convex pixel. First, we need to prove some facts about par(r)-regular sets. We begin with two lemmas and one theorem about parallel regular sets.

Lemma 7.3 *Let A be par(r, +)-regular. Then $bdA \cap B(x, t)$ is connected for every $t \le r$ and $x \notin A$. Let A be par(r, -)-regular. Then $bdA \cap B(x, t)$ is connected for every $t \le r$ and $x \in A - bdA$.*

Proof: We prove only the first part of this lemma. The proof of the second part is analogous. We show that $bdA \cap B(x, t)$ is connected for every $t \le r$ and $x \notin A$. Let this not be the case, i.e., there exist $t \le r$ and two components C and D of $bdA \cap B(x, t)$ for some $x \notin A$. Since A is par(r, +)-regular, A is also par(t, +)-regular. Applying Proposition 6.3 to C and D separately, we obtain that there exist $c \in C \cap B(x, t)$ such that $x \in n(c, t)$ and $d \in D \cap B(x, t)$ such that $x \in n(d, t)$. Thus $n(c, t) \cap n(d, t) \ne \emptyset$. This is an inconsistency, since $n(c, t)$ and $n(d, t)$ are normal vectors at distinct points $c, d \in A$. Thus $bdA \cap B(x, t)$ is connected for every $t \le r$ and $x \notin A$.   ∎

Lemma 7.4 *Let A be par(r, +)-regular. Then $A \cap B(x, t)$ is connected for every $t \le r$ and $x \notin A$. Let A be par(r, -)-regular. Then $A \cap B(x, t)$ is connected for every $t \le r$ and $x \in A - bdA$.*

Proof: We prove only the first part of this lemma. The proof of the second part is analogous. Let $t \leq r$. If $A \cap B(x, t)$ were disconnected, then $bdA \cap B(x, t) \neq \emptyset$ and $bdA \cap B(x, t)$ would be disconnected, which is impossible by Lemma 7.3. ∎

Theorem 7.10 *Let A be par(r)-regular. Then $A \cap B(x, t)$ is connected for every $t \leq r$ and $x \in \mathbb{R}^2$.*

Proof: By Lemma 7.4, it remains to consider the case in which $x \in bdA$. Assume that there exist two components C and D in $A \cap B(x, t)$ for some $t \leq r$. Then x belongs to one of them, say C. By Proposition 6.3, applied to D and $x \notin D$, we obtain that there exists $s \in D$ such that $x \in n(s, t)$. However, then $x \in n(x, t) \cap n(s, t)$. Thus $A \cap B(x, t)$ must be connected. ∎

By Theorem 7.10, Theorem 7.9 gives a simple proof that $Dig_\cap(A, r)$ of a par(r)-regular set A is well-composed.

Lemma 7.5 *Let A be par(r)-regular. Then the pattern shown in Figure 7.17 and its 90° rotations and reflections cannot occur in $Dig_\cap(A, r)$.*

Figure 7.17: This pattern and its 90° rotations and reflections cannot occur in $Dig_\cap(A, r)$.

Proof: Assume that this pattern occurs in $Dig_\cap(A, r)$. We denote the right black square by p. The neighbor squares of p are numbered according to the scheme in Section 2.1, e.g., $N_4(p)$ denotes the square to the left of p that shares a side with p. Using the ball shown in Figure 7.18(a), which has a radius smaller than r, it follows from Theorem 7.10 that that $A \cap (p \cup N_4(p))$ is connected.

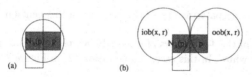

(a)   (b)

Figure 7.18: (a) $A \cap (p \cup N_4(p))$ is connected. (b) $iob(x, r)$ must intersect either $N_2(p)$ or $N_5(p)$.

Let $a \in A \cap p$ and $b \in A \cap N_4(p)$. Since the other two squares (i.e., $N_2(p)$ and $N_5(p)$) are white, there is a path joining a with b which intersects $p \cap N_4(p)$, which is the common side of squares p and $N_4(p)$. Therefore, there exists a point $x \in bdA \cap p \cap N_4(p)$. Yet $iob(x, r) \subseteq A$, but this implies that either $N_2(p)$ or $N_5(p)$ is black, since $iob(x, r)$ must intersect at least one of these closed squares (e.g., see Figure 7.18(b)). The obtained inconsistency implies that the pattern shown in Figure 7.17 cannot occur in $Dig_\cap(A, r)$. ∎

The following theorem is an important result for recovering geometric properties of an object and for noise detection. If a template occurs that is different from those enumerated in the theorem, we can be sure that it must be due to noise.

Theorem 7.11 *Let A be par(r)-regular. Then the neighborhood $\mathcal{N}(p)$ of a 4-boundary point $p \in Dig_\cap(A, r)$ can have only one of seven configurations presented in Figure 7.19 (modulo reflection and 90° rotation).*

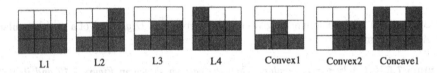

L1   L2   L3   L4   Convex1   Convex2   Concave1

Figure 7.19: All possible configurations modulo reflection and rotation which can occur on the boundary of the digitization $Dig_\cap(A, r)$ of a par(r)-regular set A.

Proof: The neighbor squares of p are numbered according to the scheme in Section 2.1. One of the 4-neighbors of p must be white, since p is a 4-boundary point. Therefore, there exists $x \in bdA \cap p$, because otherwise, $p \subseteq A$, and all 4-neighbors of p would be black. Since $iob(x, r) \subseteq A$ and since the radius of $iob(x, r)$ is equal to the diameter of a single square in $Dig_\cap(A, r)$, at least one of the 4-neighbors of p must be black. We assume that $N_6(p)$ is black.

By Lemma 7.5, only patterns (1) – (4) can occur in the neighborhood of p shown in Figure 7.20.

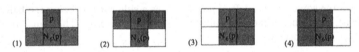

Figure 7.20: Only patterns (1) – (4) can occur in this neighborhood of p.

Since at least one of the 4-neighbors of p must be white, and we assumed that $N_6(p)$ is black, $N_2(p)$ must be white. In this case, configuration (2) in Figure 7.20 is impossible by Lemma 7.5.

Using Theorem 7.7 and Lemma 7.5, it can be checked that only the configurations shown in Figure 7.19 extend configurations (1), (3) and (4) in Figure 7.20. ∎

Observe that the set of realizable patterns in Theorem 7.11 is very small. Moreover, this set is minimal, i.e., the number of patterns which can occur as the neighborhood of a (4-)

boundary black point in $Dig_\cap(A, r)$ cannot be further reduced, since it is easy to construct a par(r)-regular set A such that $Dig_\cap(A, r)$ contains each of the patterns in Figure 7.19. Knowing that these seven configurations constitute all possible configurations (modulo reflection and rotation) which can occur on the boundary of the digitization $Dig_\cap(A, r)$ of a par(r)-regular set A, it is now a simple task to classify each of these configurations with respect to their connectivity properties. First, we identify all possible boundary configurations that are digitizations of a half plane.

Theorem 7.12 *Let H be a closed half plane. Then p is a boundary point of $Dig_\cap(H, r)$ iff the neighborhood of p has one of the patterns shown in Figure 7.21.*

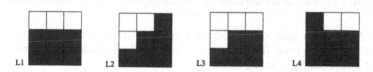

Figure 7.21: Linear digital neighborhoods.

Proof: It is sufficient to observe that i) each of the four patterns can be a legal intersection digitization of some closed half plane, and ii) the remaining three configurations in Figure 7.19 can only occur in $Dig_\cap(A, r)$ if either A or A^c is not convex. ∎

Definition: Based on Theorem 7.12, we define a **linear digital neighborhood** of p as any neighborhood configuration $\mathcal{N}(p)$ corresponding to L1, L2, L3, L4 in Figure 7.21 modulo reflection and 90° rotation. Next we define a **convex digital neighborhood** of p as any neighborhood configuration $\mathcal{N}(p)$ corresponding to Convex1 or Convex2 in Figure 7.22 modulo reflection and 90° rotation. We define a **concave digital neighborhood** of p as any neighborhood configuration $\mathcal{N}(p)$ corresponding to Concave1 in Figure 7.22 modulo reflection and 90° rotation.

Theorem 7.13 *Let x be a boundary point of a planar set A such that $A \cap B(x, 2r)$ is convex, and let p be the square of $Dig_\cap(A, r)$ containing x. If p is a 4-boundary point of $Dig_\cap(A, r)$, then $\mathcal{N}(p)$ cannot be digitally concave.*

Proof: We assume that $N_2(p)$ is a white square. Note that the squares of $\mathcal{N}(p)$ are contained in $B(x, 2r)$. If $\mathcal{N}(p)$ were Concave1, then there would exist a point $b \in A$ contained

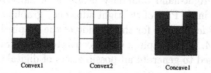

Figure 7.22: Convex and concave digital neighborhoods.

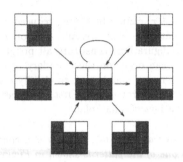

Figure 7.23: Part of the adjacency graph for digital boundary configurations.

in square $N_1(p)$ and a point $c \in A$ contained in square $N_3(p)$. Since $b, c \in A \cap B(x, 2r)$ and $A \cap B(x, 2r)$ is convex, line segment bc must also be contained in A, and therefore $A \cap N_2(p) \neq \emptyset$. Thus $N_2(p)$ would be black. ∎

Theorem 7.14 *Let x be a 4-boundary point of a planar set A such that $A \cap B(x, 2r)$ is concave, i.e., $A^c \cap B(x, 2r)$. Let p be the square of $Dig_\cap(A, r)$ containing point x. If p is a boundary point of $Dig_\cap(A, r)$, then $\mathcal{N}(p)$ cannot be digitally convex.*

Proof: We assume that $N_2(p)$ is a white square. Note that the squares of $\mathcal{N}(p)$ are contained in $B(x, 2r)$. If $\mathcal{N}(p)$ were Convex1, then $N_0(p), N_4(p) \subset A^c$. Since $A^c \cap B(x, 2r)$ is convex, the convex hull CH of $N_0(p) \cup N_4(p)$ is contained in A^c. Since p is contained in CH, it is also contained in A^c. However, then p would be white. This shows that $\mathcal{N}(p)$ cannot be Convex1.

If $\mathcal{N}(p)$ were Convex2, then $N_1(p), N_5(p) \subset A^c$. Since $A^c \cap B(x, 2r)$ is convex, the convex hull CH of $N_1(p) \cup N_5(p)$ is contained in A^c. Since p is contained in CH, it would be white. Thus, $\mathcal{N}(p)$ cannot be Convex2. ∎

The classification of the neighborhoods of boundary points given in Figures 7.21 and 7.22 can be used to both represent and recover objects. When the set of digital boundaries is fully enumerated, there are 32 patterns. Each pattern is the digitization of a local section of curve, with a range of tangent directions. We can now define a **right adjacency graph** for the digital boundary curve of a parallel regular set as a graph where the nodes are the 32 digital boundary patterns and there is a directed arc from node A to node B whenever pattern B is a possible right-hand boundary neighbor of pattern A. A **left adjacency graph** is analogously defined. Part of the right adjacency graph is shown in Figure 7.23. It can be seen that the *outdegree* = 4 for the portion of the graph shown. In fact, the entire graph has *outdegree* = 4. This graph is easily converted to a grammar and the resulting grammar can then be used to generate all possible sets of digital boundary curves.

The adjacency graph can be used directly in 3D shape recovery. Let a generalized torus be a generalization of the classic torus, where the cross-section curve (i.e., inner circle) is now allowed to be any simple, closed, twice-differentiable curve. Assuming that an object is a generalized torus (i.e., the outer curve is a circle), there is only one curve to recover, the cross-section. In Gross and Boult [54] it was shown that the contour of a generalized tube is insufficient to constrain the underlying 3D shape and that there is at least one degree of freedom. For any hypothetical non-intersecting, digital cross-section curve, we can construct a digital generalized torus. For each digital generalized torus, we can test if the contour of the generated generalized torus is compatible with the image contour. Assuming the contours are compatible, we then want to find the digital generalized torus that minimizes some intensity-based error-of-fit measure. If the maximal length of a digital cross-section curve can be bounded, this can certainly be done by enumerating the set of digital cross-section curves, but then the time bound would be exponential time, i.e., 4^n, where n is the maximal length of a cross-section curve. There are additional constraints on this problem, however, so that a complete enumeration of all digital cross-section curves is not necessary. Although the search space is large, there are few paths that actually need to be explored. Initial results are encouraging and allow to believe that the time bound for recovering the digital cross-section curve may be linear.

Our results, although stated for parallel regular objects, are also helpful to analyze the shape properties of non-parallel regular objects, as the following example illustrates. We use the legal neighborhood configurations shown in Figure 7.19 for corner detection. Assume that the object is piecewise par(r)-regular and we want to find the corners of the object. Note that good candidates for corners are sections on the object boundary where the par(r)-regular pieces are joined together. Figure 7.24(left) shows the intersection digitization of a set bounded by a superelliptic curve. In Figure 7.24(right), the boundary points having legal neighborhood configurations are colored white, while those having illegal neighborhood configurations are colored black. Thus, the black-colored boundary points correspond to sections of the object boundary that are not par(r)-regular. These points correctly identify the "corners" of the superelliptic curve.

7.5 Computing a Topology Preserving Camera Distance

In computer vision, we generally need to deal with the projection of an object surface onto the image plane. It is not the object itself, but rather its projection that is digitized. We will now prove a theorem that allows us to compute the camera resolution and a camera distance from the object such that the digitization process preserves topology. We model here the **digitization and segmentation process** of a single non-overlapping object A as follows:

(i) **Projection of the object onto the image plane**

We model this step as a scaled orthographic projection and assume that the optical axis of the camera is roughly perpendicular to the object, with a maximal angular

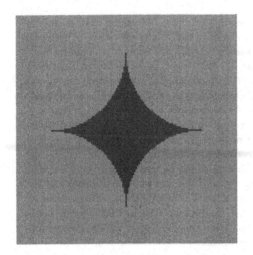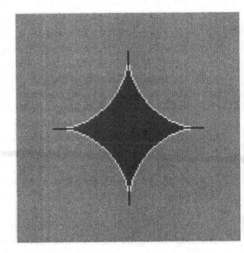

Figure 7.24: For the superelliptic object (left), the boundary points having legal neighborhood configurations are colored white, while those having illegal neighborhood configurations are colored black (right).

divergence of α between the axis and the object (see Figure 7.25). We denote the output of this projection applied to an object A as $P_\alpha(A)$.

(ii) **Camera digitization process of the projected object**

We assume a CCD camera having an image plane tessellated with a square grid, where the diameter of a square is s, and the output of the camera is a gray-level digital image. We will call s the **resolution** of the camera.

(iii) **Postprocessing step of the camera output**

We segment the output digital gray-level image of the camera by applying some threshold value to it. For some threshold value v, the output binary picture obtained by applying steps ii) and iii) to projection $P_\alpha(A)$ is denoted as $Dig_v(P_\alpha(A), s)$.

If we can estimate the curvature along the object contour, Theorem 7.3 allows us to compute the resolution of the camera that guarantees topology preservation. Thus, if we can bound the contour curvature, then Theorem 7.15 presents a straightforward way to relate the camera resolution and the camera distance such that the digitization process preserves topology. We first assume that the underlying object can be regarded as planar and its boundary is twice differentiable.

Theorem 7.15 *Let A be a planar par(h)-regular set and let α be the maximal angular divergence between the camera optical axis and the object normal as shown in Figure 7.25. Let f be the effective focal length of the camera. Then*

$$d < \frac{hf\cos\alpha}{s}$$

relates the resolution of the camera s and distance d between the camera and the object surface in such a way that the digitization process preserves topology, i.e., A and $Dig_v(P_\alpha(A), s)$ are homotopy equivalent.

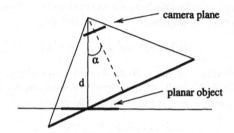

camera plane

planar object

Figure 7.25: A scaled orthographic projection.

Proof: If the optical axis of the camera is exactly perpendicular to the object, then under scaled orthographic projection, the length of the projection of a vector of length l on the object surface is

$$l' = \frac{fl}{d},$$

where d is the distance from the center of projection, i.e., pinhole lens, to the object. Since the angular divergence between the object surface normal and the optical axis is bounded by α, the minimal length of the projection l'' of l is

$$l'' = l' \cos\alpha = l\frac{f}{d}\cos\alpha$$

According to this formula, and the fact that line intersection is projection invariant, the projection of the object A is parallel regular for

$$h'' = h\frac{f}{d}\cos\alpha.$$

In order to ensure the topology preservation, the projection of the object should be r parallel regular for $r > s$, by Theorem 7.3. Therefore, $h'' > s$, i.e.,

$$h\frac{f}{d}\cos\alpha > s.$$

Thus,

$$d < \frac{hf\cos\alpha}{s}$$

is the restriction on distance d between the camera and the object such that the digitization process preserves topology. ∎

Theorem 7.15 can also be used for rigid 3D objects to determine either the camera resolution or the camera distance such that the digitization process preserves topology.

However, if there are self-occlusions of the object contour under the projection, then this theorem must be restricted to parts of the object contour without self-occlusions. We now assume a model of scaled orthographic projection. Under this model the viewing direction remains constant over the entire object. Due to Blaschke (see Koenderink [72], p. 432-433), we have the following relationship between the curvature of the contour under parallel projection and the principal curvatures on the object surface:

$$\kappa_c^{-1}(\psi) = \kappa_1^{-1}\sin^2\psi + \kappa_2^{-1}\cos^2\psi,$$

where k_c denotes the curvature of the contour, k_1 and k_2 are the principal curvatures on the surface, and ψ denotes the angle of the visual ray with respect to the first principal direction. Since $\sin^2\psi + \cos^2\psi = 1$, it follows from Blaschke's result that

$$|\kappa_c^{-1}| \geq min(|\kappa_1^{-1}|, |\kappa_2^{-1}|).$$

Since $r_c = |\kappa_c^{-1}|$ is the radius of the contour curvature, it follows from the definition of parallel regular sets that under orthography if the object is par(r)-regular then the image contour is also locally par(r)-regular. Assuming that the scaling factor s in the imaging process is either known or can be bounded *a priori*, then under scaled orthography the contour is locally par(rs)-regular. If there is no self-occlusion, then the object contour will be par(rs)-regular. Thus, we now have a straightforward way to determine either the camera resolution or the camera distance such that topology and geometry is preserved under this projection and our digitization model.

As shown in Section 7.2, there are many important object classes used in computer vision that are par(r)-regular for some r and for which the calculation of r is straightforward.

Example

We now apply Theorem 7.15 to compute a distance d between the camera and the object such that a digitized object has the same topology as the original object. This example shows the usefulness of this theorem to ensure recognition of objects based on their topological properties. The goal is to identify objects based on the number of holes. Assume that the objects can be regarded as planar and the boundaries of parts which are necessary for object recognition are twice differentiable.

For example, consider designing an inspection system for rectangular planar objects with holes moving on a conveyor belt, where the boundaries of the holes are superelliptic curves with varying eccentricities and exponents. These objects do not have to be necessarily parallel regular, e.g. due to the corners on the outside contour of the rectangles. However, it is easy to calculate a constant h such that the holes are h parallel regular. Let m_1 be the minimum of the inverses of the principal curvatures of the superelliptic curves. Let m_2 the minimum of all distances between pairs of the superelliptic curves and between the curves and the occluding contour of the object. It is sufficient to take $h < min(m_1, m_2)$.

We are given a CCD camera having an image plane tessellated with a square grid where the diameter of a square is s. We need to find a distance d between the camera and a conveyor belt such that a digitized object is guaranteed to have the same topology as the original object. We assume that the optical axis of the camera is roughly perpendicular to the conveyor belt, with a maximal angular divergence of α. Scaled orthographic projection onto the image plane is assumed. The digitized object is obtained after applying some threshold value to the gray level image of the camera. If f is the effective focal length of the camera, then by Theorem 7.15,

$$d < \frac{hf\cos\alpha}{s}$$

is the restriction on distance d between the camera and a conveyor belt such that the digitization process preserves topology.

7.6 Areas of Squares and Circles

The goal of this section is to prove the inequality (7.4) in the proof of Lemma 7.2 (Figure 7.10):

$$area(s_2 - oob(m,r)) \leq area(iob(m,r) \cap s_1).$$

We will prove this inequality in **case (a)**; the proof in **case (b)** is based on analogous arguments. We first restate the assumptions of **case (a)** in Lemma 7.2.

Let squares s_1 and s_2 have a side with endpoints C and O in common, i.e., $CO = s_1 \cap s_2$. Let the other side of s_1 that is parallel to CO have endpoints D and E, and the other side of s_2 that is parallel to CO have endpoints B and A (see Figure 7.26). We assume that vector $v = n(x, 2r)$ first intersects side DE and then CO. Without loss of generality, we can assume that the length of the sides of a square (in the square grid) is 1, and therefore, $r = \sqrt{2}$ and the length of vector v is $2\sqrt{2}$. Let M be the midpoint of v. The beginning point of v is the center of ball $iob(M, \sqrt{2})$ of radius $\sqrt{2}$, the endpoint of v is the center of ball $oob(M, \sqrt{2})$ of radius $\sqrt{2}$, and $iob(M, \sqrt{2}) \cap oob(M, \sqrt{2}) = \{M\}$. We will denote $iob(M, \sqrt{2})$ by bb (black ball) and the its boundary by bc (black circle). Similarly, we will denote $oob(M, \sqrt{2})$ by wb (white ball) and the its boundary by wc (white circle). We will denote the center of bb by Z_b and the center of wb by Z_w.

We introduce the Cartesian coordinate system such that the origin is at point O, i.e., $O = (0,0)$, and $A = (0,1)$ and $C = (-1,0)$. The goal of this section is to prove

Theorem 7.16

$$area(s_2 - wb) \leq area(s_1 \cap bb). \tag{7.8}$$

Adding $area(s_1 - bb)$ to both sides of (7.8) yields

$$area(s_2 - wb) + area(s_1 - bb) \leq 1, \tag{7.9}$$

since $area(s_1) = area(s_2) = 1$. Inequality (7.9) is trivially true when $s_2 \subseteq wb$ or $s_1 \subseteq bb$. Therefore, we assume that $s_2 \not\subseteq wb$ and $s_1 \not\subseteq bb$. We will prove inequality (7.9) for the following four cases:

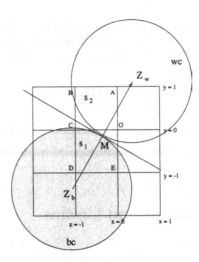

Figure 7.26:

(I.1) $((M$ is below or on line $CO)$ and $(O \in wb$ or $C \in wb))$ or

(I.2) $((M$ is below or on line $CO)$ and $(O \notin wb$ and $C \notin wb))$ or

(II.1) $((M$ is above $CO)$ and $(O \in bb$ or $C \in bb))$ or

(II.2) $((M$ is above $CO)$ and $(O \notin bb$ and $C \notin bb))$.

The inequality (7.8) for cases (I.2) and (II.2) is proved in Lemma 7.8 below. By Lemma 7.9 below, case (I.1) reduces to the case in which $(O \in v$ or $C \in v)$. By Lemma 7.10 below, case (II.1) reduces to the case in which $(D \in v$ or $E \in v)$. Lemma 7.11 below demonstrates how to prove (7.9) for these cases. We begin with the following simple geometric fact.

Lemma 7.6 *Let point X lie outside a closed ball B with center Z. Let $H(XZ)$ denote one of the closed half planes determined by the straight line XZ. Let B' be a closed ball B rotated around X such that the center Z' of B' is not contained in $H(XZ)$ and $H(XZ) \cap B \cap B' \neq \emptyset$ (see Figure 7.27(a)). Then $H(XZ) \cap B' \subset H(XZ) \cap B$.*

Proof: The circles bdB and bdB' intersect at exactly two points. The line L that passes through the two intersection points of bdB and bdB' goes through the midpoint of line segment ZZ' and is perpendicular to ZZ' (see Figure 7.27(a)). Let $H(L)$ be the half plane determined by L that contains point Z. Since two distinct circles can intersect at no more than two points and $Z' \notin H(L)$, we obtain $H(L) \cap B' \subset H(L) \cap B$. Since $H(XZ) \cap B \subset H(L) \cap B$, we have $H(XZ) \cap B' \subset H(XZ) \cap B$. ∎

Using arguments similar to those of Lemma 7.6, we can also prove

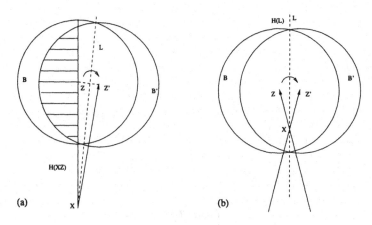

Figure 7.27:

Lemma 7.7 *Let point X lie inside a closed ball B with center Z, where $X \neq Z$. Let B' be a closed ball B rotated around X such that $B' \neq B$ (see Figure 7.27(b)). Let L be the straight line through the two intersection points of bdB and bdB' and let H(L) be the half plane determined by L that contains point Z. Then L goes through X and $H(L) \cap B' \subset H(L) \cap B$.*
∎

Lemma 7.8 *If the midpoint M of vector v is on or below line CO and $O \notin wb$ and $C \notin wb$, then $area(s_2 - wb) \leq area(s_1 \cap bb)$. If M is on or above line CO and $O \notin bb$ and $C \notin bb$, then $area(s_2 - wb) \leq area(s_1 \cap bb)$.*

Proof: We prove only the first part. The proof of the second part is analogous with wb and bb interchanged. Let M be below or on line CO and $O \notin wb$ and $C \notin wb$. First we will bound the $area(s_2 - wb)$ from above.

Since wc only intersects line CO (i.e., line $y = 0$) between points C and O, the point S with the smallest y-coordinate in wb is contained in $wb \cap s_1$ (see Figure 7.28(a)). Let wb', v', and S' denote wb, v, and S translated parallel to y-axis (by vector $\langle 0, y \rangle$ with $0 \leq y$) such that $S' \in CO$. Since $wb' \cap s_2 \subseteq wb \cap s_2$, we have $area(s_2 - wb) \leq area(s_2 - wb')$. Now we will bound $area(s_2 - wb')$ from above.

We have the situation in which $S' \in CO$ is the point with the smallest y-coordinate in wb'. If S' is different from C and O, then $s_2 - wb'$ is a union of two connected sets, say L and R, such that $L \cap R = \{S'\}$ and L is to the left and R to the right of S' (see Figure 7.28(b)). If $area(L) \leq area(R)$, then $area(s_2 - wb') = area(L) + area(R)$ can only increase if we translate wb' parallel to x-axis in the negative direction, i.e., by vector $\langle x, 0 \rangle$, where $x < 0$. Let wb'_x and S'_x denote wb' and S' translated by vector $\langle x, 0 \rangle$ such that $S'_x = C$ (see Figure 7.29(a)). Then $area(s_2 - wb') < area(s_2 - wb'_x)$, and consequently

$$area(s_2 - wb) \leq area(s_2 - wb'_x). \tag{7.10}$$

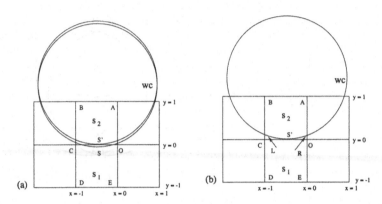

Figure 7.28:

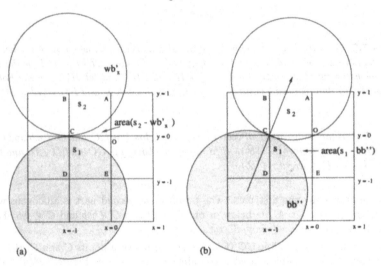

Figure 7.29:

Now we will show that $area(s_2 - wb'_x) < area(s_1 \cap bb)$. Since M is on or below line CO and $O \notin wb$ and $C \notin wb$, we have $wc \cap BC \neq \emptyset$ and $wc \cap AO \neq \emptyset$. Let $wc \cap BC = \{S\}$ and $wc \cap AO = \{T\}$ (see Figure 7.30(a)).

Let wb_α, v_α, and M_α denote wb, v, and M rotated around the center Z_b of bb by angle α. Let $wc_\alpha \cap BC = \{S_\alpha\}$ and $wc_\alpha \cap AO = \{T_\alpha\}$. Since points S and T are in two different half planes determined by vector v, we have the following implications by Lemma 7.6:

If $\alpha > 0$, then $|CS_\alpha| < |CS|$ and $|OT_\alpha| > |OT|$. If $\alpha < 0$, then $|CS_\alpha| > |CS|$ and $|OT_\alpha| < |OT|$.

Therefore, there exists angle α such that $|CS_\alpha| = |OT_\alpha|$. (Since bb does not change its location during this rotation, $area(s_1 \cap bb)$ remains constant.) Let wb', v', M', and bb' denote wb_a, v_a, M_a, and bb translated parallel to y-axis by vector $\langle 0, -|CS_a| \rangle$ (see Figure 7.30(b)). Then $wc' \cap BC = \{C\}$ and $wc' \cap AO = \{O\}$, and $area(s_1 - bb) \leq area(s_1 - bb')$. We also have that $M' \in wc' \cap s_1$, since M and M_a both lie in between lines $x = -1$ and $x = 0$.

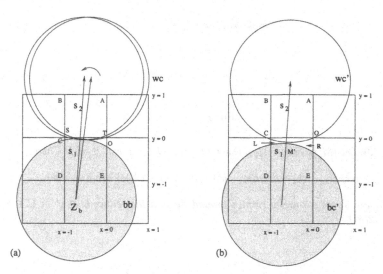

Figure 7.30:

We assume that M' is distinct from C and O. Observe that $(s_1 - bb') - (wb' \cap s_1)$ is a union of two disjoint connected sets, say L and R, such that L is to the left and R to the right of M'.

If $area(L) \leq area(R)$, then $area((s_1 - bb') - (wb' \cap s_1)) = area(L) + area(R)$ can only increase if BB is rotated clockwise around Z_w (i.e., to the left). Let wb'', v'', M'', and bb'' denote wb'_r, v'_r, M'_r, and bb' rotated clockwise around Z_w by the smallest angle such that $M'' = C$ (see Figure 7.29(b)). The configuration wb'', v'', M'', and bb'' shown in Figure 7.29(b) is uniquely determined for every starting configuration wb'_r, v'_r, M'_r, and bb', where $area(L) \leq area(R)$. Thus, we obtain

$$area((s_1 - bb') - (wb' \cap s_1)) < area((s_1 - bb'') - (wb' \cap s_1)),$$

and consequently $area(s_1 - bb') \leq area(s_1 - bb'')$. Therefore, $area(s_1 - bb) \leq area(s_1 - bb'')$, which implies

$$area(s_1 \cap bb'') \leq area(s_1 \cap bb). \tag{7.11}$$

By calculating $area(s_2 - wb'_x)$ and $area(s_1 \cap bb'')$, we obtain $area(s_2 - wb'_x) \leq area(s_1 \cap bb'')$ (this inequality is visualized in Figure 7.31). By (7.10) and (7.11), we obtain $area(s_1 - wb) \leq area(s_1 \cap bb)$. ∎

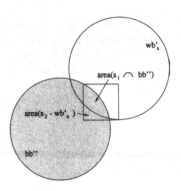

Figure 7.31:

Lemma 7.9 *Let (M be on or below line CO) and ($O \in wb$ or $C \in wb$). Then*

$$area(s_2 - wb) + area(s_1 - bb) \leq area(s_2 - wb') + area(s_1 - bb),$$

where wb' and v' are wb and v rotated around Z_b such that either $O \in v'$ or $C \in v'$ (see Figure 7.32(a)).

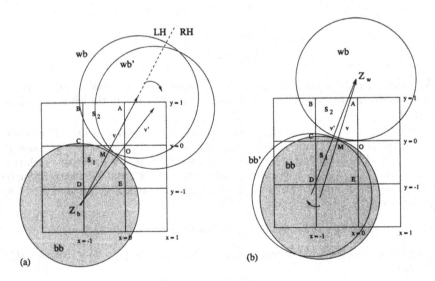

Figure 7.32:

Proof: Observe first that ($O \in wb$ or $C \in wb$) iff

1. ($O \in wb$ and $C \notin wb$) or

2. ($O \notin wb$ and $C \in wb$) or

3. ($O \in wb$ and $C \in wb$).

Since the distance between M and the endpoint Z_w of vector v is not greater than $\sqrt{2}$ and the angle of v (with x-axis) is in the interval $[45°, 135°]$, the endpoint Z_w of v must be contained in squares $s_2 \cup \ldots \cup s_7$, where $s_2, \ldots, s_7$ are closed squares named as shown in Figure 7.33. If $Z_w \in s_2 \cup s_5 \cup s_6 \cup s_7$, then one of these squares is contained in wb, and consequently their common corner A is contained in wb. Therefore, at least one of the points A and B is always contained in wb.

It can be calculated that if $C \notin wb$, then $Z_w \notin s_3 \cup s_4$, and therefore $A \in wb$. Similarly, if $O \notin wb$, then $B \in wb$. This implies that ($O \in wb$ or $C \in wb$) iff

1. ($O \in wb$ and $C \notin wb$ and $A \in wb$) or

2. ($O \notin wb$ and $C \in wb$ and $B \in wb$) or

3. ($O \in wb$ and $C \in wb$ and ($A \in wb$ or $B \in wb$)).

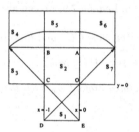

Figure 7.33:

These three cases imply the following two cases

(A) ($O \in wb$ and $A \in wb$) or

(B) ($C \in wb$ and $B \in wb$).

Below, we will show this lemma for case (A). The proof for case (B) is analogous. We thus assume case (A), which implies that line segment AO is contained in wb. Since the lemma is trivially true when $O \in v$, we will assume that $O \notin v$. Let wb' and v' be wb and v rotated around Z_b such that $O \in v'$ (see Figure 7.32(a)).

We denote by LH the closed half plane determined by vector v which does not contain O, and by RH the complement of LH. Since $O \in v'$ and the center Z'_w of wb' is the endpoint of v', we have $Z'_w \notin LH$. By Lemma 7.6, $LH \cap wb' \subset LH \cap wb$. Therefore,

$$LH \cap wb' \cap s_2 \subset LH \cap wb \cap s_2. \tag{7.12}$$

Since M is on or below line CO, the line segment $v \cap s_2$ is contained in wb. Since line segment OA is contained in wb, the convex hull of $v \cap s_2$ and OA is contained in wb. Since $RH \cap s_2$ is contained in this convex hull, $RH \cap s_2 \subset RH \cap wb$. Hence $RH \cap s_2 \subseteq RH \cap wb \cap s_2$. Since $RH \cap wb' \cap s_2 \subseteq RH \cap s_2$, we obtain

$$RH \cap wb' \cap s_2 \subseteq RH \cap wb \cap s_2. \tag{7.13}$$

By (7.12) and (7.13),
$$wb' \cap s_2 \subset wb \cap s_2,$$

which implies $s_2 - wb \subset s_2 - wb'$. Therefore,

$$area(s_2 - wb) < area(s_2 - wb'),$$

which implies

$$area(s_2 - wb) + area(s_1 - bb) \le area(s_2 - wb') + area(s_1 - bb).$$

∎

Using the same arguments as in Lemma 7.9, we can also prove

Lemma 7.10 *Let (M be on or above line CO) and ($O \in bb$ or $C \in bb$). Then*

$$area(s_2 - wb) + area(s_1 - bb) \le area(s_2 - wb) + area(s_1 - bb'),$$

where bb' and v' are bb and v rotated around Z_w such that either $E \in v'$ or $D \in v'$ (see Figure 7.32(b)). ∎

By Lemmas 7.9 and 7.10, it is sufficient to prove inequality (7.8) for the following cases:

(I.1′) ((M is below or on line CO) and ($O \in v$ or $C \in v$)) or

(II.1′) ((M is above CO) and ($D \in v$ or $E \in v$)).

Lemma 7.11 proves (7.8) when M lies below or on line CO and $O \in v$. Since the proofs for the remaining three cases are analogous, they are omitted.

Lemma 7.11 *Let the midpoint M of v lie on or below line CO and $O \in v$ (see Figure 7.34(a)). Then*
$$area(s_2 - wc) \le area(s_1 \cap bc).$$

Proof: We assume that point Z_w (the endpoint of v and the center of the white circle wc) has coordinates (p, q), where $0 \le p, q$. Under this assumption, the white circle wc satisfies the equation $(x - p)^2 + (y - q)^2 = 2$. The point Z_b, which is the starting point of v and the center of the black circle bc, has coordinates $(-a, -b)$, where $0 \le a, b$. Thus, the black circle bc satisfies the equation $(x + a)^2 + (y + b)^2 = 2$.

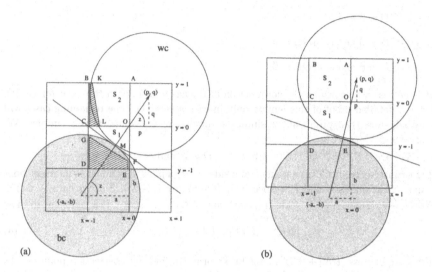

Figure 7.34:

Observe that $a \le b$ and $p \le q$, since the angle of vector v (with x-axis) is in the interval $[45°, 90°]$. Since the length of v is $2\sqrt{2}$, we have $\sqrt{a^2 + b^2} + \sqrt{p^2 + q^2} = 2\sqrt{2}$. Since M lies below the line segment CO, M belongs to line segment $Z_b O \subseteq v$. Therefore, we have $\sqrt{p^2 + q^2} \le \sqrt{2}$, which implies $p, q \le \sqrt{2}$, and $\sqrt{2} \le \sqrt{a^2 + b^2}$. Note also that $\sqrt{a^2 + b^2} \le 2\sqrt{2}$ and $a, b \le 2\sqrt{2}$.

Since the distance between M and the endpoint Z_w of vector v is not greater than $\sqrt{2}$ and the angle of v (with x-axis) is in the interval $[45°, 90°]$, the endpoint Z_w of v must be contained in squares $s_2 \cup s_5 \cup s_6 \cup s_7$, where s_2, s_5, s_6, s_7 are closed squares as shown in Figure 7.33. Therefore, one of these squares is contained in wb, and consequently its corner A. Since $O \in wb$, side AO is contained in wb. Therefore, there are the following configurations in which wc can intersect the sides of square s_2:

$s_2(1)$: $wc \cap BA \ne \emptyset$ and $wc \cap CO \ne \emptyset$ (see Figure 7.34(a)),

$s_2(2)$: $wc \cap BA = \emptyset$ and $wc \cap CO \ne \emptyset$; in this case $wc \cap CB \ne \emptyset$,

$s_2(3)$: $wc \cap BA \ne \emptyset$ and $wc \cap CO = \emptyset$; in this case $wc \cap CB \ne \emptyset$,

$s_2(4)$: $wc \cap BA = \emptyset$ and $wc \cap CO = \emptyset$; in this case $s_2 \subset wb$, since all corner points of s_2 are in wb.

Since midpoint M of v lies below line segment CO, there are the following configurations in which bc can intersect the sides of square s_1:

$s_1(1)$: $bc \cap CD \ne \emptyset$ and $bc \cap OE \ne \emptyset$ (see Figure 7.34(a)),

$s_1(2)$: $bc \cap CD = \emptyset$ and $bc \cap OE \neq \emptyset$,

$s_1(3)$: $bc \cap CD \neq \emptyset$ and $bc \cap OE = \emptyset$,

$s_1(4)$: $bc \cap CD = \emptyset$ and $bc \cap OE = \emptyset$.

It is necessary to consider the conjunction of the cases for s_2 with the cases for s_1. We will give a detailed proof of this lemma only in case $s_2(1)s_1(1)$. The remaining cases will be omitted, since their proofs follow similar arguments or are comparatively simpler. We thus assume

$s_2(1)s_1(1)$: $wc \cap BA \neq \emptyset$, $wc \cap CO \neq \emptyset$, $bc \cap CD \neq \emptyset$, and $bc \cap OE \neq \emptyset$.

Let wc intersect side CO at a point L and side BA at a point K, and let bc intersect sides CD and OF at points G and F, respectively (see Figure 7.34(a)). Since $area(s_2 - wc) \leq |BC|\frac{|BK|+|CL|}{2}$, $|DE|\frac{|EF|+|DG|}{2} \leq area(s_1 \cap bc)$, and $|BC| = |DE| = 1$, it is sufficient to show

$$|BK| + |CL| \leq |EF| + |DG|. \tag{7.14}$$

First, we express $|BK| + |CL|$ in algebraic form. To find the intersection points of the white circle with sides BA and CO of square s_2, we solve the equation $(x-p)^2 + (y-q)^2 = 2$ for $y = 0$ and $y = 1$. If $y = 0$, then $x^2 - 2px + p^2 + q^2 - 2 = 0$ and $x_{1,2} = p \pm \sqrt{2 - q^2}$. Since we need the smaller x, we obtain $x = p - \sqrt{2 - q^2}$ by $y = 0$. Thus $L = (p - \sqrt{2 - q^2}, 0)$ is an intersection point of wc with CO.

If $y = 1$, then $x^2 - 2px + p^2 + q^2 - 2q - 1 = 0$ and $x_{1,2} = p \pm \sqrt{-q^2 + 2q + 1}$. Since we need the smaller x, we obtain $x = p - \sqrt{-q^2 + 2q + 1}$ by $y = 1$. Thus $K = (p - \sqrt{-q^2 + 2q + 1}, 1)$ is an intersection point of wc with side BA. Therefore,

$$|BK| + |CL| = p - \sqrt{-q^2 + 2q + 1} + 1 + p - \sqrt{2 - q^2} + 1 = 2 + 2p - \sqrt{-q^2 + 2q + 1} - \sqrt{2 - q^2} \tag{7.15}$$

To calculate $|EF| + |DG|$, we find the intersection points of the black circle with sides CD and OE of square s_1, i.e., we solve the equation $(x + a)^2 + (y + b)^2 = 2$ for $x = 0$ and $x = -1$.

If $x = 0$, then $y^2 + 2by + a^2 + b^2 - 2 = 0$ and $y_{1,2} = -b \pm \sqrt{2 - a^2}$. Since we need the greater value of y, we obtain $y = -b + \sqrt{2 - a^2}$ by $x = 0$. Thus $F = (0, -b + \sqrt{2 - a^2})$ is an intersection point of bc with side OE. We also obtain that $a \leq \sqrt{2}$.

If $x = -1$, then $y^2 + 2by + a^2 + b^2 - 2a - 1 = 0$ and $y_{1,2} = -b \pm \sqrt{-a^2 + 2a + 1}$. Since we need the greater value of y, we obtain $y = -b + \sqrt{-a^2 + 2a + 1}$ by $x = -1$. Thus $G = (-1, -b + \sqrt{-a^2 + 2a + 1})$ is an intersection point of bc with side CD. Therefore,

$$|EF| + |DG| = -b + \sqrt{2 - a^2} + 1 - b + \sqrt{-a^2 + 2a + 1} + 1 = 2 - 2b + \sqrt{2 - a^2} + \sqrt{-a^2 + 2a + 1}. \tag{7.16}$$

In order to show that $area(s_2 - wc) \leq area(s_1 \cap bc)$, using equations (7.15) and (7.16), it is sufficient to show that

$$2p - \sqrt{-q^2 + 2q + 1} - \sqrt{2 - q^2} \leq -2b + \sqrt{2 - a^2} + \sqrt{-a^2 + 2a + 1} \tag{7.17}$$

Inequality (7.17) is equivalent to the following

$$0 \leq -2p + \sqrt{-q^2 + 2q + 1} + \sqrt{2 - q^2} - 2b + \sqrt{2 - a^2} + \sqrt{-a^2 + 2a + 1} \qquad (7.18)$$

Before we prove (7.17), we will show that if $area(s_2 - wc) \neq 0$, then $\sqrt{a^2 + b^2} \leq \sqrt{5}$ and $\sqrt{p^2 + q^2} \geq 2\sqrt{2} - \sqrt{5}$.

We first assume that $a \geq 1$. If we had $b < 1$, then $DE \cap v = \emptyset$. Therefore, $b \geq 1$. Since $bc \cap OE \neq \emptyset$ and $O \notin bb$, we have $E \in bb$, which implies (see Figure 7.34(a)):

$$a^2 + (b - 1)^2 \leq 2 \Rightarrow 0 \leq b \leq 2 \quad \text{and} \quad a^2 + (b - 1)^2 \leq 2 \Rightarrow a^2 + b^2 \leq 2b + 1 \leq 5.$$

Therefore $\sqrt{a^2 + b^2} \leq \sqrt{5}$.

We show that the assumptions $0 \leq a < 1$ and $\sqrt{a^2 + b^2} > \sqrt{5}$ imply $s_2 \subset wb$. Since $\sqrt{a^2 + b^2} + \sqrt{p^2 + q^2} = 2\sqrt{2}$, we obtain $\sqrt{p^2 + q^2} \leq 2\sqrt{2} - \sqrt{5}(\approx 0.592)$. Therefore, the endpoint of vector v (i.e. the center of wb) is contained in the square to the right of s_2 that shares a side with s_2 (see Figure 7.34(b)). Since this square is then contained in wb, its corners A and O are contained in wb.

Since the assumptions $0 \leq a < 1$ and $\sqrt{a^2 + b^2} \geq \sqrt{5}$ imply $b \geq 2$, we obtain $\frac{q}{p} = \frac{b}{a} > 2$ if $p > 0$, and therefore $2p < q$ for $p \geq 0$. Since $2p < q \leq \sqrt{p^2 + q^2} \leq 2\sqrt{2} - \sqrt{5}$, we have $2p < 2\sqrt{2} - \sqrt{5}$. The corner point C of s_2 is contained in wb iff $(1 + p)^2 + q^2 \leq 2$ (see Figure 7.34(b)), which is true:

$$(1 + p)^2 + q^2 = 1 + 2p + p^2 + q^2 < 1 + (2\sqrt{2} - \sqrt{5}) + (2\sqrt{2} - \sqrt{5})^2(\approx 1.943) \leq 2.$$

The corner point B of s_2 is contained in wb iff $(1 + p)^2 + (1 - q)^2 \leq 2$ (see Figure 7.34(b)). Since $2p < q$ and $p^2 < \frac{1}{4}q^2$, we obtain

$$(1 + p)^2 + (1 - q)^2 = 2 + 2p - 2q + p^2 + q^2 \leq 2 - q + \frac{5}{4}q^2.$$

Since $2 - q + \frac{5}{4}q^2 \leq 2$ iff $q(\frac{5}{4}q - 1) \leq 0$, which is true for $0 \leq q \leq \frac{4}{5}$, we obtain that $(1 + p)^2 + (1 - q)^2 \leq 2$. Since all corner points of s_2 are contained in wb, $s_2 \subset wc$. This inconsistency implies that if $0 \leq a < 1$, then $\sqrt{a^2 + b^2} < \sqrt{5}$. Since $\sqrt{a^2 + b^2} + \sqrt{p^2 + q^2} = 2\sqrt{2}$, we obtain $\sqrt{p^2 + q^2} \geq 2\sqrt{2} - \sqrt{5}$. We have thus shown that $\sqrt{a^2 + b^2} \leq \sqrt{5}$ and $\sqrt{p^2 + q^2} \geq 2\sqrt{2} - \sqrt{5}$.

Now we will prove inequality (7.18) when the angle z of v (with x-axis) is in the interval $[\frac{\pi}{3}, \frac{\pi}{2}]$ (see Figure 7.34(a)). Let $r = \sqrt{p^2 + q^2}$. Then $2\sqrt{2} - \sqrt{5} \leq r \leq \sqrt{2}$. In this case $q = r\sin(z)$, $p = r\cos(z)$, $b = (2\sqrt{2} - r)\sin(z)$, and $a = (2\sqrt{2} - r)\cos(z)$. In order to show that (7.18) holds it is sufficient to show that $f(r, z) \geq 0$, where

$$\begin{aligned}
f(r, z) = {}& -2r\cos(z) + \sqrt{2 - \left(2\sqrt{2} - r\right)^2 \cos(z)^2} \\
& + \sqrt{1 + 2\left(2\sqrt{2} - r\right)\cos(z) - \left(2\sqrt{2} - r\right)^2 \cos(z)^2} - \\
& 2\left(2\sqrt{2} - r\right)\sin(z) + \sqrt{2 - r^2 \sin(z)^2} + \sqrt{1 + 2r\sin(z) - r^2 \sin(z)^2}.
\end{aligned}$$

Since the second derivative of f with respect to r is negative

$$\frac{\partial^2 f(r,z)}{\partial r} = -\frac{\left(2\sqrt{2}-r\right)^2 \cos(z)^4}{\left(2-\left(2\sqrt{2}-r\right)^2 \cos(z)^2\right)^{\frac{3}{2}}} - \frac{\cos(z)^2}{\sqrt{2-\left(2\sqrt{2}-r\right)^2 \cos(z)^2}} -$$

$$\frac{\left(-2\cos(z)+2\left(2\sqrt{2}-r\right)\cos(z)^2\right)^2}{4\left(1+2\left(2\sqrt{2}-r\right)\cos(z)-\left(2\sqrt{2}-r\right)^2\cos(z)^2\right)^{\frac{3}{2}}} -$$

$$\frac{\cos(z)^2}{\sqrt{1+2\left(2\sqrt{2}-r\right)\cos(z)-\left(2\sqrt{2}-r\right)^2\cos(z)^2}} - \frac{r^2\sin(z)^4}{\left(2-r^2\sin(z)^2\right)^{\frac{3}{2}}} -$$

$$\frac{\sin(z)^2}{\sqrt{2-r^2\sin(z)^2}} - \frac{\left(2\sin(z)-2r\sin(z)^2\right)^2}{4\left(1+2r\sin(z)-r^2\sin(z)^2\right)^{\frac{3}{2}}} - \frac{\sin(z)^2}{\sqrt{1+2r\sin(z)-r^2\sin(z)^2}},$$

f is a concave function, i.e., for every $r \in [2\sqrt{2}-\sqrt{5}, \sqrt{2}]$ and every $z \in [\frac{\pi}{3}, \frac{\pi}{2}]$ we have

$$\forall t \in [0,1]\ f(r,z) \geq (1-t)f(2\sqrt{2}-\sqrt{5}, z) + tf(\sqrt{2}, z),$$

and consequently

$$f(r,z) \geq min\{f(2\sqrt{2}-\sqrt{5}, z), f(\sqrt{2}, z)\}.$$

Since it can be shown that the two one-variable functions

$$f(2\sqrt{2}-\sqrt{5}, z) = 2\left(-2\sqrt{2}+\sqrt{5}\right)\cos(z) + \sqrt{2-5\cos(z)^2} +$$
$$\sqrt{1+2\sqrt{5}\cos(z)-5\cos(z)^2} - 2\sqrt{5}\sin(z) + \sqrt{2-\left(2\sqrt{2}-\sqrt{5}\right)^2\sin(z)^2} +$$
$$\sqrt{1+2\left(2\sqrt{2}-\sqrt{5}\right)\sin(z)-\left(2\sqrt{2}-\sqrt{5}\right)^2\sin(z)^2}$$

and

$$f(\sqrt{2}, z) = -2\sqrt{2}\cos(z) + \sqrt{2}\sqrt{\cos(z)^2} + \sqrt{2\sqrt{2}\cos(z)-\cos(2z)} -$$
$$2\sqrt{2}\sin(z) + \sqrt{2}\sqrt{\sin(z)^2} + \sqrt{\cos(2z)+2\sqrt{2}\sin(z)}$$

are positive for $z \in [\frac{\pi}{3}, \frac{\pi}{2}]$, we obtain that $f(r,z) \geq 0$ for $r \in [2\sqrt{2}-\sqrt{5}, \sqrt{2}]$ and $z \in [\frac{\pi}{3}, \frac{\pi}{2}]$.

Finally we will prove inequality (7.17) when the angle z of v (with x-axis) is in the interval $[\frac{\pi}{4}, \frac{\pi}{3}]$. Let $c = \sqrt{a^2+b^2}$, i.e., c is the distance from the center Z_b of bb to point O. As we have shown, $\sqrt{2} \leq c \leq \sqrt{5}$.

By Lemma 7.7 applied for $X = O$ to wb, the left side of inequality (7.17) is maximal for angle $z = \frac{\pi}{4}$. In this case, we have $p = q \Rightarrow \sqrt{p^2+q^2} = \sqrt{2}q = 2\sqrt{2} - c \Rightarrow q = 2 - \frac{c}{\sqrt{2}}$. Therefore, the left side of inequality (7.17) is less than or equal to

$$4 - \sqrt{2}c - \sqrt{1+\sqrt{2}c - \frac{c^2}{2}} - \sqrt{-2+2\sqrt{2}c - \frac{c^2}{2}} \qquad (7.19)$$

In the following, we will bound from below the right side of inequality (7.17). By substituting $b = \sqrt{c^2 - a^2}$ in the right side of (7.17), we obtain

$$r(a,c) = -2\sqrt{c^2 - a^2} + \sqrt{2 - a^2} + \sqrt{-a^2 + 2a + 1}. \qquad (7.20)$$

Since $a \leq \sqrt{2}$ and $a = c \cos z$ implies $a \geq \sqrt{2} \cos(\frac{\pi}{3}) = \frac{\sqrt{2}}{2}$, we obtain $a \in [\frac{\sqrt{2}}{2}, \sqrt{2}]$. We will show that the function $r(a,c)$ obtains its minimum at $a = \frac{\sqrt{2}}{2}$ for every $c \in [\sqrt{2}, \sqrt{5}]$.

First, we further restrict the domain of a. Let $c \in [\sqrt{2}, \sqrt{5}]$ be fixed. Let bb_z^c denote a bb such that the distance from the center Z_b to O is c and the angle of vector v_z (which contains Z_bO) with the x-axis is z. By Lemma 7.6 applied for $X = O$ to bb_z^c, if $E \notin bb_{\frac{\pi}{3}}^c$, then $E \notin bb_z^c$ for every $z \in [\frac{\pi}{4}, \frac{\pi}{3}]$.

Since we consider case $s_2(1)s_1(1)$, we only need to consider those c for which there exists at least one z such that $E \in bb_z^c$ (see Figure 7.34(a)). Therefore, we must have $E \in bb_{\frac{\pi}{3}}^c$, which means that

$$a^2 + (b - 1)^2 = a^2 + (\sqrt{3}a - 1)^2 = 4a^2 - 2\sqrt{3}a + 1 \leq 2,$$

since in this case $\frac{b}{a} = \tan(\frac{\pi}{3}) = \sqrt{3}$. By solving this inequality, we obtain $\frac{2\sqrt{3}-2\sqrt{7}}{8} \leq a \leq \frac{2\sqrt{3}+2\sqrt{7}}{8}$, which implies that $a \in [\frac{\sqrt{2}}{2}, \frac{2\sqrt{3}+2\sqrt{7}}{8}]$ (since $\frac{2\sqrt{3}+2\sqrt{7}}{8} \approx 1.094 \leq \sqrt{2}$).

To find the minimum of (7.20), we split this expression into two parts. We observe first that the minimum of $\sqrt{-a^2 + 2a + 1}$ for $a \in [\frac{\sqrt{2}}{2}, \frac{2\sqrt{3}+2\sqrt{7}}{8}]$ is obtained at $a = \frac{\sqrt{2}}{2}$ and is equal to $\sqrt{\frac{1}{2} + \sqrt{2}}$.

To find the minimum of the remaining part of (7.20), we will treat $g_c(a) = -2\sqrt{c^2 - a^2} + \sqrt{2 - a^2}$ as a function of one variable a with parameter c. We calculate

$$g_c'(a) = -\frac{a}{\sqrt{2 - a^2}} + \frac{2a}{\sqrt{-a^2 + c^2}}$$

and

$$g_c''(a) = -\frac{a^2}{(2 - a^2)^{\frac{3}{2}}} - \frac{1}{\sqrt{2 - a^2}} + \frac{2a^2}{(-a^2 + c^2)^{\frac{3}{2}}} + \frac{2}{\sqrt{-a^2 + c^2}}.$$

We obtain $g_c'(a) = 0 \Leftrightarrow a = 0$ or $a = \pm\sqrt{\frac{8 - c^2}{3}}$. Since $g_c''(0) = \frac{2\sqrt{2}-c}{\sqrt{2}c} > 0$ for every $c \in [\sqrt{2}, \sqrt{5}]$, g_c has a minimum at $a = 0$ and maxima at $a = \pm\sqrt{\frac{8 - c^2}{3}}$.

Since the image of the function $a(c) = \sqrt{\frac{8 - c^2}{3}}$ for $c \in [\sqrt{2}, \sqrt{5}]$ is in the interval $[1, \sqrt{2}]$, the function $g_c(a)$ obtains a maximum for $a \in [1, \sqrt{2}]$. If $g_c(a)$ obtains a maximum for $a \in [\frac{2\sqrt{3}+2\sqrt{7}}{8}, \sqrt{2}]$, then g defined over $[\frac{\sqrt{2}}{2}, \frac{2\sqrt{3}+2\sqrt{7}}{8}]$ obtains the minimum at $a = \frac{\sqrt{2}}{2}$. If $g_c(a)$ obtains a maximum for $a \in [1, \frac{2\sqrt{3}+2\sqrt{7}}{8})$, then g obtains the minimum at one of the endpoints of interval $[\frac{\sqrt{2}}{2}, \frac{2\sqrt{3}+2\sqrt{7}}{8}]$. Since $g(\frac{2\sqrt{3}+2\sqrt{7}}{8}) \geq g(\frac{\sqrt{2}}{2})$ for every $c \in [\sqrt{2}, \sqrt{5}]$, function g defined over $[\frac{\sqrt{2}}{2}, \frac{2\sqrt{3}+2\sqrt{7}}{8}]$ obtains the minimum at $a = \frac{\sqrt{2}}{2}$. Since $g(\frac{\sqrt{2}}{2}) = \sqrt{\frac{3}{2}} - 2\sqrt{c^2 - \frac{1}{2}}$, we obtain that $r(a,c)$ is greater than or equal to

$$\sqrt{\frac{3}{2}} - 2\sqrt{c^2 - \frac{1}{2}} + \sqrt{\frac{1}{2} + \sqrt{2}} \qquad (7.21)$$

for every $c \in [\sqrt{2}, \sqrt{5}]$.

In order to prove inequality (7.17) it is sufficient to show that (7.19) $\leq$ (7.21), which is true, since it can be shown that the one-variable function $i(c) = (7.21) - (7.19)$ is greater than or equal to 0 for every $c \in [\sqrt{2}, \sqrt{5}]$.   ∎

7.7 Digital Supportedness

In this section we extend our theory of supported arcs presented in Section 6.3 to supported digital arcs. Based on the following results, we can define the total turn of digital arcs in the analogous way to our continuous definition for tame arcs.

We interpret $\mathbf{Z}^2$ as the set of points with integer coordinates in the plane $\mathbb{R}^2$. Any finite subset $S \subseteq \mathbf{Z}^2$ will be called a **digital set**. A **4-boundary** bd_4A of a digital set A is a set of points in A which have at least one 4-neighbor not in A, i.e., $bd_4A = \{a \in A : \mathcal{N}_4(a) \cap A^c \neq \emptyset\}$, where A^c denotes the complement of A in $\mathbf{Z}^2$.

A digitization schema that is commonly used in vision geometry literature is subset digitization, where the **subset digitization** of a planar set X is defined as the set of points with integer coordinates that are contained in X:

$$SD(X) = \{s \in \mathbf{Z}^2 : s \in X\}.$$

This schema can be easily extended to boundaries of planar sets. The result is referred to as **object boundary quantization**, and is defined as follows:

$$D_{OBQ}(bdX) = bd_4SD(X),$$

where bdX is the standard topological boundary of a planar set X. The motivation for object boundary quantization is that in computer vision digital curves generally occur as object boundaries. In particular, digital lines are considered to be the boundaries of digitized half-planes.

Definition: A set $P \subseteq \mathbf{Z}^2$ is called a **digital half-plane** if there exists a real closed half-plane $HP \subseteq \mathbb{R}^2$ such that $SD(HP) = P$. A set $L \subseteq \mathbf{Z}^2$ is called a **digital straight line** if $L = bd_4P$ for some digital half-plane P.

The black points in Figure 7.35(a) represent a digital half-plane, since they are obtained by the subset digitization of the gray half-plane. The black points in Figure 7.35(b) represent a digital line, since they are obtained by the digitization D_{OBQ} of the straight line, which is the boundary of the gray half-plane. Thus, $L \subseteq \mathbf{Z}^2$ is a digital straight line if there exists a real straight M line such that $L = D_{OBQ}(M)$ (it is sufficient to take $M = bdHP$).

Definition: Let S be a subset of $\mathbf{Z}^2$ and p a point of S. A digital half-plane P is called a **(digital) half-plane of support** of S at p if $S \subseteq P$ and $p \in bd_4P$, i.e., there exists a real

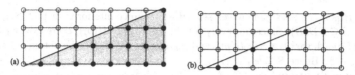

Figure 7.35: The black points represent a *digital half-plane* in (a) and a *digital line* in (b).

half-plane $H(p)$ such that $S \subseteq H(p)$ and $p \in bd_4 P$, where $P = SD(H(p))$. We will also say that S is **(digitally) supported** at p by half-plane P. In this case, point p belongs to the digital line $L = bd_4 P$. The line L is called a **(digital) line of support** of S at p.

Definition: A subset S of $\mathbf{Z}^2$ is **(digitally) supported** if, for every $p \in S$, there exists at least one digital half-plane of support of S at p.

For example, in Figure 7.36 the set of black points in (a) is digitally supported but not in (b), since there do not exist (digital) half-planes of support at points p and q.

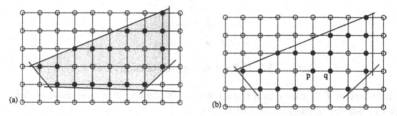

Figure 7.36: The set of black points is *digitally supported* in (a) but not in (b).

Theorem 7.17 allows us to give a new definition of a **convex digital set** as a digital set whose 4-boundary is digitally supported (e.g., see Figure 7.36(a)).

Theorem 7.17 *A finite set $S \subseteq \mathbf{Z}^2$ is digitally supported iff there exists a compact and convex set $B \subseteq \mathbb{R}^2$ with nonempty interior such that $S \subseteq bd_4 SD(B)$.*

Proof:
"$\Rightarrow$" Let $S \subseteq \mathbf{Z}^2$ be digitally supported. For every $p \in S$, there exists a real half-plane $H(p)$ such that $S \subseteq SD(H(p))$ and $p \in bd_4 SD(H(p))$. Note that $S \subseteq SD(H(p))$ iff $S \subseteq H(p)$.

Let $B = \cap\{H(p) : p \in S\}$. B is a closed and convex set as a finite intersection of real half-planes, and $S \subseteq B$. Since S is finite, we can assume that B is bounded. (If this were not the case, we can always find a convex, closed, and bounded subset of B that contains S.)

If the interior of B is empty, then B is a line segment, since a bounded convex set with empty interior is a line segment (Proposition 2.12). In this case, we can replace B by a compact and convex set with nonempty interior (e.g., a rectangle) that contains exactly the same points of $\mathbf{Z}^2$ as B. Therefore, we can assume that the interior of B is nonempty.

Thus, B is a compact and convex set with nonempty interior such that $S \subseteq B$. Consequently, $S \subseteq SD(B)$. Since, for every $p \in S$, $p \in bd_4SD(H(p))$, there exists $q \in \mathbf{Z}^2$ a 4-neighbor of p such that $q \notin SD(H(p))$, and therefore $q \notin SD(B)$. We obtain $p \in bd_4SD(B)$ for every $p \in S$. Hence $S \subseteq bd_4SD(B)$.

"$\Leftarrow$" Let $S \subseteq bd_4SD(B)$, where B is a compact and convex set with nonempty interior. It is sufficient to show that $D_{OBQ}(bdB) = bd_4SD(B)$ is digitally supported. If $SD(B)$ is the empty set, then $bd_4SD(B)$ is trivially digitally supported. Therefore, we assume that $SD(B)$ is nonempty.

Let $p \in bd_4SD(B)$ be any point. Then there exists a 4-neighbor $q \in \mathbf{Z}^2$ of p such that $q \notin SD(B)$, and therefore $q \notin B$.

Let x be a closest point to q in B. Let L be the straight line through x perpendicular to line segment xq, and let HP be the real closed half-plane of L that does not contain q (see Figure 7.37).

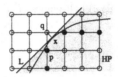

Figure 7.37: HP is a half-plane of support at x.

Since no point of B is closer to q than x and B is convex, B is contained in HP. Thus, HP is a half-plane of support at x of B.

Since $p \in HP$ and $q \notin HP$, we have $p \in bd_4SD(HP)$. We also have that $SD(B) \subseteq SD(HP)$, and consequently $bd_4SD(B) \subseteq SD(HP)$. Thus, $SD(HP)$ is a digital half-plane of support of $bd_4SD(B)$ at p.   ∎

For a planar simple closed curve C, let C^* denotes the closed bounded set surrounded by C. In particular, we have $C = bdC^*$. We define $D_{OBQ}(C) = bd_4SD(C^*)$.

Corollary 7.1 *A finite set $S \subseteq \mathbf{Z}^2$ is digitally supported iff there exists a supported simple closed curve $C \subseteq \mathbb{R}^2$ such that $S \subseteq D_{OBQ}(C)$.*

Proof:

"$\Rightarrow$" By Theorem 7.17, there exists a compact and convex set $B \subseteq \mathbb{R}^2$ with nonempty interior such that $S \subseteq bd_4SD(B)$. By Theorem 2.3, we obtain that $C = bdB$ is a supported simple closed curve. Since $C^* = B$, and consequently $D_{OBQ}(C) = bd_4SD(B)$, we obtain $S \subseteq D_{OBQ}(C)$.

"$\Leftarrow$" This is a special case of Theorem 7.17.   ∎

By Corollary 7.1, supported digital sets correspond to supported continuous sets. In particular, we can say that a digital arc is **(digitally) supported** if it is the image of a supported continuous arc by D_{OBQ}. Thus, we can extend our theory of tame arcs to digital arcs. In particular, we can define the total turn of digital arcs in the analogous way to our continuous definition. The total turn of digital arcs can be then used in digital picture processing to determine the total curvature of digital object boundaries. In the next section we show that our results also apply to other digitization models.

7.8 Object Boundary Quantization of Lines

In this section we relate object boundary quantization (defined in Section 7.7) to other digitization schemes known in the vision geometry literature. In particular, we show that intersection digitization of a half-plane (defined in Section 7.1) and object boundary quantization completely determine each other. This observation allows us to apply the results for intersection digitization to object boundary quantization, and vice versa.

In Section 7.7 we defined a set $L \subseteq \mathbb{Z}^2$ to be a digital straight line if $L = bd_4SD(HP)$ for some real half-plane $HP \subseteq \mathbb{R}^2$. There are many conditions that allow for a given digital set to determine whether it is part of a digital straight line, for example, the chord property (Rosenfeld and Kim [134]) and the (n, q, p, s)-characterization (Dorst and Smeulders [33]), but these conditions are used for different digitization models. However, they also apply to digital lines as defined here.

In order to use subset digitization for straight lines, function SD is first applied to one of the half-planes determined by a line. The boundary of the digital half-plane obtained in this way constitutes the digitization of the line. We assume first that the slope of all lines considered is in the interval $[0, 45°]$ and that a straight line L determines its lower half-plane, which we will denote by $P(L)$, i.e., $P(L) = \{(x, y) \in \mathbb{R}^2 : y \le ax + b\}$ if L is given by the equation $y = ax + b$ ($0 \le a \le 1$). In this case, object boundary quantization of L is given by

$$D_{OBQ}(L) = bd_4SD(P(L)),$$

and the following equality holds

$$D_{OBQ}(L) = bd_4SD(P(L)) = \{(x, \lfloor ax + b \rfloor) : x \in \mathbb{Z}\},$$

where $\lfloor . \rfloor$ is the floor function. For example, in Figure 7.38 the black points represent the digitization $D_{OBQ}(L)$ of the depicted line L. The digitization schema given by the last equation is used by Dorst and Smeulders [34]. Since every continuous line form an angle in the interval $[0, 45°]$ with either x- or y-axis, we can use the (n, q, p, s)-characterization for digital lines obtained by object boundary quantization. Equivalently, we can say that restricting the slope of line L to interval $[0, 45°]$ does not restrict the space of straight lines, since all other lines can be obtained by vertical or diagonal reflections (which can be described as $(x, y) \to (-x, y)$ and $(x, y) \to (y, x)$, respectively).

Rosenfeld and Kim [134] characterize grid intersection quantization of straight lines by chord property. **Grid intersection quantization** maps a continuous line to gird points closest to the intersections of the line with the grid. This gives the points $(i, [ai + b])$ for a line L given by the equation $y = ax + b$ ($0 \le a \le 1$), where $[y]$ indicates the rounding-off

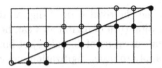

Figure 7.38: The black points represent the digitization $D_{OBQ}(L)$ of a straight line L.

function. Since $[y] = \lfloor x + \frac{1}{2} \rfloor$, we obtain that $D_{OBQ}(L)$ is the grid intersection quantization of the line given by the equation $y = ax + b + \frac{1}{2}$ (Dorst and Smeulders [34]).

Now we show that intersection digitization of a half-plane and object boundary quantization completely determine each other. Let S be a cover of the plane by unit closed squares with vertices at points in $\mathbf{Z}^2$. In the following proposition, intersection digitization $Dig_\cap$ is determined with respect to the cover S.

For a subset A of $\mathbf{Z}^2$, we denote by $Sq(A)$ the set of all squares in S that have at least one corner point in A. It is easy to see that a square $q \in S$ belongs to the intersection digitization of a half-plane HP iff at least one of the corners of q is contained in HP (see Figure 7.39). Thus we obtain

Proposition 7.1 *Let L be a straight line with the slope in the interval $[0, 45^\circ]$. Then $Dig_\cap(P(L)) = Sq(SD(P(L)))$.* ∎

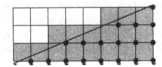

Figure 7.39: The gray squares represent intersection digitization and the black points represent subset digitization of the half-plane below the straight line.

7.9   Extension of Digitization Schemes

We gave conditions which guarantee that topology is preserved under a digitization and segmentation process. For a par(r)-regular set A, A and each of its digital images $Dig(A, r)$ are topologically equivalent. This result has many consequences for practical applications: for example, $Dig(A, r)$ is well-composed, i.e., the checker board digital patterns cannot occur in $Dig(A, r)$. For a large class of real objects, a constant r can always be computed such that the object is par(r)-regular. The definition of a digitization models a real digitization process. However, we did not consider blurring effects to the underlying objects. Thus, we modeled perfectly focused object boundaries. In the remaining part of this chapter, we extend our digitization models to objects with blurred boundaries.

Until now, we applied digitization functions to black and white 2D continuous images, which represent either a 2D object or the projection of a 3D object, i.e., an object is represented by a subset of the plane which is black and its background is white. Now we extend our model to be able to digitize intensity (gray-level or color) continuous images.

Definition: An **(intensity) continuous image** is a function $C : \mathbb{R}^2 \to I$ and an **(intensity) digital image** is a function $D : \mathbb{Z}^2 \to I$, where I is some intensity space. We assume that I is the unit interval $[0, 1]$, but the intensity space I could be any bounded subset of non-negative real numbers (e.g. $I = \{0, 1, ..., 255\}$) or any product of such subsets.

A binary continuous image C can be identified with the set C of points having value 1: $C = \{(x, y) \in \mathbb{R}^2 : C(x, y) = 1\}$. For example, in this terminology, a half-plane $P \subset \mathbb{R}^2$ is identified with its characteristic function $P : \mathbb{R}^2 \to I$, $P(x) = 1$ if $x \in P$ and $P(x) = 0$ otherwise.

The domain of a digital image D is identified with cover Q of the plane $\mathbb{R}^2$ with unit squares. We assume now that the squares in Q are centered at points with integer coordinates. Thus, $\mathbb{Z}^2$ is identified with Q by identifying a square with its center point.

Definition: A **digitization** is a function Dig which assigns a digital image $Dig(C)$ to a given continuous image C in such a way that the value of each square s in a digital image is given by the following formula:

$$Dig(C)(s) = \int_s C.$$

We will call **v-digitization** a binary digital image $Dig_v(C)$ obtained from $Dig(C)$ by thresholding with $v \in [0, 1)$, i.e.

$Dig_v(C)(s) = 1$ if $Dig(C)(s) > v$ and $Dig_v(C)(s) = 0$ otherwise.

For $v = 1$, $Dig_v(C)(s) = 1$ if $Dig(C)(s) = 1$ and $Dig_v(C)(s) = 0$ otherwise.

Observe that $Dig(C)(s) = area(C \cap s)$ for every binary continuous image C such that C is a measurable planar set, since then $\int_s C = area(C \cap s)$ for every square s. In this case, a square $p \in Dig_v(C)$ iff $area(p \cap C)/area(p) > v$, where $0 \le v < 1$ is a constant. Thus, the definition of v-digitization stated for binary continuous images is a special case of our definition for intensity continuous images.

Since we model real images, without loss of generality, we can assume that, for every continuous image function C, there exist a rectangle that is a union of squares of cover Q such that C is equal to zero outside of this rectangle and that, for every digital image function D, there exists a digital rectangle $\{0, ..., n\} \times \{0, ..., m\}$ such that D is equal to zero outside of this rectangle. For a digital image function D, this assumption means that there is only a finite number of digital points on which the function is non-zero, which is the case for real digital images. We also assume that, for a given object, the rectangles are large enough to include the relevant details of the object.

7.10 Digitizations of Half-Planes

Digital objects which are images of some real objects are obtained by a segmentation process that is mostly based on some kind of edge detection and/or thresholding. Each such process can be described as locally thresholding the value of every pixel to decide whether it belongs to the object or not. We assume that the threshold value is unknown, since in many practical applications the threshold value varies for one digital image to another, or even form one part of the same image to the other. At first glance it appears that this fact will rapidly complicate the recovery process. As we will see in Theorem 7.18, however, this is not the case for half-planes. This theorem states that segmenting a digital image of a half-plane with different thresholds will not introduce any new patterns on the boundary of the digital half-plane, since changing a threshold is equivalent to translating the real half-plane and then digitizing it. Therefore, all results obtained for recovering straight lines resulting from the digitization based on the object boundary quantization model (e.g. Dorst and Smeulders [34], [143]) can be used to recover straight lines in digital images even if the threshold v used to segment the object boundary is unknown (see Corollary 7.2, below).

In this section we assume that L is a straight line given by equation $y = ax + b$, $0 \leq a \leq 1$ and P is the lower closed half-plane determined by L, i.e., $P = \{(x, y) \in \mathbb{R}^2 : y \leq ax + b\}$.

If $t \geq 0$, then $T_t(P)$ denotes the translation of P by a vector of length t perpendicular to the line L pointing towards the outside of P (see Figure 7.40). If $t < 0$, then $T_t(P)$ denotes the translation of P by a vector of length t perpendicular to the line L pointing towards the inside of P. Thus, $T_t(P) \subset P$ for $t < 0$.

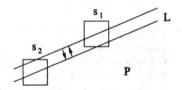

Figure 7.40: Translating a half-plane by a vector pointing toward its inside preserves the monotonicity of the area function on image squares.

The proof of the following lemma is based on elementary properties of areas of triangles and squares:

Lemma 7.12 *Let area be the area function and let s, s_1, s_2 be squares of the square grid Q. The translation T preserves the monotonicity of the area function in the following sense (see Figure 7.40):*

(1) $area(P \cap s_1) < area(P \cap s_2) \Rightarrow area(T_t(P) \cap s_1) < area(T_t(P) \cap s_2)$
if $area(T_t(P) \cap s_2) \neq 0$ and $area(T_t(P) \cap s_1) \neq 1$

(2) $t < 0 \Rightarrow area(T_t(P) \cap s) < area(P \cap s)$ if $0 < area(P \cap s) < 1$.   ∎

Theorem 7.18 shows that the set of digital lines obtained as a digitization of some real straight line is the same, regardless of the v chosen to threshold.

Theorem 7.18 *For every half-plane P and every $0 \leq w < v \leq 1$ there exists $t < 0$ such that*

$$Dig_v(P) = Dig_w(T_t(P)).$$

Before we prove this theorem, we illustrate it in the case where $w = 0$. By Theorem 7.18, we obtain that for every $0 < v \leq 1$ there exists $t < 0$ such that $Dig_v(P) = Dig_0(T_t(P))$. If we take $v = 1/2$ as illustrated in Figure 7.41, than there exists $t < 0$ such that $Dig_{1/2}(P) = Dig_0(T_t(P))$.

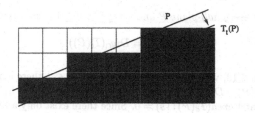

Figure 7.41: For every half-plane P and every $0 \leq w < v \leq 1$ there exists $t < 0$ such that $Dig_v(P) = Dig_w(T_t(P))$.

Proof: of Theorem 7.18

The characteristic function of the half-plane P is zero except for some rectangle. Hence, we have only a finite number of squares $s \in Q$ for which $Dig(P)(s) = area(P \cap s) \neq 0$. Therefore, all squares in grid Q can be grouped into a finite number of classes $S_1, ..., S_l$ with respect to the area of their intersection with the plane P, i.e.

$s_1, s_2 \in S_i$ iff $area(P \cap s_1) = area(P \cap s_2)$ for $i = 1, ..., l$.

We extend the area function to the classes S_i for $i = 1, ..., l$:

$area(P, S_i) = area(P \cap s)$ for some $s \in S_i$.

Observe that the rules (1) and (2) in Lemma 7.12 also hold for function $area$ extended to the classes. The following inequality chain illustrates the order of the classes with respect to the area of the intersection of their members with the plane P and the digitization constants v, w, where $w < v$:

$0 = area(P, S_1) < ... < area(P, S_i) \leq w < area(P, S_{i+1}) < ... <$
$area(P, S_j) \leq v < area(P, S_{j+1}) < ... < area(P, S_k) < ... < area(P, S_l) = 1.$

By the definition of the digitization, we obtain
$Dig_w(P) \setminus Dig_v(P) = S_{i+1} \cup ... \cup S_j.$

By the monotonicity of the area function with respect to translation T stated in Lemma 7.12, there exists $t < 0$ such that

$$area(T_t(P) \cap S_j) \leq w < area(T_t(P) \cap S_{j+1}),$$

which implies that $Dig_v(P) = Dig_w(T_t(P))$.   ∎

As a simple consequence of Theorem 7.18, we obtain the following corollary :

Corollary 7.2 *For every half-plane P and every $0 < v \leq 1$ there exists $t < 0$ such that*

$$Dig_v(P) = Dig_\cap(T_t(P))$$

Proof: By Theorem 7.18, we obtain that for every $0 < v \leq 1$ there exists $d < 0$ such that $Dig_v(P) = Dig_0(T_d(P))$. $Dig_0(T_d(P))$ can differ from $Dig_\cap(T_d(P))$ by squares $s \in Q$ such that $T_d(P) \cap s \neq \emptyset$ and $area(T_d(P) \cap s) = 0$. Since there exist only a finite number of such squares, there exists $d \leq t \leq 0$ such that $Dig_0(T_d(P)) = Dig_\cap(T_t(P))$.   ∎

According to Corollary 7.2, recovering the slope of a half-plane given its digital image obtained by an unknown v-threshold reduces to recovering the slope under object boundary quantization. Therefore, we can use the well-established techniques for slope recovery of straight line segments obtained by object boundary quantization.

7.11 Digitizations of Blurred Half-Planes

First we give conditions that characterize blurring functions with respect to half-planes that we will consider here. For example, Gaussian blurring, and generally every rotationally symmetric blurring function, satisfies these conditions. Hence, the following theorems apply to these blurring functions. After applying a blurring function B to a half-plane P, we obtain a blurred half-plane $B(P)$ which is a step-function with a uniform step of one.

We identify a half-plane P with its characteristic function $P : \mathbb{R}^2 \to \{0, 1\}$, $P(x) = 1$ iff $x \in P$. A **blurring function** is any function B which, applied to a half-plane P, produces a **blurred half-plane** $B(P) : \mathbb{R}^2 \to [0, 1]$ as the output such that the following conditions all hold (see Figure 7.42, where half-plane P is contained in the xy-plane):

(a) For every line L parallel to the boundary line of P, we have $B(P)(a) = B(P)(b)$ if $a, b \in L$.

(b) $\{(x, y) \in \mathbb{R}^2 : B(P)(x, y) = 1\} \neq \emptyset$ and $\{(x, y) \in \mathbb{R}^2 : B(P)(x, y) = 1\} \subseteq P$.

(c) $\{(x, y) \in \mathbb{R}^2 : B(P)(x, y) = 0\} \neq \emptyset$ and $\{(x, y) \in \mathbb{R}^2 : B(P)(x, y) = 0\} \cap P = \emptyset$.

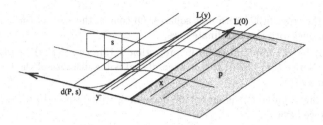

Figure 7.42: A blurred half-plane.

(d) $B(P)$ is monotonically decreasing in the direction perpendicular to the boundary line of P and pointing towards the outside of P.

In this section we show that the slope ambiguity for a blurred digital line is no greater than for a perfectly focused digital line. This follows from Theorem 7.19, which states that given a thresholded digital image of a blurred half-plane, the same image can be obtained by digitizing some translation of the perfectly focused, original half-plane. As an example consider the three digital half-planes shown in Figure 7.44.D. They are obtained by thresholding the intensity digital image of a blurred half-plane shown in Figure 7.44.B with three different threshold values. Now these digital half-planes can also be obtained by digitizing translations of the perfectly focused, original half-plane. Thus, for a given digital half-plane, it is impossible to distinguish whether the original continuous half-plane was perfectly focused or not.

By Theorem 7.19, recovering the slope of a blurred half-plane given its digital image obtained by an unknown v-threshold reduces to recovering the slope under intersection digitization of a perfectly focused half-plane. As is shown in Section 7.8 intersection digitization completely determines object boundary quantization. Therefore, we can apply the well-established techniques for slope recovery of straight line segments developed for object boundary quantization to recover the slope of a blurred half-plane given its digital image obtained by an unknown v-threshold.

Theorem 7.19 *For every half-plane P, every $0 \leq v \leq 1$, and every blurring function B, there exists $t \in \mathbb{R}$ such that*

$$Dig_v(B(P)) = Dig_\cap(T_t(P)).$$

Proof: Let P be a half-plane and let $B(P) : \mathbb{R}^2 \to [0, 1]$ be a blurred half-plane. Let $L(0)$ be the straight line that is the boundary of half-plane P. Without loss of generality, we impose a Cartesian xy-coordinate system on $\mathbb{R}^2$ such that line $L(0)$ has equation $y = 0$ and $\{(x, y) : y \leq 0\} = P$. For the illustration see Figure 7.42.

All straight lines parallel to P have an equation $y = c$ for $c \in \mathbb{R}$. We will denote a line described by equation $y = c$ as $L(c)$. If $c > 0$, then c is the distance to $L(c)$ from $L(0)$. $B(P)$ as a function on straight lines is monotone decreasing:

$$y_1 \leq y_2 \Leftrightarrow B(P)(L(y_1)) \geq B(P)(L(y_2)).$$

Let $\mathcal{Q}$ be the cover of $\mathbb{R}^2$ with unit squares. Of course, the sides of the squares are not necessarily aligned with the coordinate axes.

Let $d(P, s)$ be the minimal value in projection $\pi_y(s)$, i.e., $d(P, s) = inf(\pi_y(s))$ (see Figure 7.42). Notice that if $d(P, s) > 0$, then $d(P, s)$ is the distance of the closest point of square s to line $L(0)$.

We show that $Dig(B(P))$ is monotone decreasing with respect to d, i.e., for any two squares s_1, s_2 we have

$$d(P, s_1) \le d(P, s_2) \Leftrightarrow Dig(B(P))(s_1) \ge Dig(B(P))(s_2). \qquad (7.22)$$

For a line $L(y)$ parallel to $L(0)$ and a square $s \in \mathcal{Q}$, $length(s, L(y))$ denotes the length of the intersection $L(y) \cap s$ (see Figure 7.43). Let l be the length of the perpendicular projection $\pi_y(s)$ of any square $s \in \mathcal{Q}$ onto the y-axis. We obtain:

$$Dig(B(P))(s) = \int_s B(P) = \int_{u=0}^l length(s, L(d(P, s) + u))\, B(P)(L(d(P, s) + u))\partial u.$$

If $d(P, s_1) \le d(P, s_2)$, then for every $0 \le u \le l$ we have (see Figure 7.43):

$$B(P)(L(d(P, s_1) + u)) \ge B(P)(L(d(P, s_2) + u))$$

and

$$length(s_1, L(d(P, s_1) + u)) = length(s_2, L(d(P, s_2) + u)).$$

Therefore, $Dig(B(P))(s_1) \ge Dig(B(P))(s_2)$. The inverse implication follows from the same arguments.

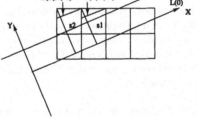

Figure 7.43: $length(s, L(y))$ denotes the length of the intersection $L(y) \cap s$ for a line $L(y)$ parallel to $L(0)$ and $s \in \mathcal{Q}$.

Since there is a finite number of squares for which $Dig(B(P)) \ne 0$, all squares in a grid can be grouped into a finite number of classes $S_1, ..., S_n$ with respect to the value of function $Dig(B(P))$, i.e.,

$$s_1, s_2 \in S_i \text{ iff } Dig(B(P))(s_1) = Dig(B(P))(s_2) \text{ for } i = 1, ..., n.$$

We extend function Dig(B(P)) to the classes S_i for $i = 1, ..., n$:

$Dig(B(P))(S_i) = Dig(B(P))(s)$ for any $s \in S_i$.

Since there is only a finite number of classes, we obtain for $0 < v < 1$ (the argumentation for $v = 0$ and $v = 1$ is similar):

$$0 = Dig(B(P))(S_1) < ... < Dig(B(P))(S_k) \leq v < Dig(B(P))(S_{k+1}) < ... < Dig(B(P))(S_n) = 1.$$
$$(7.23)$$

Thus, $Dig_v(B(P))(s) = 1$ iff $s \in S_{k+1} \cup ... \cup S_n$. Observe that if $0 < Dig(B(P))(S_i) < 1$, then $s_1, s_2 \in S_i$ iff $d(P, s_1) = d(P, s_2)$ for $i = 1, ..., n$. Therefore, we can extend function d to the classes S_i for $i = 1, ..., n$:

$d(P, S_i) = d(P, s)$ for any $s \in S_i$.

Let t be a constant such that $d(P, S_k) > t > d(P, S_{k+1})$, where

$Dig(B(P))(S_k) \leq v < Dig(B(P))(S_{k+1})$.

By inequalities (7.22) and (7.23), we obtain

$$d(P, S_1) > ... > d(P, S_k) > t > d(P, S_{k+1}) > ... > d(P, S_n).$$

If $T_t(P)$ is the translation of half-plane P by a vector perpendicular to P of length t, then $d(T_t(P), S_i) = d(P, S_i) - t$ for $i = 1, ..., n$. Hence

$$d(T_t(P), S_1) > ... > d(T_t(P), S_k) > 0 > d(T_t(P), S_{k+1}) > ... > d(T_t(P), S_n).$$

Since $s \in Dig_\cap(T_t(P))$ iff $0 \geq d(P, s)$, we have that $Dig_\cap(T_t(P)) = S_{k+1} \cup ... \cup S_n$, and consequently $Dig_v(B(P)) = Dig_\cap(T_t(P))$. ∎

7.12 Experimental Results

In Sections 7.9 and 7.10 we model a digitization and segmentation process as a relation between a continuous subsets C of $\mathbb{R}^2$ (representing a 2D object or a 2D projection of a 3D object) and its digital image. To make this model realistic, first we apply a blurring function B to a continuous 2D set C. An output is a 2D continuous intensity image $B(C)$. This image is then mapped to a digital intensity image by the formula

$$Dig(B(C))(s) = \int_s B(C)$$

for every square s of the cover of the plane $\mathbb{R}^2$. Finally, by thresholding $Dig(B(C))$ with some $v \in [0, 1]$, we obtain a binary digital image $Dig_v(B(C))$. This image can be identified with the union of squares representing black pixels, which is a subset of $\mathbb{R}^2$. We use this model to compare geometric properties of a continuous 2D object C and its binary digital image $Dig_v(B(C))$.

Now we describe an experiment demonstrating the accuracy of this digitization and segmentation model for continuous objects being half-planes.

Figure 7.44.A shows a real image taken by a CCD camera of a black half-plane on a white background forming an angle of 134.71° with the horizontal line. Figure 7.44.B shows an intensity digital image which was generated following precisely the digitization model in Section 7.9. Here we also used a black half-plane on a white background forming angle 134.71° with the horizontal line, to which we applied a Gaussian blurring function. The obtained blurred half-plane satisfies conditions stated in Section 7.11. Figure 7.44 (C and D) shows the same images thresholded with three different threshold values. The small difference between images in C and D can be regarded as due to noise produced by the CCD camera. These two images differ along the digital lines identified by the boundaries of the digital half-planes with three different gray level values. Observe that the same regular structure of the lines in image D can still be found in C. The dominating diagonal move by vector [-1, 1] in image D is still dominating in C. (For a, b integers, $[a, b]$ denotes a planar vector in the standard Cartesian coordinate system.) Of course, the lines in C are not as regular as in D; for example, we can have singular [-1,2] or [-2,1] moves, but these moves mostly cancel each other out and occur singularly.

The similarity between idealized digital lines and real sensor digital lines (i.e., boundaries of half-planes) shown in Figure 7.44, indicates that the structure of digital lines in real images is regular enough to allow for both detection and recovery. Based on this observation, we developed an algorithm for edge detection in which the digital edge characterization helps to significantly reduce the number of wrong edge responses. At the same time, this algorithm performs boundary detection, tracking, thinning, and filling gaps in the boundary. Consequently, it eliminates most of the sources of fragmentation that result from using Canny and other related edge detection methods.

This algorithm is based on the assumption that the boundaries of digital objects in real images are composed of digital line segments that are structurally similar to digital line segments in idealized images. Thus, we assume that a boundary of a digital object in real gray-level or color images is composed of digital line segments, in the sense that it can be subdivided into parts, each of which can be a digitization of a straight line segment. We emphasize that we do not assume that the underlying real objects have piecewise linear boundaries, we only argue that digital object boundaries are composed of digital line segments. This assumption allows us to use the mathematical model of real sensor digitization of blurred half-planes presented in Section 7.10 to recover boundaries of digital objects as digital straight line segments in real gray-level or color images.

In the first phase of our edge detection algorithm, we use a 5 × 5 local neighborhood of each image point to determine the strength of its edge response and to estimate the tangent direction of the eventual edge pixel. We use the digital model of a blurred half-plane to calculate the tangent angle of a digital half-plane that maximizes the color difference between the pixels in the half-plane and in its complement at every image point (Joy and Xiang [71]). The color difference calculation is based on Joy and Xiang [70] and Xiang and Joy [163]. If there is a clear maximum in color differences, the point is classified as an edge point with the tangent direction at which the maximum is reached.

Figure 7.44: (A) and (B) show two images of a blurred black half-plane on a white background forming the angle 134.71° with the horizontal line: (A) a real image taken by a CCD camera and (B) an intensity digital image generated following precisely the model of blurring and digitization described here. (C) shows the image in (A) and (D) shows the image in (B) when they are respectively thresholded with three different threshold values.

In the second phase, we extract the edge pixels which form digital line segments with the strongest edge responses (summed over the pixels in the line segment). While extracting digital line segments with the strongest edge responses, we traverse the digital boundary. Here we profit from the fact that there is only a finite and small number of digital line segments of a given length.[4]

One of the principal strengths of using digital line segments in grouping edge responses is that digital connectivity can be readily preserved in the image. Consequently, our approach to edge detection is much more suitable to recover an accurate topology of edges

---

[4]Observe that there is an infinite number of real line segments of a given length, thus fitting the pixel edge responses with real line segments of a fixed length is a much more complicated process.

from real images than Canny and other related edge detection methods. We demonstrate this by comparing the output of our edge detector with the output of the Canny edge detector and the edge detector presented in Rothwell, Mundy, Hoffman and Nguyen [137], which we will call the RMHN edge detector. Figure 7.45.A shows a histogram equalization (in order to make object edges more visible) of an image used originally by Rothwell et al. to show that their edge detector outperforms the Canny detector. Figure 7.45.B shows the result of the Canny edge detector as presented in [137], which was tuned to give the best topological results possible as explicitly stated in [137]. Figure 7.45.C shows the result of the RMHN edge detector. The comparison between Figure 7.45.B and C shows that the RMHN edge detector yields a significant improvement in topology preservation around contour junctions. However, the edge detector of Rothwell et al. did not recover the topology of the image edges correctly. In the bottom right part of Figure 7.45.C only the shadow edge is recovered but not the real edge of the object contour. This results not only in a significant contour deformation, but additionally it also makes it impossible to detect the occlusion of the central block by the other block (whose corner is seen in the bottom right part). All object edges are correctly recovered and the whole scene topology is preserved in Figure 7.45.D, which is the output of our edge detector. The use of the digital model of line segments in our edge detector not only results in correct edge topology but additionally eliminates the wiggling of edges.[5] This is so, since the images in Figure 7.45.B and C are obtained by thinning the output of the corresponding edge detectors, while the output of our edge detector produces edges composed of digital lines, which are, therefore, mostly thin (i.e., one point thick) edges. We would like to emphasize that this performance of our edge detector is achieved without using any knowledge about color quantization built into our algorithm, since the test image in Figure 7.45 is a gray-level image.

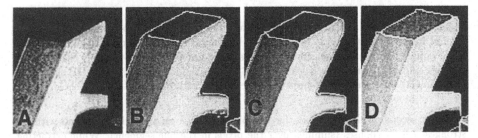

Figure 7.45: (A) shows the histogram equalization of an image used originally by Rothwell et al. (in order to make object edges more visible) (B) shows the output of the Canny edge detector. (C) shows the output of the Rothwell et al. edge detector. (D) shows the output of our edge detector, which is the only one that preserves the whole scene topology.

---

[5]This cannot be clearly seen in this figure, due to the reduction in the size of the image.

Bibliography

[1] W. H. Abdulla, A. O. M. Saleh and A. H. Morad. A preprocessing algorithm for hand-written character recognition. *Pattern Recognition Letters* 7, 13–18, 1988.

[2] R. C. Agrawal, S. C. Sahasrambudhe, and R. K. Shevgaonkar. Preservation of Topo-logical Properties of a Simple Closed Curve Under Digitization. *Computer Vision and Image Understanding*, August 1997, to appear.

[3] L. V. Ahlfors and L. Sario, *Riemann Surfaces*. Princeton University Press, Princeton, New Jersey, 1960.

[4] P. Alexandroff. *Einfachste Grundbegriffe der Topologie*. Springer Verlag, Berlin, 1932.

[5] P. Alexandroff. *Elementary Concepts of Topology*. A translation of [4] by A. E. Farley, Dover Publications, Inc., New York, 1961.

[6] P. Alexandroff. Diskrete Räume. *Math. Sbornik (Recueil Mathematique)* T. 2 (44), N. 3, 502–519, 1937.

[7] P. Alexandroff and H. Hopf. *Topologie*. Verlag von Julius Springer, Berlin, 1935.

[8] P. S. Aleksandrov. *Combinatorial Topology*, Vol. 3, Graylock Press, Albany, New York, 1960.

[9] C. Arcelli and G. Sanniti di Baja. A one-pass two-operation process to detect the skeletal pixels on the 4-distance transform. *IEEE Trans. PAMI* 11, 411–414, 1989.

[10] C. Arcelli. Pattern thinning by contour tracing. *Computer Graphics and Image Processing* 17, 130–144, 1981.

[11] G. M. Arnaud, M. Lamure, M. Terrenoire, and D. Tounissoux. Analysis of the connec-tivity of an object in a binary image: pretopological approach. *Proceedings of the 8th International Conference on Pattern Recognition*, Paris, France, 1204–1206, 1986.

[12] E. Artzy, G. Frieder, and G. T. Herman. The Theory, Design, Implementation and Evaluation of a Three-Dimensional Surface Detection Algorithm. *Computer Graphics and Image Processing* 15, 1–24, 1981.

[13] K. Azarm, W. Bott, F. Freyberger, G. Glüer, J. Horn, and G. Schmidt. Au-tonomiebausteine des mobilen Roboters MACROBE. In G. Schmidt (ed.) *Autonome Mobile Systeme*. TU München, 81–94, 1993.

[14] D. H. Ballard and D. M. Brown. *Computer Vision*, Prentice-Hall, 1982.

[15] J. Barwise and J. Etchemandy. Heterogeneous Logic. In [51], 211–234, 1995.

[16] T. Boult, R. A. Melter, F. Skorina, and I. Stojmenovic. G-neighbors. *Proceedings of the SPIE's Conference on Vision Geometry*. Boston, Massachusetts, USA, September, 96–109, 1993.

[17] L. Boxer. Digitally Continuous Functions, *Pattern Recognition Letters* 15, 833–839, 1994.

[18] H. Brunn. Zur Theorie der Eigebiete. *Arch. Math. Phys.*, vol. 17, 289–300, 1910.

[19] J. Buhmann, W. Burgard, A. B. Cremers, D. Fox, Th. Hofmann, F. E. Schneider, J. Strikos, and S. Thrun. The Mobil Robot RHINO. *AI Magazine* 16, 31–38, 1995.

[20] P. A. Burrough. *Principles of Geographical Information Systems for Land Resource Assessment*. Clarendon Press, Oxford, 1986.

[21] J. F. Canny. Finding Edges and Lines in Images. *Technical Report*, No. 720, MIT Artificial Intelligence Lab, June 1983.

[22] J. F. Canny. A computational approach to edge detection. *IEEE Trans. PAMI* 8, 676–698, 1986.

[23] C. Caratheodory. Über den Variabilitätsbereich der Koeffizienten von Potenzreihen, die gegebene Werte nicht annahmen. *Math. Ann.*, vol. 64, 95–115, 1907.

[24] M. P. do Carmo. *Differential Geometry of Curves and Surfaces*, Prentice-Hall, Englewood Cliffs, New Jersey, 1976.

[25] J.-M. Chassery. Connectivity and Consecutivity in Digital Pictures. *Computer Graphics and Image Processing* 9, 294–300, 1979.

[26] E. Čech. Topologické prostory. *Časopis pro pěstovani mathematiky a fysiky* 66, 225–264, 1937. (A translation appeared as Chapter 28 in J. Novak (ed.) *Topological Papers of Eduard Čech*, 437–472, Publishing House of CAS, Prague, 1968.)

[27] E. Čech. *Topological Spaces*. Chapter 14: Closure Spaces. Interscience Publishers, John Wiley and Sons, London, 1966.

[28] L. Chen and J. Zhang. A Digital Surface Definition and Fast Algorithms for Surface Decision and Tracking. *Proceedings of the SPIE's Conference on Vision Geometry*. Boston, Massachusetts, USA, SPIE Vol. 2060, 169–178, 1993.

[29] L. Chen and J. Zhang. Classification of Simple Surface Points and a Global Theorem for Simple Closed Surfaces in Three Dimensional Digital Spaces. *Proceedings of the SPIE's Conference on Vision Geometry*. Boston, Massachusetts, USA, SPIE Vol. 2060, 179–188, 1993.

[30] E. R. Davies and A. P. N. Plummer. Thinning algorithms: A critique and a new methodology. *Pattern Recognition* 14, 53–63, 1981.

[31] Th. Dean, J. Allen, and Y. Aloimonos. *Artificial Intelligence. Theory and Practice.* Addison-Wesley, Menlo Park, California, 1995.

[32] I. Debled and J.-P. Reveilles. A linear algorithm for segmentation of digital curves. *Parallel Image Analysis and applications. Series in Machine Perception and Artificial Intelligence*, vol. 19, 73–100, World Scientific, 1996.

[33] L. Dorst and A. W. M. Smeulders. Discrete representation of straight lines. *IEEE-Trans. PAMI*, 6, 450–463, 1984.

[34] L. Dorst and A. W. M. Smeulders. Discrete Straight Line Segments: Parameters, Primitives, and Properties. In [111], 45–62, 1991.

[35] R. O. Duda, P. E. Hart and J. H. Munson. *Graphical Data Processing Research Study and Experimental Investigation*, AD650926, 28–30, March 1967.

[36] U. Eckhardt and G. Maderlechner. Thinning of Binary Images. *Hamburger Beiträge zur Angewandten Mathematik*, Reihe B, Bericht 11, April 1989.

[37] U. Eckhardt and G. Maderlechner. Invariant thinning. *International Journal of Pattern Recognition and Artificial Intelligence*, *(Special Issue on Techniques for Thinning Digitized Patterns)* 7, 1115–1144, 1993.

[38] U. Eckhardt and L. Latecki. Digital Topology. In *Current Topics in Pattern Recognition Research, Research Trends.* Council of Scientific Information, Vilayil Gardens, Trivandrum, India, 1994.

[39] U. Eckhardt and L. Latecki. Invariant Thinning and Distance Transform. *Computing* 11, W. Kropatsch, R. Klette, F. Solina, and R. Albrecht (eds.): *Special issue Theoretical Foundations of Computer Vision*, 21–36, 1996.

[40] A. Elfes. Using Occupancy Grids for Mobile Robot Perception and Navigation. *Computer* 22(6), 46–57, 1989.

[41] R. Engelking. *General Topology.* PWN, Warsaw, 1977.

[42] B. Faltings. Qualitative Spatial Reasoning Using Algebraic Topology. In [44], 17–30, 1995.

[43] J. Francon. Discrete Combinatorial Surfaces. *Graphical Models and Image Processing* 57, 20–26, 1995.

[44] A. U. Frank and W. Kuhn (eds.): Spatial Information Theory. A Theoretical Basis for GIS. *Proceedings of COSIT'95*, Springer, Berlin, 1995.

[45] H. Freeman. Boundary Encoding and Processing. In B. S. Lipkin and A. Rosenfeld (eds.): *Picture Processing and Psychopictures*, Academic Press, New York, 241–266, 1970.

[46] Ch. Freksa. Intrinsische vs. extrinsische Repräsentationen zum Aufgabenlösen oder die Verwandlung von Wasser in Wein. In G. Heyer (eds.): Wissensarten und ihre Darstellung. Springer-Verlag: Berlin, 155–165, 1988.

[47] C. Freksa and C. Habel (eds.): *Repräsentation und Verarbeitung räumlichen Wissens. (Representation and Processing of Spatial Knowledge)*, Springer-Verlag, Berlin, 1990.

[48] B. V. Funt. Problem-solving with diagrammatic representations. *Artificial Intelligence* 13(3), 201–230, 1980.

[49] G. W. Furnas. Formal models form imaginal deduction. *Proc. of Conf. of the Cognitive Science Society*, Lawrence Erlbaum, Hillsdale, NJ, 662–669, 1990.

[50] J. Glasgow and D. Papadias. Computational Imagery. *Cognitive Science* 16, 355–394, 1992.

[51] J. Glasgow, N. H. Narayan, and B. Chandrasekaran. *Diagrammatic Reasoning. Cognitive and Computational Perspectives*. AAAI Press/The MIT Press, Menlo Park, California, 1995.

[52] D. Gordon and J. K. Udupa. Fast surface tracking in three-dimensional binary images. *Computer Vision, Graphics, and Image Processing* 45, 196–214, 1989.

[53] A. Gross. Analyzing Generalized Tubular Surfaces, *Proceedings of SPIE's Conference on Intelligent Robots and Computer Vision*, Boston, 1994.

[54] A. Gross and T. E. Boult. Recovery of SHGCs from a Single Intensity View, *IEEE-PAMI*, 161-180, February 1996.

[55] A. Gross and L. Latecki. Digitizations Preserving Topological and Differential Geometric Properties. *Computer Vision and Image Understanding* 62, 370–381, Nov. 1995.

[56] A. Gross and L. Latecki. Toward Non-Parametric Digital Shape Representation and Recovery. In Hebert, M., Ponce, J., Boult, T., and Gross, A. (eds.): *Object Representation in Computer Vision*, Lecture Notes in Computer Science 994, Springer-Verlag, Berlin, 313–325, 1995.

[57] A. Gross and L. Latecki. Modeling Digital Straight Lines. *13th International Conference on Pattern Recognition (ICPR)*, Volume II, 156–160, Vienna, Austria, August 1996.

[58] A. Gross and L. Latecki. A Realistic Digitization Model of Straight Lines. *Computer Vision and Image Understanding*, to appear 1997.

[59] Ch. Habel, Cognitive Linguistics: The Processing of Spatial Concepts. In *T. A. Informations - ATALA (Association pur le Traitement Automatique des Langues)* 28, 21-56, 1987.

[60] Ch. Habel. Repräsentation räumlichen Wissens. In G. Rahmstorf (ed.), *Wissensrepräsentation in Expertensystemen.* Springer-Verlag, Berlin, 1988.

[61] Ch. Habel. Prepositional and depictorial representations of spatial knowledge: The case of path-concepts. In R. Studer (ed.): *Logics and Natural Language.*, Springer-Verlag, Berlin, 1990.

[62] Ch. Habel. Discreteness, Finiteness, and the Structure of Topological Spaces. In C. Eschenbach, Ch. Habel, and B. Smith (eds.): *Topological Foundations of Cognitive Science. Papers from the Workshop at the FISI-CS*, Buffalo, 1994, Graduiertenkolleg Kognitionswissenschaft, Hamburg, 1994.

[63] H. Herrlich. A Concept of Nearness. *General Topology and its Applications* 5, 191-212, 1974.

[64] G. Herman, Discrete Multidimensional Jordan Surfaces. *CVGIP: Graphical Models and Image Processing* 54, 507-515, 1992.

[65] C. J. Hilditch. Linear skeletons from square cupboards. In B. Meltzer and D. Michie (eds.): *Machine Intelligence IV*, American Elsevier, New York, and University Press, Edinburgh, 403-420, 1969.

[66] K.-H. Höhne and W. A. Hanson. Interactive 3D-segmentation of MRI and CT volumes using morphological operations. *J. Computer Assisted Tomography* 16(2), 285-294, 1992.

[67] K.-H. Höhne, M. Bomans, M. Riemer, R. Schubert, and U. Tiede, and W. Lierse. A Volume-based Anatomical Atlas. *IEEE Comput. Graphics Appl.* 12, 72-78, 1992.

[68] K. Ito, ed., *Encyclopedic Dictionary of Mathematics.* MIT Press, Cambridge, MA, 1987.

[69] K. Jensen and D. Anatassiou. Subpixel Edge Localization and Interpolation of Still Images. *IEEE Trans. PAMI* 4, 285-295, March 1995.

[70] G. Joy and Z. Xiang. Center-Cut for Color-Image Quantization. *The Visual Computer* 10, 62-66, 1993.

[71] G. Joy and Z. Xiang. Reducing False Contours in Quantized Color Images. *Computers and Graphics* 20, 231-242, 1996.

[72] J. Koenderink. *Solid Shape*, MIT Press, Cambridge, 1990.

[73] E. Khalimsky, R. Kopperman, and P. R. Meyer. Computer Graphics and Connected Topologies on Finite Ordered Sets. *Topology and its Applications*, 36:1-17, 1990.

[74] O. Kia, D. Doermann, A. Rosenfeld, and R. Chellappa, Symbolic Compression and Processing of Document Images. Technical Report CAR-TR-849, Center for Automation Research, Univ. of Maryland, College Park, January 1997.

[75] C. E. Kim and A. Rosenfeld. Digital Straight Lines and Convexity of Digital Regions. *IEEE Trans. PAMI* 4, 149–153, 1982.

[76] R. Klein. *Algorithmische Geometrie*, Addison-Wesley, Bonn, 1997.

[77] T. Y. Kong. A digital fundamental group. *Computers and Graphics* 13, 159–166, 1989.

[78] T. Y. Kong. On the problem of determining whether a parallel reduction operator of n-dimensional binary images always preserves topology. *Proceedings of SPIE's Conference on Vision Geometry*, 69-77, 1993.

[79] T. Y. Kong and A. W. Roscoe. Continuous Analogs of Axiomatized Digital Surfaces. *Computer Vision, Graphics, and Image Processing (CVGIP)* 29, 60–86, 1985.

[80] T. Y. Kong and A. W. Roscoe. A theory of binary digital pictures. *Computer Vision, Graphics, and Image Processing (CVGIP)* 32, 221–243, 1985.

[81] T. Y. Kong and E. Khalimsky. Polyhedral Analogs of Locally Finite Topological Spaces. *Proceedings of Northeast Conference on General Topology and Applications*, 153–163, Marcel Dekker, New York, 1988.

[82] T. Y. Kong and A. Rosenfeld. Digital topology: Introduction and survey. *Computer Vision, Graphics, and Image Processing* 48, 357–393, 1989.

[83] T. Y. Kong and A. Rosenfeld. If we use 4- or 8-connectedness for both the objects and the background, the Euler characteristic is not locally computable. *Pattern Recognition Letters* 11, 231–232, 1990.

[84] T. Y. Kong and A. Rosenfeld. Digital topology: a comparison of graph-based and topological approaches. In G. M. Read, A. W. Roscoe, and R. F. Wachter (eds.): *Topology and Category Theory in Computer Science*, 273–289, Clarendon Press, Oxford, 1991.

[85] T. Y. Kong, R. Kopperman, and P. R. Meyer. A topological approach to digital topology. *American Mathematical Monthly* 98, 901–917, 1991.

[86] T. Y. Kong and J. K. Udupa. A Justification of a Fast Surface Tracking Algorithm. *CVGIP: Graphical Models and Image Processing* 54, 162–170, 1992.

[87] J. Koplowitz and A. P. Sundar Raj. A robust filtering algorithm for subpixel reconstruction of chain coded line drawings. *IEEE Trans. PAMI* 9, 451–457, 1987.

[88] J. Koplowitz and A. M. Bruckstein. Design of perimeter estimators for digitized planar shapes. *IEEE Trans. PAMI* 11, 611–622, 1989.

[89] S. Kosslyn. *Image and Mind*. Harvard UP, Cambridge, Mass., 1980.

[90] V. A. Kovalevsky. Finite Topology as Applied to Image Analysis. *Computer Vision, Graphics, and Image Processing (CVGIP)* 46, 141–161, 1989.

[91] Z. Kulpa. Diagrammatic Representation and Reasoning. *Machine Graphics and Vision* 3, 77–103, 1994.

[92] L. Latecki. *Digitale und Allgemeine Topologie in der bildhaften Wissensrepräsentation.* DISKI Dissertationen zur Künstlichen Intelligenz 9, infix, St. Augustin, 1992.

[93] L. Latecki. Topological connectedness and 8-connectedness in digital pictures. *CVGIP: Image Understanding* 57, 261–262, 1993.

[94] L. Latecki. Multicolor Well-Composed Pictures. *Pattern Recognition Letters* 16, 425–431, 1995.

[95] L. Latecki. 3D Well-Composed Pictures. *Proceedings of SPIE's Conference on Vision Geometry*, San Diego, California, 196–203, 1995.

[96] L. Latecki and S. Pribbenow. On Hybrid Reasoning for Processing Spatial Expressions. *Proceedings of the European Conference on Artificial Intelligence (ECAI 92)*, Vienna, Austria, August 1992.

[97] L. Latecki and R. Röhrig. Räumliches Schließen und Berechenbarkeit. *Künstliche Intelligenz.* Ch. Habel (ed.): *Special Issue on Spatial Representations and Spatial Reasoning.* 4/93, 35–43, 1993.

[98] L. Latecki, U. Eckhardt, and A. Rosenfeld. Well-Composed Sets. *Computer Vision and Image Understanding* 61, 70–83, 1995.

[99] L. Latecki, A. Rosenfeld, and R. Silverman. Generalized Convexity: CP_3 and Boundaries of Convex Sets. *Pattern Recognition* 28, 1191–1199, 1995.

[100] L. Latecki and A. Gross. Digitization Constraints that Preserve Topology and Geometry. *Proceedings of the IEEE International Symposium on Computer Vision (ISCV 95)*, Florida, USA, November 1995.

[101] L. Latecki, Ch. Conrad, and A. Gross. Conditions that Guarantee a Digitization Process Preserves Topology. *Proceedings of 17. DAGM Symposium Mustererkennung in Bielefeld (Pattern Recognition Conference)*, Springer-Verlag, Berlin, 210–217, 1995.

[102] L. Latecki and F. Prokop, Semi-proximity Continuous Functions in Digital Images. *Pattern Recognition Letters* 16, 1175–1187, 1995.

[103] L. Latecki and C. M. Ma, An Algorithm for a 3D Simplicity Test. *Computer Vision and Image Understanding* 63, 388–393, 1996.

[104] L. Latecki and A. Rosenfeld. Supportedness and Tameness: Differentialless Geometry of Plane Curves. Technical Report CAR-TR-838, Center for Automation Research, Univ. of Maryland, College Park, September 1996.

[105] L. Latecki. 3D Well-Composed Pictures. *Graphical Models and Image Processing*, to appear.

[106] L. Latecki, Ch. Conrad, and A. Gross. Preserving Topology by a Digitization Process. *Journal of Mathematical Imaging and Vision*, to appear.

[107] R. K. Lindsay. Images und Inference. *Cognition* 29, 229–250, 1988.

[108] T. Lozano-Pères. Spatial planning: A configuration space approach. *IEEE Transactions on Computers* 32, 108–120, 1983.

[109] H. E. Lü and P. S. P. Wang. An improved fast parallel thinning algorithm for digital patterns. *Proceedings of the IEEE Conference on Computer Vision and Pattern Recognition*, San Francisco, CA, 364–367, 1985.

[110] D. Marr. *Vision. A Computational Investigation into the Human Representation of Visual Information*, Freeman, New York, 1982.

[111] R. A. Melter, A. Rosenfeld, and P. Bhattacharya (eds.), Vision Geometry. *Contemporary Mathematics*. American Mathematical Society, Vol. 119, 169–195, 1991.

[112] K. Menger. Some Applications of Point Set Methods, *Ann. Math.* 32, 739–750, 1931.

[113] H. Minkowski. *Geometrie der Zahlen*. Leipzig, Berlin, 1910.

[114] M. Minsky and S. Papert. *Perceptrons. An introduction to Computational Geometry*, The MIT Press: Cambridge, Mass., 1969.

[115] E. E. Moise. *Geometric Topology in Dimensions 2 and 3*, Springer-Verlag, 1977.

[116] D. G. Morgenthaler and A. Rosenfeld. Three-dimensional digital topology. *Information and Control* 51, 227–247, 1981.

[117] G. L. Naber. *Topological methods in Euclidean spaces*, Cambridge University Press, Cambridge, 1980.

[118] S. A. Naimpally and B. D. Warrack. *Proximity Spaces*. University Press, Cambridge, 1970.

[119] S. E. Palmer. Fundamental aspects of cognitive representation. In E. Rosch and B. Lloyd (eds.) Cognition and categorization. Lawrence Erlbaum, Hillsdale, NJ, 1978.

[120] T. Pavlidis. *Algorithms for Graphics and Image Processing*, Springer-Verlag, Berlin, 1982.

[121] T. Pavlidis. An asynchronous thinning algorithm. *Computer Graphics and Image Processing* 20, 133–157, 1982.

[122] F. P. Prokop. Neighbourhood Lattices-A Poset Approach to Topological Spaces. *Bull. Aust. Math. Soc.* 39, 31–49, 1989.

[123] F. P. Prokop. A Step Beyond Topology. In *Papers on General Topology and Applications*. N.Y. Academy of Sciences, Vol. 728, New York, 96-113, 1994.

[124] G.J.E. Rawlins and D. Wood. Ortho-convexity and its generalizations. In G.T. Toussaint (ed.) *Computational Morphology*, Elsevier, Amsterdam, 137-152, 1988.

[125] F. Riesz. Stetigkeitsbegriff und abstrakte Mengenlehre. *Atti IV Congresso Internazionale dei Matematici*, Roma, 1908, Vol. II, 18-24, 1909.

[126] C. Ronse. Minimal test patterns for connectivity preservation in parallel thinning for binary images. *Discrete Applied Mathematics* 21, 67-79, 1988.

[127] A. Rosenfeld. Digital straight line segments. *IEEE Trans. Comput.* C-23, 1264-1269, 1974.

[128] A. Rosenfeld. A characterization of parallel thinning algorithms. *Information and Control* 29, 286-291, 1975.

[129] A. Rosenfeld, Digital topology. *American Mathematical Monthly*, 86:621-630, 1979.

[130] A. Rosenfeld. *Picture Languages. Formal Models for Picture Recognition.* Academic Press, New York, 1979.

[131] A. Rosenfeld, 'Continuous' functions on digital pictures. *Pattern Recognition Letters* 4, 177-184, 1986.

[132] A. Rosenfeld and J. L. Pfaltz. Sequential operations in digital picture processing. *Journal of the Association for Computing Machinery* 13, 471-494, 1966.

[133] A. Rosenfeld and A.C. Kak. *Digital Picture Processing*, Academic Press, New York, 1982.

[134] A. Rosenfeld and C. E. Kim. How a Digital Computer Can Tell whether a Line is Straight. *American Mathematical Monthly* 89, 230-235, 1982.

[135] A. Rosenfeld and T. Y. Kong. Connectedness of a Set, Its Complement, and Their Common Boundary. *Contemporary Mathematics*, Vol. 119, 125-128, 1991.

[136] A. Rosenfeld, T. Y. Kong, and A. Y. Wu. Digital Surfaces. *CVGIP: Graphical Models and Image Processing* 53, 305-312, 1991.

[137] C. Rothwell, J. Mundy, B. Hoffman and V.-D. Nguyen. Driving Vision by Topology. *International Symposium on Computer Vision*, 395-400, Coral Gables, Florida, November 1995.

[138] D. Rutovitz. Pattern recognition. *J. Royal Statist. Soc.* 129, 504-530, 1966.

[139] H. Samet. The Quadtree and Related Hierarchical Data Structures. *Computing Surveys* 16, 187-260, 1984.

[140] J. Serra. *Image Analysis and Mathematical Morphology*, Academic Press, New York, 1982.

[141] K. Siddiqui and B. B. Kimia. Parts of Visual Form: Computational Aspects. *IEEE Trans. Pattern Analysis and Machine Intelligence* 17, 239–251, 1995.

[142] K. Siddiqui, K. Tresness, and B. B. Kimia. Parts of Visual Form: Ecological and Psychophysical Aspects. *Proceedings of the IAPR's International Workshop on Visual Form*, Capri, Italy, 1994.

[143] A. W. M. Smeulders and L. Dorst. Decomposition of Discrete Curves into Piecewise Straight Segments in Linear Time. In [111], 169–195, 1991.

[144] M. Spivak. *A Comprehensive Introduction to Differential Geometry*, Volume Two, Publish or Perish, Boston, 1970.

[145] J. Star and J. Estes, *Geographic Information Systems*. Prentice Hall, Englewood Cliffs, New Jersey, 1990.

[146] R. Stefanelli and A. Rosenfeld. Some parallel thinning algorithms for digital pictures. *Journal of the Association for Computing Machinery* 18, 255–264, 1971.

[147] H. S. Stiehl. Issues of Spatial Representation in Computational Vision. In C. Freksa and C. Habel (eds.): *Repräsentation und Verarbeitung räumlichen Wissens.*, Springer-Verlag, Berlin, 83–98, 1990.

[148] J. J. Stoker. *Differential Geometry*, Wiley, 1969.

[149] L. N. Stout, Two Discrete Forms of the Jordan Curve Theorem. *American Mathematical Monthly* 95, 332–336, 1988.

[150] Th. M. Strat and G. B. Smith. The Management of Spatial Information in a Mobile Robot. In A. Kak and S. Chen (eds.) *Proceedings of the Workshop on Spatial Reasoning and Multi-Sensor Fusion*, Morgan Kaufmann, Los Altos, 240–249, 1987.

[151] H. Tamura. A comparison of line thinning algorithms from digital geometry viewpoint. *Proceedings of the 4th Int. Conf. on Pattern Recognition*, Kyoto, Japan, 715–719, 1978.

[152] H. Tietze. Bemerkungen über konvexe und nichtkonvexe Figuren, *Journal für die reine und angewandte Mathematik* 160, 67–69, 1929.

[153] M. Unser, A. Aldroubi, and M. Eden. Enlargement or Reduction of Digital Images with Minimum Loss of Information. *IEEE Trans. on Image Processing* 4, 247-258, March 1995.

[154] F.A. Valentine. A Three Point Convexity Property, *Pacific J. Math.* 7, 1227–1235, 1957.

[155] F.A. Valentine. *Convex Sets*. McGraw-Hill, New York, 1964.

[156] P. Veelaert. Digital Planarity of Rectangular Surface Segments. *IEEE Trans. PAMI* 16, 647–652, 1994.

[157] P. Veelaert. Designing Perceptrons for the Recognition of Digital Straight Lines. *Proceedings of the 4th Conference of Discrete Geometry for Computer Imagery.*, Grenoble, 1994.

[158] B. A. Verkov. *Elementary Number Theory.* Wolters-Noordhoff Pub., Groningen, The Netherlands, 1970.

[159] K. Voss. *Discrete Images, Objects, and Functions in Z^n*, Springer–Verlag, Berlin, 1993.

[160] Y. Wang and P. Bhattacharya. Digital Connectivity and Extended Well-Composed Sets for Gray Images. *Computer Vision and Image Understanding*, to appear.

[161] H. R. Wilson, D. Levi, L. Maffei, J. Rovamo, and R. DeValois. *The Perception of Form.* In L. Spillmann and J. S. Wener (eds.): *Visual Perception. The Neurophysiological Foundations.*, Academic Press, San Diego, 231–272, 1990.

[162] M. Worring and A. W. M. Smeulders. Digitized Circular Arcs: Characterization and Parameter Estimation. *IEEE Trans. PAMI* 17, 587–598, 1995.

[163] Z. Xiang and G. Joy. Color Image Quantization by Agglomerative Clustering. *IEEE Computer Graphics and Applications* 14, 44–48, 1994.

[164] I.M. Yaglom and V.G. Boltyanskii. *Convex Figures.* Holt, Rinehart and Winston, New York, 1961. Translated from the Russian original (1951) by P.J. Kelly and L.F. Walton.

[165] T. Y. Zhang and C. Y. Suen. A fast parallel algorithm for thinning digital patterns. *Communications of the ACM* 27, 236–239, 1984.

Index